Other Books by Tolly Kizilos

Trips to the Soul: Poems
Recollections: Poems
Zeal: A Memoir
God and the Problem of Evil
Once Upon a Corporation
Decision at Golgotha
Tradition and Change
Dwarf's Legacy

CHANGED
FOR
GOOD

—— THE DISCOVERY OF PURPOSE ——

APOSTOLOS "TOLLY" KIZILOS

CHANGED FOR GOOD
THE DISCOVERY OF PURPOSE

iUniverse books may be ordered through booksellers or by contacting:

iUniverse
1663 Liberty Drive
Bloomington, IN 47403
www.iuniverse.com
844-349-9409

ISBN: 978-1-6632-1769-1 (sc)
ISBN: 978-1-6632-1770-7 (e)

Print information available on the last page.

iUniverse rev. date: 01/30/2021

Dedication to the Essential Workers who Sustained Us During the COVID 19 Pandemic of 2020

I had started writing this book when COVID 19 struck humanity and spread sickness, death and fear on us. In the early weeks of the spreading pandemic, nobody knew the damage this virus could inflict, or which segment of the population might be the most vulnerable, or how it spread its poison, or anything else about it. Humanity needed people to risk their lives in medical, nursing, and other first responder jobs as well as people in cashiering, groceries' delivery, garbage-collection and other essential jobs, so we could all survive. Many courageous people, took the risk and kept us alive. They are the heroes of our time. Their labors have meaning, and their life, an enduring purpose in God.

Disclaimer

The stories in this book reflect the author's recollection of events from his life. Some names, locations, and characteristics have been changed to protect the privacy of people. Some names of organizations, systems, operations and devices have been changed to avoid any unintended disclosure of business-related information. There were also persons that intersected my life, who had names that I never knew or have long forgotten and have given them new names to complete the narrative. Dialogue has been re-created from memory, guided by the truth of the topic and the theme of what had meaning in the events of my life.

Table of Contents

D
STUDENT, STEEWORKER, HUSBAND

E
STEERING IN AND OUT OF ENGINEERING

F
INTO WRITING AND O.D.

G
ENJOY, SUFFER AND REJOICE

Preface

"Seek first his kingdom and his righteousness, and all these things shall be yours as well." (Matthew 6:33)

This book is an attempt to piece together some significant parts of my life, previously neglected or nonexistent yet, to convey the experiences I've had in my journey for finding meaning in the pursuit of my goals and a purpose that could endure to my journey's end. The book is also an attempt to gain a deeper understanding of my life as a whole, made greater than the sum of its parts, after experiencing God's love in a spiritually intense turning point in my life.

Modern scientists believe that we tell stories to make up the reality of the universe because physical measurements are insufficient to do the job. People have also been telling their stories to connect with each other and form a community without the gloom of loneliness and enjoy the bonds of friendship. Sometimes, when someone tells or writes a story from his or her bewildering life, listeners or readers enter the world being created and ask questions that the storyteller hadn't thought about, and are guided to search and find answers that enlarge their understanding not only of the story but also of their world as well. Thus, my stories become portals to the reader's life.

Some of us have a lot of stories with meaningful experiences, i.e. experiences that reveal the kind of people we are, the kind of world we are trying to build, and the journey we have been on. Our stories may enable others to expand their sense of reality and reach deeper into their hearts and minds. Some of the stories portray the challenges and the ingenuity of surviving during the Nazi occupation of Greece, the Communist insurrection in Greece and the courage needed to grow and mature in times of famine, fear and hazard in a culture of mystery, tradition and miracle.

My experiences of moving a lifetime from one continent and its culture to another is unusual enough, but it becomes a metaphor for an explorer's resilience, when it is followed by the pursuit of widely diverse careers achieved by hard work in the pursuit of goals, and a strangely manifest providential help.

Recent shifts in perspective after my wife's illness and a continuing spiritual transformation after her death, have enabled me to see the intimate connections of my life's experiences more clearly, and inspired me to probe them from a more mature, systematic perspective in this book. Some of the stories may be examples of the grace we hope for, as we struggle inside us and in the world, hoping for the gifts of love, peace and joy, which, for me, mean happiness.

As I reach the later years of my life, I continue to reflect on how I "ended up" where I am, and the work that needs ahead. We all know that life is a hodge-podge of success and failure, studded with unknowing and mystery. The book is intended to show that the kind of persons we are at first, and the kind of persons we choose to become, using our free will and following God's guidance, can move us closer to an enduring purpose, which for those who have faith, is closeness to God.

When I examine the decisions that I made at critical junctures of my life, I wonder whether luck, coincidence, fate, logic, or faith had something to do with what happened, or is happening. I often sense the benevolent presence of God, and I am thankful for the freedom and peace that follow his guidance.

I went through several stages of development, adjusting my goals to meet new responsibilities, set more mature goals, and devoted myself to things I valued more. My renewed faith in God has instilled in me a greater sense of contentment with my life and hope for the future.

I feel more compassion for others and have understood that a worthy purpose in life gives us the gift of a happy and serene life.

There have been many occasions when I sensed that I was moved to take a different path than the one I had intended to follow. And there were times when I felt the world was too generous to me, and times when it was miserly and made it difficult for me to do what I desired to do. These situations arise, if one keeps in mind that God is always around and no one knows what he will contribute for our benefit now or later on.

"Life must be lived forwards, but can only be understood backwards," Kierkegaard wrote. Looking back on the seminal experiences of my life, I find a common link. There is often a strangeness about the experience, perhaps an eerie feeling, an omen or a premonition, a wondering of what it may mean, not only in the present situation, but also for the development of our inner life. Often, these experiences are jarring and challenge us to change our ways, to "start living or give up." These shifts in awareness may become turning points in our lives. We experience a strangeness in ordinary events that jolts us into a new state of awareness that stamps itself on our consciousness and causes us to change our habits, our values, even our beliefs. We all would benefit by being aware of who we are and what world we are experiencing.

Sometimes, years must pass before we realize the meaning of a particular event; sometimes only minutes. Some years back, I made a point of spending a few hours a week visiting George, a Greek-American friend of mine, who was gradually becoming paralyzed by a protein-related degenerative disease. On these visits, I'd push his wheelchair to the garden of the nursing home where he lived, light a cigarette for him and hold it so he could inhale. He was full of life before his illness, enjoyed Greek music and, even though he could hardly talk as the disease advanced, he loved to tell stories of his experiences during the Communist insurrection in Greece, and found reasons to laugh, even when death was grim and menacing. I enjoyed George's company and felt I was doing something good, something that added relief and pleasant company to my friend George with a little effort from me. Every time I went to see George, I tried to do something that would help him escape the depressing environment in which he had to live. On one occasion, I hired a local Greek music band to play for George at the Gathering Hall of the nursing home. Wanting it to be a surprise, I didn't tell George in advance. Next day I got a phone call from George's son who told me that George had died two hours ago.

Years later, it dawned on me that, in addition to comforting and befriending George, my involvement in his life had another purpose: I learned how to be more attentive, more helpful to my wife when illness ravaged her body and I was her sole caregiver for three years.

We are all on a journey, pursuing goals we hope will give meaning, make us happy and give a purpose to our lives. Most of us want to make the world a better place for all and become happier and wiser in doing it.

Ever since I was a child I have believed that approaching God was a kind of purpose, and meaning was given to my decisions and actions by trying to do what makes the world even a little better place. Writing this book is an opportunity for me to testify to the value of these simple principles. The book reflects the life I have stitched together solely from many true experiences, some of them mysteriously providential and far stranger than I could have planned. Besides, the book offers many opportunities for telling truthful stories which may be not only intriguing and amusing, but also revealing what helps or hinders the building of a meaningful and happy life from the experiences we have. Sometimes, telling the story is enough.

Without consciously intending it, I also see part of the impetus for writing this book is a desire to better understand and integrate a wide range of discrete life experiences and recurring themes that form a greater whole that emerges only with the benefit of hindsight. One could regard this book as an attempt to put Kierkegaard's observation into practice—to live forwards and backwards at the same time, so as to see how the whole of a life is mysteriously greater than the sum of the parts. The ability to see this larger meaning and purpose, of course, assumes the existence of an all-powerful and loving God, a

God constantly nudging us to become the people he created us to be and live now with all the gifts he gave us.

From a psychological point of view, one could also see this book as an attempt to grapple with the central challenge inherent in the human condition—to stare death in the face and find comfort in knowing that our existence mattered. In Erik Erikson's theory of adult development, this successful resolution of the crisis with which we are confronted at the last of the eight stages of psycho-social development is crucial to the development of a fulfilling life.

In the end, the greatest gift we can leave posterity is the blessing of a life lived with an adoring love of God, and love of human beings. Anyone can start moving toward God any time; all one needs to be closer to God is his say-so and his commitment.

A

CHILDHOOD IN TIMES
OF WAR AND PEACE

1

Jumping over Saint John's Fires

I was squatting in the dirt square my mother had marked out for me on the dirt, next to our rented apartment, and drew the shape of a bridge because my mother said that I would be a great civil engineer when I grew up and that's what they do. All I know is that a bridge is a good thing to have, because it helps people go where they want to go and return, but it's not a thing I want to do. I know that this is Saint John's Day and tonight there will be fires on our street, and I'll try to jump over a little one as all boys do. I don't know if I will be able to do that, but I'll try. My mother told me that there will be a fire engine around and it will be exactly like my toy. Frosso, our landlady, is telling a story to another woman from the outer reaches of our neighborhood, an alien, Frosso calls her, because of her egg-shaped head and her big black-button eyes.

Frosso is telling her alien friend that the "Freedom" newspaper reported in the news that they found a teenager-stowaway in the bowels of the Ocean Liner, Nea Hellas ("New Greece"), just before it sailed from Piraeus for New York. Then, Frosso offers her one of her special cookies, but the "alien" refuses it politely. I'm not surprised. I never liked Frosso's cookies, nor did the alien. But, the offers were made.

I want to hear the details of the stowaway's story and listen carefully when Frosso says that, according to the rumor she heard at Botsis' Bakery, if a steward hadn't been looking in the bowels of the ship on his inspection, the stowaway would have never been found and he would have been on his way to America, "the land of golden sidewalks," she said. I'm there, in the bowels of a great ocean liner, alert and ready to run, dash and escape from anyone looking for me. I have no idea what ship bowels look like but I can imagine a huge dark, gallery, smelling a little like my uncle-doctor's garage. I feel sad that the teenager wasn't fast enough or strong enough or willful enough to escape and sail to his dream. That boy is in pain.

I've been sick with rheumatism and earaches, and have experienced fear, left alone in the dark in my room at night. I've heard my parents talk about the rumors of war, which is what drops clouds of silence, wipes out smiles, drives skeletons out to the streets. They worry about the cold, the hunger and death. Going to America stayed in my mind, waiting for some other event to bring it out to the real world, and make sense of it. The events of that day are among the earliest memories I have. I was four to five years old.

I became aware of the world that day because it is the earliest interaction with the world that I remember. Maybe I remember so well because the fires, were lit all over in the street next to our apartment. When the time came, they said that Saint John's fires were ready. If you jump you have protection all year long from all evils that attack the body. I saw men jumping and big boys running and leaping. I started my run and picked up speed and I was ready to fly over the flames and stay healthy all year long, but somebody grabbed me by the waist and lifted me up on his shoulders and we both went over a fire, then another fire and another, seeing our shadows running like raiders up against house walls, until we saw my mother waiting for us and the big boy, Gregory, who carried me on his shoulders brought me down and presented me to her. I was furious and thankful for the ride, but I didn't say anything. I had jumped over the fires of Saint John and that was what counted.

My father was sure that Frosso's apartment was too damp and contributed to my rheumatism and my earaches. Humidity was the enemy. We had to go. We moved just before the fascists of Mussolini attacked Greece. I went to school in the new neighborhood of Neos

Cosmos, in October, 1940 and the war started, soon after our move. I was five, no doubt about that.

After I had been in grade school for a while, my father said the teacher told them I was a good student, and finished my homework on time, but I was "disobedient". I wasn't very pleased by that first report. I had expected praise rather than criticism for trying to learn as much as I possibly could by asking or answering questions when I could. I protested to my father for the punishment I got in school because the teacher didn't want to respond to my questions or wanted me to wait my turn and answer when she gave me permission. I didn't want to wait and listen to things that were obvious. I had to learn more things and couldn't wait. I had important things to do in this world and you just didn't do them by being the teacher's pet. I got used to the "disobedient" part. Year after year in grade school, I got the same report and my father always signed it proud of his son's academic performance while recommending "more discipline" for my "rough edges". On my last year, I started fighting for change. Why did they lock the bookcase with the School Encyclopedia? Couldn't they allow me to read it in the library room, if I asked permission? And why didn't they build another bathroom rather than have to push and shove outside the only one they had for boys? I was a rebellious kid that needed to be educated, but the system had its way and didn't want to go along with mine. The square-inch-section wood ruler with steel imbedded in the corners landed on my palm and knuckles harder every year, until I left grade school and was never punished again for being "disobedient".

I was happy that our new apartment was on the second floor of a grand-looking building with a fortress face, and I could keep track of people several streets away by traversing the 30 feet or so of our balcony up front. The trouble was that my mother could do the same thing and, later on, she would be tracking my movements and, if she couldn't see me, she would call out my name and hundreds of people or thousands, for all I knew, would hear my name bellowed as if she was a Muslim muezzin singing the word "Tolly" from a strange Koran.

The first day of the war against the Mussolini's fascists came suddenly one morning. Mother and I were on our balcony and some people stopped briefly and told us what they knew about the government's brave stand against the Italian fascists. There were rumors of thousands of young people joining the army and being transported up north on trains. The radio cautioned people to keep their limbs inside the windows, because one young man had lost an arm reaching out of his open window. I just made a note of this, but I had no idea that I would retain it for 80 years. It was part of a noble war, and I felt proud of the volunteers and admiration that extended over all the people who united to crush the enemy.

I remember an old man passing by, under our balcony. I noticed his wobbly walk, but didn't yet know any of the problems that come with drinking. It was the first time I had a chance to examine a totally bold head from above. There was a sense of centrality to that head. I wasn't sure why the old man raised up his head and looked at my mother. He might have greeted her first, or she might have given him one of her cheery "good mornings", but before the exchange of greetings could be completed, the old man lost his balance altogether and dropped on the dirt road, hands, butt and elbows all at once. My mother took off and I followed her downstairs. She wasn't the kind of person who could watch anyone in trouble without rushing to help. There were a few people gathered by the time she made it down to the scene of the accident and started to check the old man's head talking compassionately to him all along. I remember a burst of joy in everyone's face when the old man opened his eyes, winked and smiled.

An angelic face of a girl, a few years older than me, stopped laughing, and said to me,

"You live here, don't you?" I nodded. She wanted to know how the old man fell, and I told her I didn't know. "What's your name?" she asked and I told her. "I'm Cleo," she said and then, "You are Apostolos; why don't you leave it alone and stop calling yourself Tolly??' I didn't know what to say.

I had never thought about my name, but I liked what she aid, how she said it.

"It's too long!" I said and stood up. The old man took the hand of one of the people around him and crawled to the stoop of our house and sat down.

"Do you know Katina, on the first floor?" she asked.

"She doesn't go out, but my mother says her daughter visits her."

"You'd like her," Cleo said excited. "She's so wonderful, you'll never forget her, if you ever meet her."

"I'm not Cleopatra, by the way. Just Cleo, the Muse, you know?" she said and smiled and run toward her house. I waved to her. I couldn't take my eyes away from the brown plait that moved as she run away. Cleo was a good friend to have in this tough neighborhood at this unpredictable time. Cleo would be a great friend any time.

As far as I was concerned that incident was somehow a harbinger of the quick victory we expected from the war. Man drops down; my mother helps the old man, and the old man rises up and walks. Girl finds me; girl becomes a good friend. My mother stood up, grabbed my hand and surveyed the street around us with a penetrating gaze. There was worry in her dark, sparkling eyes and her furrowed forehead. "There will be trouble," she said, her eyes conveying a grim foreboding. She wished the old man something like "Stay sober, grandpa, and make Greece proud!" as we headed back up to our perch.

Everything would be all right. Before long kids with bleeding noses would seek my mother, because she knew how to stop a nosebleed; mothers would bring their children to her to feel their hurting arm bones and find out if they would heel or should be taken to the local clinic. Helping others made her happy. One time she spent a week helping a friend of hers with typhoid fever and drove my father to despair with worry "because we could all get the disease and die," he said.

The Greek army was mobilizing. There was excitement all around the neighborhood. Young men and women were joining the army in droves. I remember Kyr-Argyris, the candy and tobacco storeowner, a few doors down the street from us, next to the iconographer's workroom, saying that there were trainloads of people going north, and some enthusiastic young recruits, who were riding on top of the wagons, were injured when the trains went through tunnels and people forgot to duck. My parents would talk about the war more often now.

We would talk a lot about the wounded, the frostbitten and the dead -- the evil we couldn't kill.

Why couldn't I be in the army someday? I could feel the wind blowing on my face as the train sped north, toward Thessaly, Macedonia and Epirus, some of the northernmost reaches of our land, and then into Albania, where the Italian army was coming from. Sometimes I was sure I could take care of myself, no matter what the danger was. Some people were ready to celebrate victory. My father, always cautious and measured in his ways, didn't like what was going on. He saw dark clouds gathering around us. He wanted my mother and me to be extra careful out in the streets. He became concerned about scarcity in food in the months ahead and started a hidden pantry by turning sideways the wardrobe at the corner of the bedroom, so we could gather some canned food – beans and peas and olive oil — for the days of the lean cows.

My mother was on top of all the news from the neighbors, the radio, the magazines and the newspapers. If the internet was around they would have hired her for the News along with the BBC. She was the hub of communications for the neighborhood, tracking the moves of the enemy and helping others cope with the sadness of loved ones leaving for the front, or consoling women who were left behind with children and poverty and men without legs removed by frostbite and gangrene. It was that balcony that put her on center stage, but if it wasn't there, mother would have erected a stand to look ahead and care for us all.

There was more to war than the joy of the first day. One word, one look, one move and the way you used to look at the world could be forever changed. The Nazis were coming down to help the laughable Italian Army. The start of living under Fascists and Nazis was dawning on me through the hazy sky. Why not fight at sea? That's what my uncle Vassos Laskos, my mother's brother, the submarine captain, had been doing, and that's what I wanted to do. Dreaming of fighting for freedom was exhilarating. Freedom is a crazy word we learned from cradlesongs and stories we studied in school, or when we fell asleep reading the history of Greece that always included three words, "Freedom or Death", or "Come back with your shield, or on it".

I knew the names of all the commanders who fought to liberate Greece from the Ottoman Turks in the 1820s. Many of them were Albanian Greeks, ancestors of my mother's relatives. I thought of going to the Naval Academy and become a combat officer like my mother's two brothers had done, but when I found out, at twelve, that I was nearsighted and the Navy didn't allow that for combat, I scuttled that dream and focused on science, math some poems and thoughts of going to college in America. There was no time when I picked easy things to do, or living without exploration and discovery of something. I always imagined that changing myself by learning, or the world by doing something meaningful and good, required work. I found a way to be happy doing things that made me learn more and the world, somehow, better.

Our soldiers needed socks and gloves and sweaters and my mother was good at knitting and sawing and went to work. When she finished one of her projects – a sleeveless sweater, a pair of socks – we would wrap it up, put them in small boxes with walnuts and raisins, add a couple of packs of cigarettes and get it written up for uncle Paul or other soldiers, and mail it to the war zone. I tried some knitting, but I wasn't good at it, so I stuck to packing the boxes and writing addresses.

Some days the bells of Saint Mary's would ring the joy we all felt when our soldiers conquered some Albanian city from the fascists and we raised the flag and sung songs ridiculing Mussolini and his troops. This was the joy of David hitting Goliath. But the humiliation was too much for the Nazis, so they came down to help the Italians. The Greeks held them back for three weeks, fighting sometimes barefooted, against the relentless snow and the Nazi panzers. And so, the Germans broke through and the occupation of the land of freedom began. We would have to suffer a lot to keep the hope of freedom alive. And we never lost faith that God would help us win.

2

Archangel Michael's Motorcycle

It is cold now, and marble feels icier on the skin than air. I hold the bottom of my gray coat tight over my bare legs wishing that I was ten rather than eight, so I could pester my parents and maybe get a pair of golf pants to protect my skin like Nunak does in the North Pole, instead of wearing shorts in this icy world. Never mind; that time will come. So, I'm counting up to the thousands, chewing up time, so I can run upstairs, when I reach a number as close to ten thousand as I can and eat a slice of bread with a few drops of olive oil sprinkled on top of it. Most of the time, that was half of my mother's daily ration of five ounces of bread per person, as ordered by the Nazi Directorate, which run the city of Athens at the time. I already had my portion by noon and was still unbearably hungry. I am aware that we live in hard times, but I don't know how much harder they'll become. I wonder if there will be beans from our stash behind the bedroom wardrobe and a couple of sardines, but I doubt it. Beans are for special occasions. There will probably be spaghetti, made from stinky, tasteless flour or collard greens with drops of olive oil, and a piece of feta cheese to make everything else tolerable.

I know that the iconographer is in his little room across the street, still working on a Saint, because his light is on. I could stop by for a visit and spend some time watching him work on the holy man's blue phelonion as I have done many times before, but cold and hunger are not much different there right now than where I am perched.

Eleni, the old woman next to the iconographer's room-studio, has a couple of hens and sells eggs to those she likes, to "sympathetic people" she says. Once in a while my mother prevails upon her and buys an egg or two from her for my "proteinic health" as she calls it. Kyr-Argyris, the candy-and-tobacco-store owner closes his place early and goes home when the temperature drops. The cold wind puts a lid on all thoughts of business. Further down is Cleo's house, and she feels to me like a warm breeze, mysteriously present, but nowhere to be seen. Probably taking English lessons at some school, as she told me once she wanted to do. Today, I imagine her reading some history book in her room. She told me that she was "intellectually" in love with Thucydides, but I hd no idea what that meant at the time.

I feel the cold and dreamt the hot hibachi we may fire up tonight, if my father has found any useless pieces of wood or some chunks of coal for fuel from the company he works for. He has permission to carry them out, after they search his briefcase. I can put up with the hunger and the cold, but if the Nazis come rolling on their hogs as I saw them do in Aigion once, or sent a tank in the neighborhood, which they had already done, to scare us in the boulevard because somebody stole some gasoline from one of their monster trucks somewhere in greater Athens, or because somebody killed a soldier on some mountainside nearby and ten people in our neighborhood must be caught in a "blockade", and exiled or executed, then I would be terrified.

I counted up to a few thousand numbers that evening – I know I didn't get to ten thousand – and as the light faded out of the sky, and a very cold winter night made me shiver, I run upstairs and ate whatever goods my mother had prepared for me. I thanked God at the dinner table for the food he gave us, but I don't remember how much I believed that he was responsible for those gifts. Then my parents started a coal fire in the hibachi and the world started feeling pretty livable again. The wind was howling and the north wall of our bedroom was like ice to the touch and dripping water when I breathed near it. Nobody knew anything about insulation back then. The wet concrete walls made me fear that my father might think the place was unhealthy for me like the previous apartment we had, which was supposed to be bad for my rheumatism, and decide to move again. I liked this house and wanted us to stay put. The heat from the hibachi couldn't have raised the bedroom temperature more than a few degrees, but the hot coals were a life-giving sight and did provide some warmth sitting close by. We all wore a couple of sweaters, and it took a lot of maneuvering to move from this bedroom to the other colder rooms in the apartment. We slept with a couple of heavy wool blankets and I used a chamber pot at night, rather than take a trip to the bathroom without any heat and, sometimes, without any lights, because electricity was also regulated. I remember listening to my parents' rhythmic breathing and feeling peaceful and secure.

I have no idea what I was thinking that night before I fell asleep, but I often thought of my mother travelling to the countryside to barter shoes for food. My father would buy shoes from various shoemakers in Athens and my mother would load herself up with shoes in sacks, find some friendly truckers from her native city of Eleusis, climb up on top of whatever load they carried and head for the northern villages, perched up in the open air and the elements in the summer. When the truck stopped, she would trade shoes for whatever staples the villagers had available. She brought home olives and olive oil, some small bags of wheat, beans and lentils, and one time a head of cheese, which we had to cut in pieces and keep in a large terracotta urn filled with brine so it could last a long time. It was comforting to know that the corner behind the bedroom wardrobe was never empty. I prayed that the Nazis never find our secret pantry and set us up on a wall to execute us.

In the evening, we would gather in the bedroom, and my mother would tell us stories about the people she met and the trades she made. She was gutsy, insistent and stood up for what was fair in a deal. If the merchant was particularly difficult, my mother would trump him by telling him that he was trying to starve her little child at home. She wasn't arguing for gain but for the life of her son. And she was good at this. She would tell us how she was able to travel on top of the trucks, holding onto ropes and the truck sideboards. She would tell stories of other travelers up high on the loaded trucks, or bouncing hard on an empty truck. She would tell us that the last trip was more comfortable than the previous one, whether the truck driver had a co-driver or had a seat in the cub for her, and how she managed to get through the various checkpoints the Nazis set up to catch saboteurs and black marketers. Her bright smile, her quick wits, and her ease in social interactions were all that stood between us and starvation. She was so happy with her accomplishments. Her labor had purpose and gave meaning to her life, no matter how dangerous and how hard it was. I must have fallen asleep that cold winter night with such thoughts in my mind. I was safe. My stomach was full. I would thank God for whatever help he gave my mother, no matter what role he had played in our lives that day.

During my mother's travels I was alone at home while my father was at work. If I wasn't sick, I would spend my time reading and playing in the apartment, or go out in the street and join my friends for a multitude of games with a wood sword hanging out of my belt, and various items like marbles, beer-bottle tops and candy wraps all of which were used to gamble and win or lose depending on skill, luck and occasionally by a fight. Sometimes, when I was done with my schoolwork, and it was cold outside, I would put on a robe and a cape as bishops of the Orthodox Church do, fastening with safety pins my mother's gold embroidered table runners and pillow coverings to make a phelonion and look as regal as a bishop does, and I would sing hymns from the Orthodox liturgy of Saint Chrysostom in front of the wardrobe mirror, making all the appropriate moves for censing, blessing and sprinkling of holy water. Every time my mother was gone I prayed that she would return to us unharmed. She always did.

As I take myself back to that part of my life, I find that God was normally found within the web of rites, rituals, sacred objects and images of the church. It seems to me now that Jesus Christ was contained within the space and time of the church by the clergy's position and authority. Religion was seamlessly interwoven to the national dreams and aspirations of the people, regardless of their faith. The rule of Christ over the church wouldn't become real for me until I was a young man. When I was close to my retirement years I became very interested in the role of the church and wrote a book with a critical appraisal of the Orthodox Church in America, which would apply to Greece as well. It wouldn't be outlandish to find a connection between my later view of the Church organization in the book I wrote and the thoughts passing like clouds in my childhood dreams until the sun shone through them. A priest of the neighborhood was owner or teacher in my grade school and I always would find something to discuss, debate, disagree or confess.

Now I return to that cold night as I lay in my bed, drifting to sleep seeded by dreams of my mother's daring travels for food and my parents' breathing. I had been asleep for quite some time when screams crushed my dreams and woke me up. Mother was screaming. She was shaking my father, trying to wake him up. But he wouldn't move.

"Open the window," she shouted. I jumped and opened the door, terrified. "Open the window!" she screamed.

I didn't know why. Did we want the freezing night in our bedroom? It sounded crazy, but I obeyed. She was beyond mania. The cold wind filled the room. I approached the bed and saw my father's ashen face. One of his arms was hanging down his side of the bed. I took that arm and started shaking him, screaming at him to get up. My mother slapped him over and over again. My head felt heavy, hard to turn it. My mother jumped out of bed and opened the door and another window in the other room to get a breeze. My head was throbbing. Wind rushed inside. I breathed the icy air with lust. I felt cold but my head was clearing up. My mother run with the hibachi out of the room to the kitchen sink, cursing the coals, until the sizzling water she poured over them drowned her anger. She took it out to the tiny back yard we had and slammed the door.

We managed to wake my father up and helped him sit in bed. He was babbling. We turned him over, tried to lift him. I don't know how, but we forced him to stand up next to a chair for support. Then he took a few steps. He was sick, and we helped him to reach the bathroom. A faint light, from a flashlight with a dying battery was turned on, and for a moment, I watched him drop on the toilet. When he stirred, I closed the door. We didn't want him passing out again. My mother told me to wait outside. As long as I could hear him breathe and cough and move,

I wasn't afraid. Terror was in the stillness of his sleep, in the silence of the dark, not in the sounds of sickness.

We helped him back to bed. After a while, some color returned to his face, and his eyes became calm, focused. We shut the windows and the bedroom connecting door again. I went beside him and watched him breathe and felt hope trickle in me. We had won this round. My mother was putting cold, wet compresses on his forehead, because that is what she always did when headache struck any person for any reason. I would like to write that he placed his hand on my head and smiled at me, but I'm not sure that this happened, so I cannot say it. Then, he turned toward my mother and I thought he smiled to her. I also imagined my mother saying "Try and get some sleep. It'll be fine now." She would say something like this and plead and smile back at him. She leaned over him, removed the wet compress and kissed his forehead. After a while he fell asleep, but my mother kept her vigil by his side. I went back to my bed, thanking God for having kept us alive. He had shown me one way he could help. The cold, somehow, seemed very friendly now. As long as I felt cold I knew no one would die.

The next day, I learned all about carbon monoxide poisoning. My mother swore never to allow the use of the hibachi for any reason whatsoever inside the house again. She straightened my hair that morning with more than her usual tenderness and told me how she came to be awake just in the nick of time to save us all from certain death.

"I was asleep," she said. "I was dreaming that my cousin, Michael, was riding his motorcycle when I was a girl. It was a big monster machine and made a lot of noise, but he was a gentle man and I wasn't afraid," she said and stopped. She seemed to need courage to go on. "In my dream he was headed straight at me. I felt I couldn't move. I believe that he wanted to run me down He was trying to kill me," she whispered in disbelief. "Stop! Stop!" she screamed, just as she had done in her nightmare. "But he kept coming, like Death himself," she said. "The apprehension receded from her face. "I woke up and he was gone. Then I felt my splitting headache and the hibachi coals stunk," she said.

"It wasn't my cousin Michael," she said as if she could see a new world now. That was the Archangel Michael, who woke me up!" she said in holy veneration, her voice becoming a whisper as she crossed herself in the way of the Orthodox Christians. I tried to understand how one Michael could turn to another one. "The Archangel wasn't trying to run me down; he was trying to wake me up!" She turned her head up at the icons high on the wet wall. "Thank God!" she said and crossed herself again. I crossed myself, admiring the power of the winged motorcyclist.

3

Grade School Rebel

I went to school at The United Pedagogical Grade School, a little dinky private school, run by Father Haralambos, the senior priest of the local Saint Mary's Greek Orthodox church. All the teachers I had were lay people, except for the fifth and sixth grade's combined class, which was taught by another priest, Father Constantine, or Papa-Kostas, for short. Papa-Kostas was the assistant priest and became the senior priest and schoolteacher after the Communists killed Father Haralambos during the December uprising. Most of the teachers were big on discipline, but they were also caring and knew their stuff well. Papa-Kostas was a judgmental, authoritarian, who believed that his way of teaching was the best way to educate his students. He wanted us to succeed and would use all his resources to that end. He tempered his autocratic style with humor and a healthy desire to explore whatever subject came up in class, as long as he had the last word. All teachers were determined to pound the fundamentals into our heads, one way or another and I was always ready to show them that only things that made sense would be accepted by me. Acting this way, I learned that there were boundaries that could only be crossed at a cost. I was never aware of spiritual errors in my ways, so I would jump to answer any question the teacher asked, before any other student had a chance to answer, as if that was my duty. I was disciplined with a ruler for my misbehavior or given long writing assignments, like "write the first five lines of a poem a hundred times with no error". If you make an error you have to do it all over again for the next day.

I believe, that I got a first-class primary school education, which includes a good start in critical thinking and problem solving as well as understanding the basics of ethical and responsible conduct. By the time I graduated from that little grade school I had a good grasp of the Greek language and children's literature, orthodox theology, the history and geography of the country, and I could deal with decimals, fractions and all the basics of arithmetic. I was hungry for knowledge, but we had no books around, and the school kept the encyclopedia locked in the school office, and wouldn't let me in. Several years later I would walk a few miles to borrow a book from the library of one of my father's friends, or read old magazines my father gathered from his colleagues at work and brought home to me. I knew more about Luther, Sigmund Freud and happenings in the Argentine pampas than I knew about Plato and Aristotle, because the pamphlets were randomly given. And there were a couple of novels with a couple of chapters read and many more imagined.

When I started getting an allowance, or earned some dollars singing Christmas Carols, I started buying my own encyclopedia in magazine form. By the time I left for America I had reached the letter E of the "Helios" Encyclopedia and had learned all about Aristotle's fixation on facts as the beginning of all knowledge, but had no idea about Plato's Cave, so I had only a slight advantage in my first humanities class at MIT, which covered both.

From the start, I was a good student, combining several qualities of success: hard work, adequate smarts, imagination, resilience and good sense in taking risks. My way of learning was to ask questions, lots of questions, about every aspect of any topic, and study hard, even though I would usually start late, and leave a lot of things for the last minute. In class, there were times when I knew I ought to remain silent, but felt I owed it to myself, the class and the teacher to speak out; and there were times when I knew I should have kept my mouth shut, but didn't and paid for it one way or another, including humiliation. Inquisitiveness was sometimes perceived to be disrespect, or rebelliousness, and was punished by additional work. When I recited the Nicene Creed and made a mistake on one word of the last sentence I paid for it with writing the creed, I don't remember how many times.

Teachers sent reports to my parents, praising my academic performance but regretting my disruptive behavior in class. My father had a standard response: "Thank you for your efforts to instill excellence in my son, but I recommend stricter discipline to correct his disruptive behavior." I stepped over the line, but never because I hurt anyone physically, or cheated anyone, or because I was in any way unethical or hated anyone. I knew my parents didn't like the distinction of having the most rebellious son in the school, but I sensed, as kids, somehow, always seem to sense, that having such a smart and sassy kid didn't dismay them. Besides, wasn't my uncle Vassos, the Captain of a Submarine, who was admired by everyone in the family and loved by my mother, his little sister, the man who was later killed in a naval battle by a Nazi corvette, a rebel all his life? And what about his brother the poet, who jumped over the wall of the Military Academy of Greece he was attending and roamed Africa to see the world he didn't know and write poetry against the Fascists?

The teachers, feeling justified by my father's encouragement, would renew their efforts to crush my so-called rebelliousness, but to no avail. I would raise my hand, and answer the question before the teacher called on me, because I wanted to be first. And if the teacher asked the question of someone else, and he or she didn't have a quick response, I was there with an answer that was usually right on and out of order. Nobody told me that my competitive way had some drawbacks I might find o be deplorable. These moves were unacceptable not only to the authoritarians in the school, but also to the teachers who cared for our development, and I would be called to the front of the class for disciplinary action. I would be asked to stretch out my hand, palm up, so the teacher could land two, four or however many blows, with a two-foot-long oak ruler with a square section, he or she thought would make me behave properly. Some teachers hated this part of their job and delivered gentle blows; but, there were others, who struck with conviction, sometimes raising the ruler up high as if they were going to attack menacing Turkish soldiers.

When the teacher was Papa-Kostas, the priest, the rod whizzed through the air and the strikes he delivered were hard enough to make me wince and act more defiantly than ever. Nobody attributed my misbehavior to pride and envy, and nobody criticized me for these character flaws, an omission that would have spared me pain when I was humbled and taught me how to admire the rights of others. I had to be guided from within to learn about my humanity.

When other students asked questions, I listened with the same expectation of revelation that I had for answers to my questions. Because I found myself in this unusual situation of exploring under a more-or-less benevolent dictatorship, I have generally fond memories of my teachers and my student life. I always believed that Papa-Kostas, admired my guts and respected me as a person, so his harsh ways were born without lasting resentment. I had several friends in class and was always included in the games we played in the schoolyard and beyond. So, overall, in spite of the strict enforcement of rules by my teachers, and especially by Papa-Kostas, I feel that they did right by me, given what they knew about educating children at that time. I felt free to play by the rules or not, and that feeling empowered and helped me to be the kind of person I wanted to be: I felt free to do what I thought was the right thing to do, but always responsible to the authorities and to God. They were teachers who cared about us and showed it many times by answering our questions or praising our work. This reward and punishment regime I went through, taught me that sometimes you have to take the risk of being punished or being ridiculed, so you can learn what you want to know, and act the way you want to act, so others may learn what you know, rather than learn what the teacher or the boss or the authorities want you to know and conform to the rules of conduct without exceptions. That was me in the early years of my life. Taking the risk of speaking my mind when most people remain prudentially silent has always been my way of doing the best I can in the search for answers to real problems. But, as I was getting ready to make the transition to high school, I realized that I needed to become more deliberate in my actions. I set out to train myself, to postpone gratifications of all sorts. I remember practicing self-control by placing a piece of chocolate in front of me as I studied and let it stay there for hours before I decided to eat it. When I had just enough money to buy my favorite Eskimo ice-cream bar, I would purposely skip it and save the money for another day. It took me a couple of years of saving the money I earned singing carols on Christmas, going door to door in the neighborhood and later in busses, to buy the chess set I had always wanted. I was seven or eight. I applied this self-control of my impulses to all sorts of situations until I was good at it. And when I had it down to a science, I felt free to be impulsive or cautious at will.

In spite of my rebellious way, my parents believed that I was responsible and exceptional all along. They trusted my ability to know and do the right thing, but didn't trust me to choose and do what they wanted me to do.

My mother had many ways and means of finding out where I had been and what I had been doing. She was a master networker, before networking was conceived. She talked to my friends and their parents about all sorts of little things, always fishing for details on my conduct. People liked to confide in her and my friends were easy pray for the clever ways she had for picking their brains. When I disobeyed her rules to stay safe and took a tumble or two on the gravel pits, or climbed barefoot the mounts of broken glass from beer bottles to collect bottle caps for gambling games in the streets, as I did a couple of times, my mother knew and threatened to let my father know of such daredevil acts, but she never did. I usually would present her with arguments that convinced her that I had thought about all the dangers she was dreaming of and had come up with solutions that made sense.

When I came home with a bruise or a scraped knee because I got into a fight, my mother would invariably blame me for being the instigator and never saw me as the victim. Somehow, it would never occur to her that some bully in the streets could get the best of her precious intimidating son. Ergo, I was the perpetrator of all misfortunes in the streets of Neos Cosmos.

I was, indeed a fierce defender of all my body parts, but never an attacker. Once, I got into a fight with Vous, one of the older and tougher kids that hung around the neighborhood and played in the streets with us. He was built like a bull. He was much too strong for me to tackle when he kicked me in a soccer game we were playing. Moments later, I found my head being squeezed between his knees. I remember the utter silence I felt because my ears were completely plugged up. I tried to wiggle out of the lock but he kept pushing me down and squeezing my head. And, then, out of desperation, I did something I had never done before and would never do again: I sensed a moment when he eased his hold and I turned my head just enough to get my teeth around the tendons at the side of his knee and bit him. He howled and let me go. I stood up and we stared at each other fuming with fury.

The Nazis and the Fascists left us alone in school, but when the Communists took over and were running things in the neighborhood, they made us sing the communist *Internationale*, and started giving us some indoctrination that they hoped would attract us enough to join the youth organization of the party. I remember that most guerrilla soldiers had beards, carried machine guns that hang from their shoulders and called each other "comrade" in the streets. After the government wrested control from them, and the Truman Doctrine was implemented in 1947, we sung the Greek National Anthem and learned a lot about the friendliness of American sailors and the help we got from the American people. I remember clearly that I was in a cub scout meeting when someone burst in the room and announced with a joyous cry that uncle Truman, leader of the free world, had decided to help Greece fight the communists. The Greeks wanted to befriend Americans in uniform, and the kids would gather around the sailors from the fleet that docked in Piraeus as if they were groupies following movie stars.

Later, Greece became one of the great supporters of the Korean War effort, fighting with the Americans. Immigration to America was an opportunity most Greeks considered a godsend. The word "nylon" came to symbolize the latest advances in technological progress and became the "cool" thing to have or be in the Greek Fifties. America was admired as the savior of Europe for its inspiring constitution, its helping hands of AID and USIA, and its Fulbright Scholarships and Grants of all kinds. America was the hope of the world through its leadership in founding the United Nations with the life-sustaining agencies of UNRA and UNESCO and WHO later on; and America was the guarantor of a future through the NATO alliance, which was committed to the defense of the free nations in Europe. No one could ever imagine that anyone would tear down the love and admiration we felt for the land of Liberty.

Right after our liberation from the Nazis, grade school students, learned all about the generosity of the American people by surviving on the K-Rations that the American military distributed at the school. We didn't know English, but it took only a day to figure out that the best box of food to get was the blue one with the word "Dinner" on it. Capitalism was in full swing among the street-smart school children of a more or less free Greece. Everyone wanted blue boxes and knew how to calculate the relative value of any two kinds of boxes in an exchange. So, we came to like the Americans, because they brought us freedom and were generous in helping us survive when our country was down. I dreamed of going to America someday and doing my best to excel.

Papa-Kostas wasn't only a demanding teacher and a strict disciplinarian but also a man who enjoyed lively exchanges of ideas with students. Unfortunately, he didn't know that his approach to education could frighten some of the timid souls in class and, perhaps, cause them to perform poorly. I didn't mind the harsh discipline or being put on the spot because I always wanted to explore ideas, but I'm not sure others felt the same way. And, I might have learned more about obeying authority than I did by fear.

Even so, I didn't rebel in class the one time I should have done so, and I regret my silence to this day. It happened when a teacher decided to punish Krokas, probably the poorest and most troubled kid in the class. Krokas was big for his age, but a little clumsy and slow. He seemed unable to learn much, because he couldn't answer the questions the teacher asked him in class. He was scruffy, and a repulsive odor emanated from his nose that forced you to stay away from him.

Anyway, no one had much to do with Krokas, and he was usually left to himself. Everyone suspected that he was a church charity case and tolerated him. The teachers had tried to get him to learn every way they knew how, but had no success. So, when Krokas did something in the back of the room that disrupted the class for the third or the fifth time, one of the teachers decided to punish him in a way I had never seen before. He took out two smooth pebbles from the ceramic pot that held a plant by the window near his seat, placed the pebbles on the floor and ordered Krokas to kneel on top of them in front of the class. We all winced, and I felt a great scream arise in my mind, but I said nothing. I thought that this was torture, and I wanted to protest, but I was as inert as a stone. Krokas took the punishment without showing pain, but I knew he was in pain and I was angry at the teacher and myself. Fear must have tamped down my anger and compassion, and I was left with the shame that comes when we fall short of the expectations we have of ourselves. I thought about this failure of myself and vowed not to repeat it. The coward knows when he fails and makes up all sorts of reasons to prove that he was wise in doing nothing. Sometimes I wonder what happened to Krokas. I never spoke to him, either before or after his punishment, but I have thought of his courage and his dignity in taking his punishment more often than I have thought about many other things that seemed important back then.

I often gave a voice to what others wanted to say but didn't want to risk saying it. Later in life I tried to understand why it was so hard for me to be more obedient in grade school. As I matured, this rebelliousness was appropriately channeled and became disciplined inquisitiveness, probing, exploration and, most of all, an impulse to dig in until the hidden was revealed. In math, I would labor to solve classic problems Jesuits had formulated hundreds of years previously; in literature, I wouldn't close the book, until I also understood the theme, the reason for the existence of the book and its connection to other, similar books. In class, I asked questions until I had some answer to the why of a battle, or the cause of a famine, or the reason God might have had for asking Abraham to sacrifice his son, Isaac. In a class on religion, I asked professor Keramidas what the difference was between morality and lawfulness. He said that lawfulness was doing the right thing because you were afraid of being "caught by the pincer of the prosecutor," whereas morality was doing the right thing because you chose to do the right thing. I also asked stupid questions and was ridiculed by my professors or was humbled by my laughing classmates. Long ago, I had decided to live on the edge and did so.

In later years, when I was a Director in a large corporation, I spoke out against authoritarian managers, and argued with executives for changes in company policies to improve the work life. These actions made me feel that I was doing something worthwhile. I have always been the person who asked questions, and when asked, I answered questions as openly and passionately as I could. Often, I feel that if I don't expose a speaker's one-sided arguments I am negligent, fearful or cowardly.

When I heard for the first time upon coming to America, the expression, "You have to stand up and be counted," I felt that I had found an old pair of missing shoes that fit me perfectly and would always feel comfortable wearing them. There were times when I even thought that I would put on my gravestone the words "He stood up to be counted." I must also admit that many years ago, taking a stand against the power brokers was heroic, and fed my voracious ego. Feeling the glory of goodness when you cut down monsters, robs you of the bits of goodness you gained in the battle. You lose when you win that way. It's hard being good all the time. Perhaps, impossible.

And, my motives haven't always been as noble, as it may appear: Sometimes I wanted the recognition of people I respected and acted in ways that gather their respect or, if doable, their admiration. Wanting hard to win, to excel, to stand out and be recognized, were important to me back then. I've always wanted to become better than I was. But, I cannot deny that I'm also selfish, victim of a deadly pride. I want to ditch it and do what I am good at doing without inflation of my ego. There are many of us straightening out the world. And a loving and powerful God is working on our side. But, pride sticks like Velcro on my skin.

4

Surviving the Occupation.

"The best political weapon is the weapon of terror. Cruelty commands respect. Men may hate us. But we don't ask for their love, only for their fear."
Heinrich Himmler, leading member of the Nazi Party

"Gentleness is the antidote for cruelty."
Plato

"But to you who are listening I say: Love your enemies, do good to those who hate you." (Matthew 5:44)
Jesus Christ

T he hunger I felt every evening, sitting on the marble stoop of our apartment building, intensified as the food supplies dwindled. The Nazi army got most of the food in the country for itself, and the population had to live with the leftovers. Statistics from a study of the US Department of Defense show that in the winter of 1941-1942 infant mortality in the Athens area, according to the Germans, rose from 6 percent to 50 percent. It was reported in a USA Department of Defense Report that of every ten children born during that time, only one lived more than a month. More people were dying in the streets from starvation, or were frozen to death than from any disease. The black market was one of the ways to get food by those who could afford it. People sold everything valuable they had to get enough money to afford buying food in the black market. We heard that people sold their homes for five gallons of olive oil. But, becoming involved in any way with the black market or bartering increased the odds of getting caught and being hanged in public by the Nazis. My parents decided it was too dangerous to continue bartering for food, and my mother's traveling days ended. We had to focus on finding food around us. Soup kitchens for children were set up in schools and factories, and we had to wait patiently our turn for a bowl of lentil soup and a slice of bread. My father was prowling the streets looking for philanthropic groups, catholic nuns, the Red Cross and some foreign Philanthropic organizations which distributed spaghetti, beans and other staples from time to time.

Some kids with even less food from home than I had, needed more than the soup kitchens could provide. They waited for shopkeepers to empty their garbage and rummaged in the cans for anything that one could eat without dropping dead from spoiled food. Finding the rind of a lemon was hitting the jackpot. I had never thought much about lemon rinds, but Little Beggar, one of the kids in my neighborhood group, who stopped by the stoop of Kortessis sometimes, a garbage connoisseur, told us that lemons had vitamins to give you a healthy body. He also told us that there were some German officers, who found it entertaining to throw their leftovers to barefoot children in the street and watch them fight over them. They would point to the one who managed to get some chicken leg or the leftover of a pork chop and cheer him on, while jeering the losers.

Beside depriving us of our food supplies, the Nazis imposed punishing rations. The bread ration in the winter of 1941-1942 in the Athens-Piraeus area, normally 406 grams per day in peacetime, averaged between 84 and 137 grams that winter. Although Hitler himself had gone to pains to pay tribute to Greek heroism and to assure the Greeks that he respected their classical heritage, Axis food policies made it only too obvious that the victor was willing to let the Greeks starve. We were expendable. We couldn't understand that at our young age, but we were afraid of the Nazi presence, even when they were just passing by. It took me years to relax when I happened to smell leather, because the smell of Nazi leather boots had stamped fear on my soul.

Many years later, I read an article based on a psychotherapist's research that showed the Nazis were the most fearful people on earth and to avoid their "angst" terrified people everywhere. Fear spread in many directions. Like a deadly gas. I remember the time when a horse-drawn cart from city hall went past the iconographer's room, and Cleo's house, beyond the yard with the empty bus with rotting seats that stunk, until it reached the two-room apartment of kyr-Argyris, the candy maker, and stopped at a house beyond it. I waited outside, taking in the stench that oozed out of that cart. I hadn't known the smell of death in human beings. Then, I saw the body of a young woman being brought out the door on a stretcher. Two workers drew the tarp to the side, covered the body with the tarp, and tossed it on top of other bodies, as if it was a sack of potatoes. Somebody said that she was the poor relative of kyr-Argyris' family, working as a maid for his neighbor's family, as if that would explain the absence of any crying and lamentations. I run away.

There were reports at the time that people in their despair buried the dead out in the open fields without reporting the deaths, so they could continue using their food coupons and collect their portion of food and bread. And for every dead person there were a dozen others sick, limping or freezing in the streets. There were reports of people dropping off and dying in basement wells and the open streets. Sometimes, a passerby would fall down and stay down. The newspapers reported that passersby would stop and minister to the fallen, and other times they would look down and walk away, as helpless to act as the fallen. The mood of the population grew darker, and a horrible thought began to take hold of our consciousness: the Nazis didn't care if we all died. Death came without a reason; it came because we were Greeks. Yet, the struggle to survive went on. But, this will to wipe out life itself, gave meaning to our going on with life. I remember no time that I felt hopeless. I cannot recall any people who committed suicide, though I'm sure there must have been some.

The inflation skyrocketed. You needed a bundle of money to buy a loaf of bread and a shoebox full of bills to buy a pair of shoes. The price of a newspaper climbed from two drachmas to thousands of drachmas in one year, and by the time the war ended, four years later, it cost 25 million drachmas to buy a newspaper. People realized that survival was worth all the possessions they had. The Nazis wanted to find Greeks to blame for the scarcity of food and found a few black-marketers, now and then, to be suitable scapegoats. They hanged several from posts in public places to discourage the practice and show the people that they were just protecting their interests. The people hated the black-marketers, but knew that the siphoning of food by the occupiers was the main cause of their misery, not the few dozen people the Nazis hanged from electricity posts.

There were long lines outside grocery stores, butcher shops, bakeries and any other places where rumor had it that food was being sold. People waited their turn in long queues, but vigilantly, which means that they were always trying to cut corners and move a little closer to the food distribution point, if nobody stopped them. They knew that whatever goods were for sale would run out before all the potential buyers could buy what they needed to survive, and tried to make it before the cutoff point was reached.

You had to be alert, ready to defend your place and nip in the bud by loud protest, by shoving and elbowing and kicking any attempt by anyone to get ahead of you. And you had to make sure no one was attempting to get in line by "tangential attachment," which started with greeting someone on the line, progressed to discussion of news and other pleasantries and ended up with the newcomer attaching himself or herself to the person greeted, usually, way ahead of where that friend would have had to stay in the queue, if he or she had any sense of fairness and civility left in that world of urgent need, deception and brokenness. I used the second person too many times above and I know why: I wanted to be friendly and kind and gentle and compassionate, but "you had to be alert" and aggressive, and angry, ready to get but never to give, so that the "you" could, perhaps, hide the shame of the creature I was becoming. Fighting against a "glue-on" wasn't much of a noble goal, but it was a meaningful experience, especially if it included benefits for others in the family.

When I told some of these stories to my American friends in college, they always felt sorry for us. I always tried to explain: yes, we suffered a lot back then, but we weren't depressed or suicidal; I never felt lonely or lost hope. There was always something to get – call it achieve; a way to get the last potato in the grocer's barrel and win; make a trade of zucchini with the lady in the back, who liked them and would probably be gone by the time she got to the bin, if she would get a cauliflower, (or two?) for us. And, there was also banter, humor and laughter on the line that made time pass more tolerably. The darkness of our situation was smudged because we made a kind of game of it.

I caught a glimpse of Cleo ahead of me on one of the waiting lines. She never turned back to look. She was talking to another girl her age and wasn't paying attention to her line placement. I saw a man trying to push himself ahead of her. "One small step for him and no step from anyone else.," I thought. I knew his game and I was troubled. I was ready to leave my place, rush ahead and protest, but Cleo, turned toward the "attached-on" and smiled at him. The man backed away and crawled to the place where he had come from. Cleo was in the last years of high school and all I could do was admire her, wish that she learn English and wait until I was ready for a trip to America.

During those days of lean cows in Athens, funerals were another good happening for us kids. Somehow, people always managed to send off their loved ones with a generous serving of kolyva, which consist of boiled wheat grains with plenty of sugar frosting, red pomegranate seeds and candied almonds, as is the custom in the Greek Orthodox Church. We would fight over our portion of a handful of kolyva and attack anyone who dared go after a second serving before we did. Kolyva was the only candy we could get in those days of scarcity and grief, and we blessed the dead from the heart and the belly.

We were determined to survive one way or another and learned the costly ways of doing so. We learned to hide, protect and cherish what we had both as individuals, but also as a group. The dire needs we all felt forced us to mistrust strangers, keep secrets, take risks that help us win contests without stealing or lying. We wanted to be good, because we were afraid of the priests and God. I was a much older man when I realized that I wanted to be as good as I could be, because I felt God was my friend and wanted to please him. It was a revelation I wish I had understood in my early years. I had no idea that it's so much easier to be good if you want to be that way, rather than having to be so. But, it's not that simple and it took some years to put it all together.

5

But for One Boiled Potato

When German soldiers appeared in the streets, the kids would run for cover and the adults would bow their heads down and look busy with whatever they were doing. Rumors of arrests for black marketeering, for espionage, for stealing from the "protectors of the homeland" and other offenses and crimes would sweep the neighborhood and intensify the fear that weighed down our lives. The newspapers always showed photographs of those who had been found guilty of crimes against the people, hanging from poles or set up blindfolded against walls waiting for execution. The Nazis called themselves "protectors of the Greek people" and were quick to blame five or ten crooks every once in a while, for the famine raging in Athens, rather than tell us that they were the ones sucking off the lifeblood of the population. The crimes reported were always such that the people would be satisfied with the punishment: stealing foodstuffs from public warehouses, gouging people with exorbitant prices in selling olive oil, bringing to market spoiled legumes, selling dog meat and calling it goat meat and other such violations hated by the starving citizens. Some believed the propaganda, but most were silent and kept their fury hidden from the conquerors. Some thought that there were people out there who sabotaged the occupation forces but when they were caught were branded as black marketers instead of being celebrated as heroes.

There were rumors that people were taking to the mountains and starting to organize a resistance movement. Most of the rebels were communists or leftists; some were royalists and right-wingers and organized separately. The newspaper I was now able to read was full of stories about victories of the Axis forces and defeats of the Allies. I learned the word "propaganda" from the neighbors' whispers as they talked about the large, gaudy and ever-present newspaper pictures. The most widely available news magazine of the Axis Forces was called "synthema", which means password, in Greek. A password was used in the Eleusinian Mysteries at Eleussis by the initiates, indicating their willingness to be part of the rites. The Nazis stole the Greek and I spent a lot of time reading that propaganda rag because it was cheap. That's when I started cutting out pictures from the magazine and learned the German uniform insignia as I had learned all of them for the Greek army and navy ranks. I also learned the names of all the allied and German aircraft used in the war – the Spitfire, the de Havilland, the DC-3 or "Dakota," the Stuka, the Younkers the Fokker and the rest. After the victory of the Allies, I threw away the Nazi insignia and learned all the insignia for the American armed forces, studying the pamphlets my father brought home from work.

All of us were careful not to provoke any German soldiers in any way while playing in the streets. We were afraid of them not only for what they did, but mainly for what they could do. I was too young to know how the Nazis robbed and killed innocent civilians, but the evil was in the air around them, and even children like me could smell it in their boots, belts and stares.

Later, many historians and chroniclers documented the brutality of the German military during their occupation of Greece. Mark Mazower in his book, "Inside Hitler's Greece", based on hundreds of supporting documents, recounts some of the events that show the hatred these people had for the people they enslaved. I paraphrase below his description of some of the atrocities committed by the solders of "the master race" as the occupation went on and the people started to resist. I do this to show that the deprivations my family and I had to put up with were small compared with the horrors many other Greeks suffered.

In June 1944, in one of the worst atrocities of the entire war, a Waffen-SS unit on patrol against the guerrillas entered the village of Distomo and ran amok, massacring several hundred people in their homes. A Red Cross team which arrived from Athens a couple of days later even found bodies dangling from the trees that lined the road into the village. The SS commander Fritz Lauterbach claimed that his troops had been fired upon with mortars, machine guns and rifles, but the German Secret Field Police agent, Georg Koch, had accompanied the troops that day and revealed that this was untrue.

In Kalavryta, a town in northern Peloponnesus, the Wehrmacht troops shot 696 Greeks and burned twenty-five nearby villages. Greek Government sources, (as reported in the USA Department of Defense Report AD 272833, "Case Study in Guerrilla War: Greece During World War II," by D. M. Condit), state that 1770 villages lay in ashes by the end of the occupation in 1944. The massacre was done according to the reprisal policy laid down by the German authorities . . . Near the beginning of the occupation the German Command had issued precise quotas for reprisals: 50 to 100 hostages were to be shot for any attack on, or death of a German soldier; 10 if a German was wounded, and so on. In practice such horrific guidelines proved unworkable, but the tenor of the order was adhered to. As early as December 1942, Field Marshal Keitel had issued the reprisal policy, which included the following: "The troops are therefore authorized and ordered in this struggle [against the Resistance] to take any measures without restriction even against women and children if these are necessary for success. [Humanitarian] considerations of any kind are a crime against the German nation . . ." The massacre at Kalavryta horrified even the German Ambassador Neubacher. He had the German consulate general report from the scene and demanded an investigation by the Theater Commander. "It is much more comfortable," he wrote to him with some irony, "to shoot to death entirely harmless women, children and old men, than to pursue an armed guerrilla band."

Of course, not all German soldiers were killers. My father continued to work at the munitions plant, which had been converted to a maintenance depot for aircraft engines headed for Rommel's army in North Africa and used to say that the Germans left you alone, if you did your job and obeyed their rules. The officers occupying my maternal grandmother's house and my uncle's house in Eleusis, were also said to be ordinary people who missed their families back home.

I recall the time when mother and I were going to visit my mother's friend, Pinio, and a strange thing happened to us on the way there. As we were passing by a fenced yard where German soldiers had their barracks, we saw a giant stirring something with a ladle in a black kettle over a woodfire. We stopped to watch, and I wondered what marvelous food might be in that steaming kettle. The giant turned and saw me hanging from the wire fence. He smiled, and my mother motioned to him that I was hungry. She first pointed at me and then, bunching her fingers together, she pretended to devour whatever they were supposed to hold, including their present nothingness. I stared with suspicion. The man was a soldier, wearing the trousers of his uniform, held by wide suspenders, but having only a khaki long-sleeve undershirt. He dug into the black cauldron with his ladle and brought up a huge steaming boiled potato. He smiled looking at us and came toward us slowly, swinging the cradled potato to cool it. He stood behind the fence, cupped his hands together to show us what to do, then forced the potato through the grid with his hand and the handle of the ladle. My mother and I caught the crumbling pieces in our cupped hands on the other side of the fence and thanked him. The potato was still hot, but we were hungry and we blew on the pieces and tossed them from one hand to the other and ate what could be eaten without burning our mouths. The soldier pointed at me and said something in German that we couldn't understand. Then he reached into his back pocket, and pulled out of his wallet the picture of a woman and a child about my age. He pointed to the picture and then to himself several times to indicate togetherness, and my mother gave him the sign of approval for the wonderful family he had.

"Heinrich," he said pointing to the child in the photo.

"Tolis," my mother said, tapping me on the head. Tolis is my

Greek nickname before one of my English teachers Americanized it to "Tolly," when I was getting ready to leave for America. "Hans," he said and we joined palms on either side of the fence.

We thanked him several times and he kept saying that it was nothing, raising his huge hands up by his shoulders and waving them at us, as if trying to erase the writing on some imaginary blackboard with wide sweeping strokes. We were still eating the potato pieces as we walked away. "Nice man," my mother said. "He must miss his wife and son." I looked at her but I didn't understand. I couldn't imagine a "nice" German soldier at the time. But, the "Potato-Man" was a good man and one of "them." I couldn't quite fit both thoughts in the morality of the universe I knew, and that seemed to be a good problem to have.

6

A Chapel Made of Love and Junk

Before the Nazi occupation, my father was promoted to a supervisor of the materials section at the munitions plant where he was employed. He took me along once and showed me the huge presses that shaped bullets out of brass "buttons," and the power saws which cut off the brass rods to make the brass "buttons". I liked the smell of the lubricating fluids that kept the rod and the saw blade cool. Sixteen years later I would be writing my Master's thesis in Mechanical Engineering at MIT, based on the temperature measurements I was making on the spinning workpiece in various lathe operations. The smell of the lubricating oil was the same, but the world was different. We also visited the underground secret shelters of the factory, where, I imagined, they stored ammunition, huge long tunnels, well lit, apparently impenetrable. Inside the plant, my father wore his red, round, security badge on his lapel, and I had a green visitor's badge on and held my father's hand proudly. He introduced me to people he worked with, and they all were very welcoming as they explained what they did. I must have been less than seven years old because after that the Germans were using the factory to repair their fighter planes and there was no way I could have been allowed there.

We stopped at the guarded gate and my father told the guard that we would go to the "Project" for a few minutes. The guard greeted me and urged me to take off my beret. I used to wear a beret all the time, "to protect my ear from the cold," I was told. I took off the hat and felt naked, but I was ready to explore and didn't mind it. My father showed me his "Project" with a joyful smile I rarely saw in him.

"I'm building a little chapel for Saint Barbara," he said as we went inside and admired the little church. "Saint Barbara is the protector of artillery people and heals ear aches," he explained.

I wondered how significant this dual purpose was, but I figured it out after a few minutes.

"We have a lot of packaging equipment that we can use for building instead of tossing things out as garbage," he explained. He was proud of his work. I knew then that my dad had a goal to leave a lasting gift behind. My father also used his accounting knowledge to rebuild a much larger community church for us in Neos Cosmos. I know he felt that he was leaving another good thing behind. I have to say that I didn't feel I left any good thing behind when I worked as an engineer for a few months at a munitions plant. I knew at that time the Vietnam war was pointless and should have taught us a lesson about the time to fight, and the time to rest, but it didn't.

My father went on to explain the details of his "Project". "They gave me permission to build this little church," he said, as if he had to respond to some invisible guard and convince him that he had done nothing wrong.

It was a good day for both of us and always reminds me how he took care of me when I was sick and supported me in any way needed to show he cared. He came to all review meetings with my teachers at school and was present when I recited poems, and saw me every year when I received the first prize of the Ministry of Education for academic excellence. We had many differences when I was growing up, but I know he was proud that he contributed to my success. It happened that he understood grading and numbers, so we talked a lot about that, but he rarely engaged me on any topics other than performance in academics. He knew nothing about sports; he had no hobbies or other pastimes; he had seen only one movie in fifteen years and got all his news from the paper. And, he never talked to me about sex, or relationships with girls at any time, relying, perhaps, on my mother's social skills to handle such topics. Sometimes we discussed politics, but only in general terms because he didn't believe that it was prudent to disclose his voting preferences to anyone, though I knew he was at the center of the political spectrum. He didn't know the weight his high expectations for my performance piled on my back.

He was often preoccupied with problems at work and talked to my mother about them, expressing his feelings of disappointment and frustration with mediocre performers, slackers, retired military officers who acted dictatorially and people's disregard of ethical standards. From some discussions I overheard, I think he also felt mistreated by some of his superiors because they valued political skills and pleasantries more than results. He was determined to prove to the bosses above him, including the owner of the plant, that he deserved recognition and should be trusted with greater responsibilities. He never achieved the goal of becoming a director at the company.

Before the Nazis occupied Greece, my father, who was Section Chief of the Materials Section, buried all precious industrial diamonds and other expensive tools of the plant in caskets and buried them to protect them from the Nazis. After our liberation he dug up all the tools and presented them to Bodosakis, the owner of the company on New Year's Day. He had hoped for a promotion as a thankful gesture. Instead, he got to see Bodosakis, the great man, get a little extra cash and a few yards of cloth for a fancy suit from one of the owner's textile factories.

He came home that day and showed us the new bills he had received. It was a day drenched in sunlight and the bills were in mint condition with the striking reddish colors of higher denomination drachma bills. My mother and I hugged him and congratulated him hoping that a promotion would follow. He gave us a generous bonus and we spent some time talking of bigger and better things to come.

Every year my father would pay a visit to Bodosakis at the headquarters of the company, wish him a "Happy New Year," report to him the progress he had made, receive a bonus in cash, sometimes enhanced by a bundle of expensive cloth for a coat or a suit, and leave with promises of better things to come, which never did. One time a colonel got the promotion he had hoped for, and another time, a metallurgist. He didn't feel free to quit, as, I know, he would have wanted to do. He suffered and cried inside, but like many working people today, he stood at his post and took the pounding of the sly, the slickers with connections and the mighty owner. And the pounding took its toll and shrunk his emotional world, as it does for many working people everywhere. He finally had a heart attack at 53, due to stress, and left that rat race, quit smoking and lived another 33 years, many of them working productively, in good health and relative peace.

After he retired from the munitions plant, he worked for a contractor and helped to organize and control the finances for the construction of the largest steel mill in Greece. He was very sharp in accounting and knew tax law so well that in later years, after he retired from the contractor's company and had some free time, people from miles around would seek him out at his favorite kafenio and ask for his advice with their taxes, which he was glad to offer freely.

I know my father loved me, but he expressed his love with controlled warmth. As I became more independent and there was less need for his support, he gradually withdrew. He had a sense of humor, but we didn't see it very often. On the other hand, he was easily angered and could hold his anger for days. When my parents fought and distanced themselves from each other, I was often fearful and depressed. My mother would sometimes try to break the pall, but it wasn't always guaranteed that he would drop his utter isolation and rejoin the family. As a last resort, my mother would ask me to approach him in his solitary gloom and try to get him to reconcile. It was then that I learned some valuable skills of conflict resolution which were essential for the OD job I had later in life. Sometimes, my father would find a graceful way to break the isolation, and we'd all be back together again, laughing at any stupid thing that happened around us. Seeing my parents talking to each other again felt like Easter. I have always felt happiness come as a cloud engulfing me when angry people forgot their inner turmoil and laughed together. When I understood better who my father was and why he behaved so irrationally at times, I forgave him. Life had not been kind to him, and he carried the scars of his upbringing and his work life ordeals.

Many decades later, when I traveled to Greece and spent some time with him in his old age, I saw how frail and tender he was inside, and I could forget the anger and isolation with which he tried to cope in his earlier years and love him as a dear friend. We talked about some of the things I had always wanted to discuss with him – politics, economics, women, ethics, religion, work, writing, careers, life and death, the whole spectrum of the interests we shared but never discussed before.

One time he confided in me that he was disappointed because I had not been promoted from Director to Vice President at the company where I worked. I assured him I didn't choose to advance because I wouldn't be able to work close to people who loved power more than people. I tried to educate him that I wanted to create work life systems that gave workers more freedom and satisfaction at work. "And," I added poignantly, "If I became a Vice President, I wouldn't have any time left to be with my family, or write and teach, all of which are dear to me." I wanted time to solve problems that helped people, and be free to think, write and teach. And I wanted to enjoy life with my wife and children before they were growing up and would leave home someday soon. He looked at me mournfully but didn't respond. I don't think he ever believed my reasons for not wanting to ascent up the corporate ladder. He was sure that I wanted to advance but wasn't able, just as he had not been able to do. He was still sure that nobody would stop trying to get more money and recognition from those above him, if, with greater effort, he could. He didn't feel that, as a supervisor, he had the freedom to act, to create a dynamic and caring workplace, or just leave and get another job. I think he had lived some of his dreams of success through me and wasn't ready to drop the dreams he gave me and dream my own dreams for a while. He was one of millions of working people, who live many years of their lives without experiencing love for the work they do, or the friendship of their co-workers. I think that after he retired, he was recognized for his ingenuity by a small contractor with big dreams who made him the builder of one of the largest steel companies of Greece. He was at last recognized and free to create a great workplace. I think that some of my career choices later in life were made with the desire to empower the people who had to dream what they were not allowed to achieve.

7

Looking for Miracles

Our apartment was two blocks away from Saint Mary's Church in our neighborhood. The church was the biggest building in the neighborhood, had the most traffic of any other public place, and had become the assembly hall and center of communications for the entire neighborhood. When something happened in the community, any unusual action, criminal or heroic, threatening like a fire, or joyous like a victory in battle for the Allies, the news would spread from the courtyard of the church to the outer reaches of the neighborhood. Before the occupation of Greece by the Nazis, ringing the church bells heralded the victories our army scored against Mussolini's Fascists. After the occupation the church bells were muted, but we spread the news just as fast by noise and whispers.

I was playing a table game at the house of one of my neighborhood buddies when his mother came in and announced that there were people running to the church because there was a miracle happening inside. We all stopped playing and took off for the church. The rumor had spread like wildfire beyond our neighborhood that one of the icons in the church had tears running down from the face of a saint. I cannot remember whose icon it was – it could have been a saint, Holy Mary, John the Baptist or Saint Nicholas. Long lines formed outside the church. Many people were praying silently and crossing themselves. I must have been about ten years old at the time. Some older people were searching for the reasons of the miracle. They said these were tears of sorrow, shed for the ills our country suffered during the Communist Uprising, a fratricide, really, of 1945, after the Nazis were defeated. Others were saying that the tears were for the horrible sins we had committed and for which God had imposed a harsh punishment on us. The saints were lamenting our demise. I wanted to ask what sin had I committed which caused the tears on the icons, but I didn't want to create an incident, so I kept quiet. My goal was to witness a miracle, so I remained quiet.

I went to the church and waited in line with great anticipation and fear for what I might see. God knew I had doubts about miracles and he could punish me for that. I didn't try to hide. It took a long time for the queue to inch forward, and find myself in front of the icon. I crossed myself and lifted up my head so I could see. There were so many things going on around me – people talking, people lighting candles with smoke spreading all around, people shoving, shadows moving, people crossing themselves and whispering prayers, genuflecting and squeezing past one another, holding prayer beads, and feet shuffling and children crying. There was so much commotion that I was never able to study the icon carefully. One look and I was pushed past the icon, past the chance to experience a strange event that could shed light to my thinking. It would take decades and intensive study of the Bible to understand that God's miracles are everywhere, if only one knows how to look for them. In spite of my inability to secure the proof of a miracle, I never ceased to believe in the possibility of miracles, because I never ceased to believe that we were created by a powerful and demanding, God. Sometimes I loved God, but it didn't think that God would love me

At first, I believed that God would punish me on the spot, if I didn't obey his commands. He could scramble my speech, if I cursed; he could paralyze my hand, if I shoplifted; and, he could twist my head so I could only see behind me, if I looked at lewd things as some people said that he had done to a young man in Kallithea, another neighborhood of Athens. I was relieved to think that God did nothing to me for doubting his miracle, if there was one that I didn't see. But, I couldn't quite drop the idea that God would do something horrible to me, if I went astray. I took all that in and tried my best to obey.

God is the only person I have never wanted to rebel against. It seemed to me that it was pointless to rebel against an omnipotent God. I haven't figured out yet whether any Being can be God without being omnipotent, but I know there are some people who believe that God doesn't have to be omnipotent to govern his Creation. He doesn't overpower it, but woes it to move in ways that are best for all.

I'm not going to describe here all my attempts to witness and affirm some miraculous act, but I want to describe another event having to do with rumors of a miracle, because it all but extinguished my desire to keep searching for miracles and I started thinking of other ways that God may be using to guide his world toward the goals he has set.

I was older now, but I still visited the churchyard to see some of my old friends and play a table game in the little garden the church had created for the neighborhood kids. One sunny day, we stopped the game and half a dozen or so of us went to the Candle Workroom to watch the church sexton making candles. Shortly after that, a deacon came in the workroom and announced in an officious manner that there were miracles happening at last in downtown Athens. "The Lord is entering the battle," he said, with a voice that didn't allow questions. He said there were crosses that people saw in the windows of one of the tall buildings downtown Athens and crowds had gathered to see them. He was sure there would be an announcement in the paper. I left the candle-making operations with a couple of other guys and took a bus for Syntagma Square, trying to locate the building by what people might say or by spotting a crowd gathered outside some tall building. That was the way I used to go to my high school and I knew the area well. I was as alert as I could be. The sun was going down and I found people looking up at tall buildings for shiny crosses. I joined one of the crowds and saw people pointing at windows and claiming that they were seeing Crosses. I heard such things as "Fourth row from the top, five windows from the sunny side corner!" Once I saw a shining window, but I couldn't see the sign of the Cross. I asked where a man saw a cross. "Look at the Center of the building! It's where the sun is less bright and the Cross is at the center!" One of my friends said "I don't see anything but sunlight." A few people argued and some agreed and pointed in the same direction.

"There, there! Do you see it?" another friend said, all excited.

"Where? Where?" the rest of us screamed.

"There ae some straight lines on the window close to the middle of the fifth floor." I stared at the shaded windows, and the sunny windows, but couldn't see any straight lines in the middle of any window. Perhaps, I saw some parallel lines that might have been imperfections in the glass, but nothing like a Cross. I wasn't sure. I never could trust my vision anyway. Even with the glasses I was now obligated to wear, I couldn't see well. I relied on people, especially my friends, to agree, but they couldn't. There was no agreement in the crowd either. When most people could see the Fokkers and the Hurricanes chasing each other in the sky during the war, I was lost in stray clouds. My myopia required thick lenses, my vision was never reliable. I was depressed on my way back home. By the time we got back home, no one was sure that he had seen a cross on a window. I was deep inside myself as I imagined bright, luminous crosses on specific windows of a tall building. Wasn't such a Cross the vision of Constantine that made him a believer in Christ and started Christendom sixteen hundred years ago? I felt that God didn't want me to be included in the group of people who see his glory.

I thought of talking to Papa-Kostas, who was still my priest, but I was sure that the discussion would lead to some argument and I would come out of it feeling guilty of some sin or other which prevented me from seeing any miracles. I looked and looked for a long time, but I never was sure that I saw anything like a cross. I thought I saw a glimpse of a rainbow as from a film of oil on a glass surface – or was that my imagination, desperately trying to shore up what I thought was my shaky faith?

Regardless of the poor vision I had, I was all set to see a miracle. I had been looking for a miracle more persistently than most, but I wasn't sure what a miracle is. Isn't a baby's birth a miracle? I wasn't sure of anything. The possibility of things happening in the world in violation of physical laws was and is fascinating to me. But, it never occurred to me until I had experienced the world more fully as a young man and as an adult that there are other strange things that happen against all odds, that go beyond reasonable expectations, things that happen even though they have close to zero probability of happening. I have often thought of some of the things that happened to me in this way more as miracles than coincidences or rare events. I often thought that someday I'll lay bare my thoughts and write about the things I used to call coincidences, and other things, the times I had thought I had been lucky and the times when I realized that God had something to do with my life.

Sometimes strange events become the stuff of our sorrows or our joys. I was always interested in what was happening and what did it mean for the world, for people and for me. I wanted to know what makes life such a puzzle and what is the character of God who runs the show with us having some freedom to mess things up. I was with my friends in the field we called Alana, where we played all field games. That time, several of us had gathered, to play soccer with a ball made out of old socks, when Antony appeared and screamed that there was a killing near the gate of the Park of Byron. We all took off running north. None of us had seen a street killing before, but we all wanted to know what such an event looks and feels like. Who does such horrible things and how do people suffer such evil deeds?

There was a large crowd gathered by the gate of the park. I wiggled through a couple of rows of people arrayed in circles and froze in place. There was blood, a lot of blood on the ground.

"It's Cleo and Nikitas," a young man said as he arrived on the scene with a woman on his side. Immediately he turned around and blocked the view of the woman who was with him.

"Let me see!" she shouted. He pushed her back out of the circle in spite of her loud protests. I heard all that while I was trying to see the faces of the bodies on the ground.

"I know the guy," came the words of someone much taller than me. "He's a policeman; crazy about Cleo!" one of the people in front of me said as if a reporter was passing information.

"He knifed her first and slid his throat after," the man continued as if a senseless creature spewed facts to him. By this time, I knew whom they were talking about, but refused to believe it. Cleo was my friend and I didn't want her to be hurt.

"They are gone!" someone said and I was ready to kick or punch him. I asked God to save her. Antony found me in the tangled crowd and whispered to my ear:

"It's our Cleo." The ambulance arrived and the two fallen lovers disappeared. I never was able to see their faces, but I kept looking at the two pools of blood and feeling crushed by the presence of two people gone forever and what happens to the blood when it stays on the ground. I was angry and hated death. Not Cleo! I said again and again, as if the repetition would get rid of the evil done.

It was only a few weeks later when the word was out that Cleo was alive and well with a bandaged throat, and Nikitas, the cop, had been seen walking in the streets of Kallithea. I had a great feeling of being more than alive when I heard the news. I thought there might be a miracle somewhere in there. I called it a strange event, however, because I couldn't see any violation of natural laws, even though Antony and Domo disagreed with me. They insisted they could see that Cleo's head was split apart from the body and were angry with me and called me "Four Eyes" and bonehead. Before we split that night to go home, we agreed to thank God for fixing the evil deed his way. Could God have really heard the people who prayed for these two lovers?

Years later, when I visited Mount Athos I heard of many miracles taking place, but again, I never witnessed one myself. I was told that they opened the crypt of a saint in one of the monasteries there and found a candle that was burning for decades without being burnt out and without any oxygen in there. Then there were reports of a saintly monk seen by different people, hundreds of miles apart, but at the same time. One of the monks told us that every year on a certain date they filled a tank outside the monastery with water and a day later they found the water turned to olive oil. I asked if they ever had the water and the oil chemically examined, but the monk scoffed at me and told me they don't do such faithless acts up there. Then the same monk told our group that a sinner tried to kiss the icon we were looking at and was punished by having his lip stuck to the glass of the icon. I wasn't sure what to believe and what to dismiss.

One of the monks who had heard my questions followed me when I went out to the yard, getting ready to leave, and said with a judgmental voice: "You educated people should be more careful because you'll be harshly judged if you cause others to lose their faith with your questions. I was still young and I didn't know what to say. Now, I would have told him that the mind and all its discerning apparatus are gifts of God and we would be remiss if we didn't use them to get to the truth. We were told by Jesus, "'Love the Lord your God with all your heart and with all your soul and with all your mind."

Our mind is a gift of God and we cannot dismiss it when it come to gauging reality, truth and nature. There are miracles, alright, but we need discernment to point them out.

Later, I came up with a "Micro-Miracle Theory", which explains that we have many miracles, but they are in bits and pieces, here and there, connecting myriads of action points over time in infinite space in a way that makes it difficult to identify the miraculous action. We may think of Providence as the system of actions produced by the Micro-Miracles. As I gathered more experiences I realized that we all experience strange events in our lives, but we don't believe them, don't notice them, dismiss them and hold our prideful neck straight. God isn't about to prove to us the million ways he acts in the world. Many years later, I found out that we have to get close to God and be aware of his guiding presence before we grasp the truth of his miraculous actions. If we get close to God and love him, everything that happens with us is a miracle, and we know it and thank him.

8

Memory of Mortars and Dreamers

There were several times when I escaped deadly dangers, scared in basement shelters while bombs exploded outside, and a couple of times, daring death in the streets when planes dove down over the rooftops and rained brass shells on us and bullets further out. There was a time when the people were terrified and a couple of dozen neighbors came inside our building and stayed in Katina's first-floor apartment. My mother was pregnant with my sister and I would go downstairs every morning with her for safety from bombs, while my father stayed upstairs at our apartment grinding wheat with a hand-held coffee grinder, so we could make a pita or two for dinner. He couldn't work down there and didn't like crowds.

One evening a mortar exploded outside our house breaking all our front windows with one shrill blast, as my mother, pregnant with my sister, screamed and crawled trying to make it to the back of the house, where my father and I were busy grinding wheat. I had the feeling that God didn't want anyone to get hurt that time, but what did I know?

The next day, I went downstairs and stared out of a window in Katina's apartment as a woman was setting a few potato-size rocks on a square plot of black-looking dirt. Some of the rocks had red streaks on them. I stared at her, trying to figure out what she was doing with the strange looking rocks when I felt a hand on my shoulder and I turned and saw Katina, the beautiful old woman with long silver-white hair down to her waist I had seen only once before.

"Her brother was killed with the mortar last night," she said, looking at the woman working on the dirt plot across the street. She had just torn pieces of a bread from a loaf and passed them to a bunch of kids having snatched it from the sack some men had brought after their risky run to the neighborhood bakery. I drew back and stared at her. "He was a Communist soldier, but he was a good man," she said, as if I had interrogated her. "She's trying to make a cenotaph with the bloody stones." I didn't know what that was and kept looking at her and at the sister of the missing man outside. "They won't give her the body," my guide said. I crossed myself and left the scene to find something to eat. My mother, the perennial policeman of her restless son, wanted to know what I was up to. I told her that the mortar had killed a good communist and his sister was burying his blood. "He's with God now," she said and crossed herself. She was pleased that I wasn't stirring any trouble and said that there was some food in the kitchen and when I was done there, I should go upstairs and help my father grind some more wheat.

I went to the kitchen and ate oatmeal with watered milk. Outside the kitchen I run into Katina again. "Here is some bread for you too," she said and handed me a chunk of bread. I shoved it in my pocket to avoid a quarrel with other hungry kids and give it to my mother.

Katina took my hand and held it between her hands. "You are Tolis from upstairs?"

"Apostolos," I said, as if I wanted to prove her wrong.

"Don't be afraid," she said, as if I had shown fear. "There will be more deaths in the days to come, but in the end, we'll be fine," she said and let my trapped hand escape. I run upstairs to help my father grind some more wheat. Cleo had told me that Katina was her friend and I should listen to her because she dreams tomorrows.

Several days later, while gathered at Katina's apartment, listening to the news somebody was telling us about a Red Cross ship loaded with food and coming toward Piraeus, we heard that Lena, the pregnant wife of the tavern owner next door was killed early that morning. We all prayed that the doctors could save her baby girl at the hospital.

I knew Lena well. She was my friend. The neighbors used to run down to her basement tavern in a hurry, whenever the air raid alarm howled with terror. It was our designated shelter for all air raids before the Nazis occupied us. She was always so glad to see us. Sometimes when I was alone at home, I would go to her basement tavern and have some lunch. She was such a welcoming human being. I imagined her climbing the stairs, trying to figure out how she could climb out and keep her baby safe. My mother was crying and praying at the same time. Men went out to smoke their cigarettes in silence.

Later that day the people stopped praying for Lena's baby, and I knew she was dead too. I hated death because I couldn't see it and destroy it. I saw Katina, and asked her if that was the end of the killing in the street. "Was Lena your friend?" she asked. She held my hand and said: "The good people live happy in another world without death anywhere around." She let my hand go and said with a smile: "There'll be no killing there or here, anymore". When I told my mother, she said that Katina is a dreamer and they are usually right.

B

VARVAKEION MODEL HIGH SCHOOL

9

The Big Game Hunter

W hen I was in the sixth grade, I prepared for the entrance exams of the elite high school Varvakeion Model High School, or Varvakeion, for short. I knew that it attracted the best students and was difficult to get in. Many leaders I had heard about had studied at the school. I wanted to test myself and I made passing the exams my goal. It was a hard goal to achieve, but it was a worthy goal and, somehow, I sensed that one finds out what is the best that one can do, by competing for worthy goals. Besides, my uncles, Vassos and Agesilaus, and my cousin Omeros had attended the school before me, and all of them were known to be the "brains" in my mother's family. My cousin Nondas and I were going to find out whether we were able to follow on their footsteps.

Everybody in Greece, upon completion of the sixth grade, was required to attend a public or a private high school. There were no examinations for entry into these high schools, but Varvakeion was the exception. To attend Varvakeion, one had to pass very stringent written and oral entrance examinations in math and language.

Varvakeion was a public school for boys, founded by Ioannis Varvakis around 1860, one of the great benefactors of Greece, who made his money doing business in Russia. The school employed the top teachers in the country, and was used to educate not only top students for the professions needed for the country's progress, but also to train teachers, who came to observe various classes as they were being taught, or practiced teaching the students of Varvakeion on rare occasions. Attending Varvakeion was totally free.

Some 500 students were competing for the 80 available positions, and most of the 500 were at the top of their school classes. It was a competition for excellence, if there ever was one. Three of my classmates from my grade school class and I participated in the exams, Kefalas, Yannis and Sotos. Three of us, were neck and neck in class. Kefalas was not a top student, but he was determined to follow the rest of us and compete in the exams. I think he got the motivation to try for Varvakeion from my mother, who used to coach him and me together, sometimes. The four of us were kids from middle class families and we were there to match wits with the children of the rich and famous, whose parents, one might say, run the country. We knew that if we were admitted, we had a chance to reach as high as we could. I was ready for the competition. I believed then, as I believe now, that everyone who wants should have a chance to get to the top, if he or she has what it takes and works hard for what is needed.

My cousin, Nondas, was also preparing for the exams, under his sister Maria's guidance. She was a law student and was considered the intellectual in the family. Everyone in my mother's family was lining up behind us. I can't vouch for that, but I wouldn't be surprised to learn that they were betting on one or the other of us, in secret. I remember the anxiety I felt, but also the excitement. Varvakeion was located in downtown Athens and, if I were to attend school there, I would be spending a lot of time traveling every day by bus and on foot around the big city. This would be a big change for a kid used to having a three-block-long radius of operation in one of the second-rate neighborhoods of Athens. When things were closing in on me I prayed to God to guide me.

I took the exams believing that I would succeed. I kept thinking that one of those eighty spots was mine. In the Modern Greek examination, I wrote an essay about my career plans that in some fantastic way paralleled the successful careers of Greek benefactors, like Ioannis Varvakis, the founder of the school, whose example I wanted to follow. It was a tale, full of daring-do and lofty goals, cast in a dreamlike narrative that showed in no uncertain terms what an ambitious little rascal I was, and how determined I was to work hard and succeed in the world. When I handed the essay to the supervising teacher, I remember, I had second thoughts. Had I taken this matter seriously enough, or had I just written a story for fun at the most critical time of my life? I felt embarrassed by what I had written. What on earth was I doing, dreaming of mythical success out in the open? Well, what was done was done. I consoled myself with the hope of excelling in the coming oral exams. If I couldn't ace the orals, nobody could, I told myself. After all, what had I been doing all these years in grade school, but competing in hit and run oral exams? Wasn't standing up and expressing myself my forte? Thinking back, I can say for sure that I was worried, but also ready for the competition. I wanted to be good, but I didn't act in a humble pietist way.

A couple of days later, the oral exams were upon us. I did well in Math and then I had to cope with the essay I had written. I entered the examination room and faced half a dozen senior teacher-examiners sitting around a large table. I wasn't relaxed, but I was confident that my nature would see me through the ordeal. They had read my essay and wanted to know more about my plans for the future. Was I really interested in hunting wild animals in the jungles of Africa while searching for gold and diamonds, as I had written in my essay? How was this beneficial to society? And why would I give all the profits from goldmining to Greece, rather than have a rich and pleasurable life? Was there something wrong with having a lot of money? What if I didn't find gold, but instead was gored by a rhinoceros while searching for gold? I could see that they wanted to have some fun with me, and I was ready to oblige.

Well, I answered with some defensiveness, but also with chutzpah, that the hunt is the search, and the gold is the lofty goal everyone ought to have for his life's work. The wild animals are the obstacles we encounter in our search for the objective; killing animals is overcoming obstacles. What one does when he achieves his objective varies among people, but I admire our founder and the other benefactors and philanthropists of Greece, and I want to be like them and give most of my money, as they did, to create institutions of excellence. I said that it would satisfy me to do that, and perhaps to be remembered by future generations for my contributions to our society. I didn't give a very good response when they asked me why I saw myself sitting on an ivory throne in some jungle palace, but I muddled through by saying something almost like that, I think, that the magnificent seat was a sign of authority gained by the power of persistence and wisdom.

Of course, I don't remember the exact words I used, but the words I use to describe this distant past experience right now reflect nearly all that was happening in my brain, heart and trembling body. I thought fast and I gave these unexpected answers, which called for more questions, which I answered with even more extravagant answers. I made sure to stay on course and never retract from my story. I was committed to the course without ever calculating the odds of success. Something inside me knew where I was on the map. I know that I believed the essence of what I said, and I must have convinced them that I was serious about making something worthwhile out of my life. My imagination had started to create and would continue doing so in the years to come. I took chances, coming across a little more defiant, perhaps, than I should have. I needed their approval so bad, that I didn't give a hoot for their approval. With a chance for success close to one in ten, I instinctively knew, that I had to take chances. Somehow, I felt that I had to stand out as an imaginative thinker and go-getter, even at the risk of being taken to be a deluded and prideful child. Thank God I grew out of that. We all know that adults with these traits can kill thousands of people and never miss par at the golf course.

I felt good after I got out of the oral examination room. For a few minutes I felt that every part of me was entirely free and had used freedom wisely. I figured that what I wrote made more sense with the oral commentary I provided. I finished with my logic tamping down my elation. I stopped the self-evaluation, with the conclusion that I had done a good job – neither great, nor poor., distinct for sure. A lot would depend on how well my competitors had done. Nondas also reported that he had done well. Kefalas, one of the four of us from my grade school wasn't sure, and I didn't find out what the other two guys from our grade school thought of their performance. I think I was trying to find out how crazy the others had been.

The summer of 1947 was almost over when the newspapers announced that the results for entrance to Varvakeion were out. When I got to the schoolyard, the crowd around the rosters, pinned on a wall, was huge. I remember pushing through the crowd to get close enough, so I could read the names. I found my name: Apostolos Kizilos #44; and then, Nondas Laskos #26. Kefalas was also within the eighty who made it, and so was Sotos from my grade school. Yannis who hardly opened his mouth in class and was thought to be the top student in class by Papa-Kostas, didn't make it. He was always cautious, an example of propriety and correctness, and never broke any rules, never got into a fight and, probably, never dreamed that he would ever be a big game hunter in the jungles of Africa. It would have been too much if four of us had made it to Varvakeion from that little grade school in the backwoods of Athens. But, Nondas had scored higher than I had, and the competition between us, I knew, would heat up. Our friendship was so deep that it made competition a joyful game.

The winners of the competition began the school year with a spirit of confidence. It never crossed our minds that we were lucky, or favored in some way by God, as well as being smart and diligent, but it should have. I was delighted to be in the science section of forty students, and my goal was to do my best. I became a model of good conduct and studied hard to excel. I asked questions when I didn't understand something, or when I was curious about something, and I answered questions when I could offer something worthwhile. I tried to never disrupt the class as I used to do in grade school and succeeded. Somehow, my grade-school rebelliousness was gone.

I always sat on the first row of desks, because I couldn't see very well, but also to avoid the distractions, that sometimes took place at the back of the class. The desks were made for two students, and often, the two boys who sat together for six years remained friends for life. I sat next to Takis, a quiet, very studious boy, with strong Christian values and a prodigious memory, who became a very noteworthy medical doctor in Greece. Nondas sat next to Andreas, a sharp kid with a great sense of humor, who became an M.D. and a General in the Medical Corps of the Greek Army. We were an exceptionally motivated class, and just about everyone participated in the discussions and gave his best. When they held back too long, teachers would ask them for their view. And they always managed to contribute something better than they thought they could.

Because I had the top grades in class, some of my fellow students, I imagine, thought that I was the smartest student in class. I never thought so. I thought there were several students who were better than me in various subjects. Demetrios was almost silent in class, but I suspected that he was the top student in Physics, and Lakis, always nearly silent and invisible, I thought might be the best Mathematician. I thought I was the best in Modern Greek and writing.

There wasn't a girl to be seen for miles around the school, and we often talked about finding out where the girls were, as if they were a rare, precious resource, like palladium or platinum. Of course, girls were everywhere and nowhere. The best place to find beautiful girls was in each boy's imagination. Some public high schools were separated by gender but others, like the high school in Eleusis, were not. We were always envious of the lucky dogs that didn't have to look further than the desk next to them to talk to a girl or get an uplifting smile. We were as bereft of girls as some city monks are. Some of the guys could meet girls through family acquaintances, through siblings, in clubs and organizations that they or their families belonged to, but I had none of these ways available to me. So, I found myself without any kind of relationship with a girl. Since I had to spend most of my day out of the neighborhood, I even lost track of the few neighborhood girls that I might have had some relationship with since they spent most of their time in the local school and befriended boys who were students there. I saw Cleo a few times after her boyfriend tried to kill her, and was happy to see that she had another boyfriend to whom she got married a few months later.

In the first two or three years, this deprivation of female friendship didn't matter a lot, but later the need for relationships with girls grew and, as usual, I searched to find places for meeting girls, like The Young People's Center associated with The Young Hellene, a young people's magazine with a lively literary life for various groups, or the Alliance Française school, which was an Institute for learning French for both boys and girls, or an Academy for learning English in mixed classes, and so on. But for the first few years I was focused on doing well in school and enjoying the big city with my school friends. I reached the top of the class right away and stayed there, scoring high on both technology and literature classes. I sometimes wondered if my grade record of the present year affected the grade record I would have for the next year. But, I found out that the teachers knew what they were doing, by getting bad grades when I slowed down for a while.

All the guys I had spent the early years of my life in daily contact with around the stoop of Kortessis, Antony, Vous, Beanpole, Koula the Tomboy, the Little Beggar and Katie our meticulous nurse, or the Abyssinian and Stellian and Kalamata and all the rest of them except for Kefalas, faded in the background. I wrote about all of them in "Zeal" a Memoir I wrote for my early years. Only the events we faced and some of the experiences we shared together in the harsh years of war, and occupation remain with me. We grew apart and weeks would go by without meeting any of them. Once in a while I would see the Devil hustling newspapers in Plateia Klathmonos (which means Square of Lamentations) and I would say hello to him. I think that most of the other guys continued getting together because they attended the same school, but the world had changed for me, and I had to cope with different circumstances than they did. Sometimes, I wonder how my friends remember the same events that shaped our young lives. What memories did they retain? What did they learn from our common experiences? I'm sure that all of us built different worlds in our minds using the same facts, and all these worlds are real and true for us even though they are different. The memory of facts changes, but the feelings upon which they stand are common and unite us.

Varvakeion high school had to hold classes in the afternoon and evening at a Grade School building far from home because the Nazis had burned down the original Varvakeion building that the founder of the school had built, and no funds had been made available for reconstruction, yet. That meant that I spent six years going to school from about one in the afternoon to about six or seven in the evening. I had to take two busses and walk about half a mile, or take one bus and walk more than a mile. I often went to school with Kefalas because we lived close to each other. We were often joined by other guys on the way back and made up quite a raucous teenage gang that carried on in the streets, the arcades and the squares of Athens with shouts, laughter and all sorts of fun and games. Sometimes, we would stop at one of the specialty stores for tiropitas and a glass of beer, or a bougatsa, or loukoumades and engage in long, loud discussions about the political parties running in the coming elections or the standings of the three or four great soccer teams in the country, or the weird personality of a new teacher, or the clumsiness of one of the geography teachers being trained last week in our class, or the antics of the class clown, or the next day's physics problem that no one had figured out yet.

There were of course many discussions of Hollywood movies and life in America and stories of movies that were not for teenagers, but one of us had managed to sneak in and watch and was very enthusiastic reporting what he saw. There was always a medley of risqué jokes and an occasional account of a budding relationship that one of the guys had with the girl of his dreams and wanted to tell us all about her. Theodore, one of the guys, who later came to America for graduate studies, knew dozens of jokes and told them so well that no one else could top him. He became the official joke teller of the group while the rest of us listened and laughed with abandon. Theodore remembered all his jokes and identified each joke with a number, which he announced every time before telling the joke. After several repetitions, instead of wasting time and energy telling the joke of the shoemaker and his fat wife who beat him up when he glanced at another woman, he would say, "Remember Thirty-Four?" and everyone would burst out laughing at the joke of the shoemaker and his fat wife. "Do you guys remember Number Forty-Three?" Someone else would counter, and everyone would laugh, "Wow! I remember – the albino monkey with his redheaded lover!" someone else would add, proving to everybody that he knew the code and was, therefore, a bona fide member of the gang. Joke number "Sixteen" was my favorite, but I cannot remember it!

Sometimes on the way home we'd encounter street peddlers, usually selling "super" razor blades, or "extra nylon" stockings or "Chinese silk" ties, all of them with fake shoppers buying what they sold to prime the pump of commerce. These "boosters" would crowd around them and create the impression that these were indeed very hot items on a fire sale. Our pastime was to stand back, watch the fake shoppers circle around and identify them as fast as we could. And, when the police would break up the operation, often to the dismay of the country bumpkins who were disappointed that they missed buying the whole year's supply of Gillette blades or Zippo lighters, we would move on to the windows of Lambropoulos, the best department store in the capital and find out which one of the dummies modeling the latest dress or suit was a real human being, posing as a dummy. There would be arguments and debates about who, how, and for how long and how much would one want to bet on him or her to stand still. Once we reached a consensus on the real human, we did everything we could to distract him or her, and make the "dummy" come to life by yelling, laughing, making faces and acting in bizarre ways in front of the window. Most of us never made a dent on any "dummy's" poise, pose or posture. The only one who managed to get one manikin to smile and change pose with gusto, was Basoukos, one of the students from the Classics Section, who started the Brotherhood of Disturbed Juveniles as satire for the despotic teachers we had and came close to being expelled.

Basoukos did it by having frosting and lemonade coming out of his nose and saliva dripping down his chin, while reciting the first line of Homer's Odyssey in ancient Greek: "Tell me, O Muse, of that ingenious man, who travelled far and wide after he sacked the great city of Troy." We held our breaths while Basoukos howled, scrutinizing every inch of that model's figure. The beautiful blond woman in the green dress, green pumps and green handbag held her pose as long as she could.

She clenched her fists and tried to stifle the rising laughter inside her, but she finally succumbed to the puffy, dripping, round clown-face that Basoukos had conjured, and her entire body relaxed. When Basoukos managed to animate the doll in the window, we broke out with howls too and laughed ourselves silly. She smiled at us and assumed a slightly different pose but as ethereal as ever. "Perhaps, the green lady took pity on him and saved him from ridicule," someone mused later, when the green lady entered one of our many conversations. Basoukos went to the military academy and became an officer in the armed forces, a colonel, someone told me. I bet the green lady still poses in the memories of the young bucks who made her laugh and change position.

When these nomadic evening tours were finished, there would be time for me and a couple of others guys to visit one or two Travel Bureaus and pick up some travel folders of places to dream of going someday, or time to stop by at the American Information Center, the USIA agency had established, and browse some of the many magazines they had. There were countless places to visit and learn from, or just enjoy the sweet waste of time. We were glad to be students at the top school in the country; to be in the city that gave birth to Western Civilization; to be alive after the Nazis were wiped out by our great friends, led by the United States of America. It was a blessing to be alive and free at that time and have so many friends planning for a great future. We knew we had found the best platform for launching our dreams into reality and enjoyed every moment of it.

10

The Buss Plug Bursts

When I was sixteen, a street-smart kid growing up in a tough neighborhood of Athens, tops in my high school class at the most prestigious public school in Greece, strong and headed straight for his goal of excellence as an arrow headed for a bullseye, I felt that nothing could stop me. Many of us feel that way, I suppose, when body and mind work well together and parental nurturing moves us in loving ways that also promote discernment of right and wrong and train us to choose the better path ahead.

I was going to study in America. It was my idea from the earliest times of my awareness. I had no money, no clue what to do to get from there to here, no English language to go further than "How do you do" and say "Hey, good looking, what's cooking," to a pretty girl, if I ever met one and she happened to listen to a scrawny youth who was not only shy, but also painfully afraid of rejection by girls, had no clue of English idioms, but was ready to explore the world and change whatever could make it a little better.

It took some hard knocks to learn that it was pride that made me so brave and so vulnerable. I convinced myself that failures were not important. My goal wasn't having a gorgeous girlfriend My goal was going to America to study and do some good there too. That meant I had to learn English, find a University that would grant me a scholarship, get my father, who was not well off and on the tight side with money, to dole out some of the living expenses, while I worked somewhere in America to earn the rest.

I was a junior and decision time was upon me. I had to move fast, in making connections of all kinds, establishing a network, one would say nowadays, learning what I could about the acceptance of foreign students, discover the travel possibilities as a sailor on some merchant ship and take care of the travel with work for the ship fare, learn the requirements for admission to every school before I applied and a dozen other things that would help me achieve that goal, while I maintained my performance as the top dog in my class.

I had to take two busses to get from my house to school and walk for half a mile in downtown Athens. Sometimes, there was no time to lose and wait for the next bus so, when the bus was full and taking off, I would grab the bar of the rear side door, gain a foothold on the doorstep and wedge myself in, as people accommodated themselves inside. It was tight near the door. It was risky. I t wasn't a smart thing to do, but it had worked for me many times before, and I was sure it would work for me again. But, this was a day that the crowd in the bus couldn't be contained. The push and shove intensified, and I felt the force in my stretched arms as I hung with my satchel for dear life out back.

I was the plug that kept several bodies from bursting out the door. The bus was already moving at a good speed. I couldn't jump with my back facing the road. No room to turn and jump. One more push and I could be dumped out of the bus, like a potato sack from the back of a truck. Some human body somewhere inside moved and the steel bottle plug burst out.

I said I didn't pass out. I sensed that I was being transported and when the movement stopped, I opened my eyes. My mother's shape, then her face formed slowly by my bedside. Someone asked if I was alright.

"What happened?" someone else asked.

"Don't try to raise your head." "Your boy was very lucky, Ma'am," a heavy male voice said with authority.

"His Guardian Angel saved him," someone said with conviction

"The Holy Spirit is always with us," someone else insisted. Will they have an argument? I wondered.

There were people leaving, and my mother was thanking them. My mother prayed. I was being transported again. A nurse said "They are tough these boys. They think nothing can hurt them."

My mother thanked "My Little Jesus," and "The Little Holy Mary" as she called Christ and Mary lovingly. I thanked God for my life as well, but I didn't really believe that God had reached out and saved me from death or a crippling disability. I didn't think God would bother with a stupid guy who hangs out of bus doors. I was the one who made a mistake, the one who happened to fall in such a way that I didn't get hurt too bad. I believed in myself and didn't think that God bothers with the happy and the horrible events unfolding all around us every day. I had to suffer a lot more than a simple concussion, earaches and rheumatism before I could understand, let alone believe, that God is always around and barely able to hold back his mighty hand and lay me down on a pillow.

11

Questioning Authority

"Life is either a daring adventure or nothing at all."
Hellen Keller

Probably, the most knowledgeable, most famous, most demanding and feared teacher we had in high school was Alkinoos Mazis, the brilliant physics professor, who threw me out of the class once because I said that one of my classmates had the hair of a Neanderthal man. When Mazis entered the classroom, silence would roll like a heavy tarp over us. His after-shave lotion was always strong and pleasant and we would have known he was with us, even if our eyes were shut. He was a short man, bald, with a short, well-trimmed moustache, exactly the length of his upper lip. He was always impeccably dressed and walked with deliberate movements like a diver slogging underwater. He would sit on a chair in front of his desk, cross his legs, and survey the class, as if trying to detect which one of us was least prepared that day, so he could call on him to come up to the board and test him, teach him, ridicule him, encourage him, enlighten him, empower him, humble him or, somehow, wake him up to the fascination of science and the values he ought to have in order to achieve meaningful things in his life. We would sneak looks at him, never making a daring eye to eye contact with him for fear of calling attention to ourselves that might land us up on the blackboard in retaliation for disrespect, bravado, challenge his authority or any other unfortunate interpretation of our uninhibited behavior.

Some of us thought that he had a slight limp, and it was rumored that he had a wooden leg, but none of us was sure of that. I sat in the front row, no more than ten feet away from him, when he chose to sit with crossed legs in front of his desk and I examined his leg almost every time. I had his disputed leg in my field of vision for the better part of the duration of every class. I would often fantasize that I got up, stood before him, smiled politely and started tapping on his sock-covered leg with my knuckles, expecting to feel unyielding wood and hear its telltale hollow sound. But, we were all cowards, more or less, and none of us thought that we would ever verify the rumor, even though all of us were on the lookout and cast countless probing glances at that stocking-protected leg.

Mazis had written several books on physics and was admired by every high school teacher and student who tried to grasp the basic laws of physics. The young teachers who came to our school to learn held him in high esteem and were coached kindly by Mazis

Every teacher taught us something beyond learning the subject matter he taught, but Mazis gave us, probably, the most valuable lessons for life. We were juniors and then seniors, taking physics in the Science Section of the best high school in the country, taught by the top teacher in the country, and we were all highly motivated, because physics was a crucial subject in the entrance exams we would have to pass before qualifying for admission to the Polytechnic, the top technical university for engineers, or the University of Athens, which was the top school for scientists. All of Mazis' classes were electric in one way or another, because someone would do something and excel beyond all expectations, or fail miserably against all hopes. But on one particular occasion something extraordinary happened, and I remember it with exceptional clarity Because it affected my life.

We were seniors, taking the first semester's written examination in physics and all of us were apprehensive because the material had been difficult and essential to our future career success. As always, we had to answer two out of three theory questions and then solve one out of two problems. The grade depended equally on the quality of answering the theory questions, and on solving one of the two problems correctly. I had no problem answering the theory questions, and then, I read the first problem. It was an easy problem, but I wasn't sure I understood it well enough, so I read the second problem. It was a tough problem, and required a lot of detailed calculations with plenty of chances for error in the limited time remaining in the exam. I went back to the first problem and read it very carefully. I understood it well now and thought it wouldn't take a lot of time to solve it, so I started working on the first problem. I froze when I realized that there was a mistake in the information given. The problem couldn't be solved the way it was stated! Yet, the problem was stated the way it was stated by professor Alkinoos Mazis, the teacher who had told us that he reserves the top grade on the scale of 0 to 20 for God, the next grade for himself and the third grade for the student who turns in a flawless exam. I felt cold sweat running down my sides. I was the top student in the class, which had ten to twelve subjects in various areas of knowledge, but I abandoned the first problem and immediately shifted gears and started to work on the second problem. I had just enough time to arrive at a solution but there was no time left for review or make any correction to any possible errors. It would have been so easy to do the first problem, if it had only been stated correctly . . . Or, was it stated correctly, but I hadn't been able to see how to read it? I handed in my exam and got out in the schoolyard. Every student I asked had solved problem number two, because, as most of us put it, "there was something wrong with problem number one."

When professor Mazis came to class with the examination papers the first week of the second semester, we were all anxious as always, to see how well we had done, but more than that we wanted to find out how he, Mazis, the Magician, had created such a conundrum for us. This time, Mazis didn't pass out the exams to the students right away. He just pulled out the bundle of exam papers from his leather briefcase and set it on his desk. "You can pick up your papers at the end of the class," he said. Standing before the class, he asked what we thought of the exam. Several of us spoke, saying that it was difficult, but fair for the time allotted.

"Which problem did you solve?" he asked pointing to someone in the back of the room.

"Problem Number Two, Sir," came the weak voice of Karakitsos, a six-foot two giant with an Adonis face, at the last desk, who shook like a leaf when he was up for oral presentations.

"And you?" he asked Spathis, the restless joker of the class.

"Problem Number Two, Sir," Spathis responded.

"And you, Kizilos?" he asked, and I heard the accusation and the hurt in his voice. I was after all the top student in the class on overall grades for five consecutive years.

"Problem Number Two, Sir." I just couldn't keep from adding, "There was something odd with Problem Number One."

"Were there any others who thought that there was 'something odd' with Problem Number One, as the distinguished Mr. Kizilos puts it?" he asked caricaturing my words to show his disdain for them. We all raised our hands. Mazis stared at us without showing any sign of recognition. We might as well have been withered flowers in an arid field.

He was silent as he strolled like a caged lion before the class. He brought his chair in front of his desk, sat down and crossed his legs.

"There was something wrong, but only one of you dared to write that in his exam paper." He let his words sink in, deep into our hearts and minds.

Many heads turned around searching for that one student who dared to confront the mighty Mazis with his error or his gut "test".

"There are forty of you, who took the exam, and thirty-nine did Problem Number Two. Yet, most of you – all of you – figured out that the other problem was stated incorrectly. You didn't have the guts to write that down on your paper. You played it safe . . ." He stopped as if he wanted to leave the rest of his thought unspoken, but his emotions won out. "You played it safe like all cowards do," he said and changing his mind, grabbed the bundle of exam papers and handed it to one of the students to distribute to the class.

He had worked hard; he had given everything he had to make this a class of star performers. It was this class that would lead Science and Technology, in the Colleges and Industry of Greece. He couldn't accept that our ability to take risks and confront authority was so low. He had no stomach for people who couldn't speak the truth that they were smart enough to discover. We had insulted Science and him by playing it safe. His granite face seemed scratched, and his eyes were dark, tired, it seemed, of staying open. Silence was the best we could hope for now, but Mazis hadn't finished teaching.

"Solving problems somebody gives you isn't the most important thing in life; you'll need courage to find the problems that matter before you can accomplish anything worthwhile. You'll come across many things that are wrong, unfair, second rate, and you'll have to fix them, improve them or end them. And for that, you need the courage to take a risk. Courage was what counted in your exam." We felt the weight of his accusation and took note of his words. "Only Demetrios Kouremenos dared to tell me that Problem Number One was stated wrongly," he said and cast a thankful smile toward him. "He corrected the error by restating the problem correctly, and solved it. One out of forty of you is not a good enough record for any class, and certainly not for my class. You must stand up and be counted!" He replaced his chair behind his desk and then, turning slowly, as if he carried a load on his back, said to the class, "I am disappointed in you, gentlemen." Then, he dismissed the class early and slogged toward the exit, holding his empty briefcase.

It took a few minutes to recover from the blow Mazis had delivered to us, and when we were back in action, the question all of us discussed in the schoolyard that day was this: "Did Mazis make a mistake in Problem Number One, or did he purposely introduce the mistake to teach us a lesson?" Most of us thought that Mazis was not able of making such a stupid mistake and quite able of resorting to unusual methods to teach us something important.

I believed that Mazis made a mistake. When he realized his mistake, he took advantage of the situation to teach us a greater lesson like the great teacher he was. I could never believe that he introduced a mistake purposely into the exam. But why would he not do so, if he felt that this was the only way he could teach us a very valuable principle? Now I say that he made a mistake because he was a wise man and knew that a dishonest act should never be mixed into the honest and wise efforts of a wise teacher. The only other lesson I wish he had added to his teaching, was to tell the class that "sometimes you will not know why things happen the way they do".

We were all proud of our fellow student, Demetrios Kouremenos, who on this occasion represented the best of the class. I was delighted to hear, many years later, that he had become a full professor at the Polytechnic, the most coveted academic position an engineer could attain in Greece. Later, he held important leadership positions in Greek companies and had other responsibilities. He was a good student overall, but starting a year or two before this incident he had apparently been quietly scoring big in math and physics. I was the first to acknowledge his excellence in these subjects and have praised his performance and his courage in another book I wrote.

I learned a lot from that experience and took risks to speak what others knew but were silent. There are every day examples which point to tragic mistakes that happen because n one has the guts to unearth the error and start a discussion or oppose it outright. Sometimes we have to take a risk, not because we'll be effective, but because we believe that what we do is the right thing to do.

My critique of the Greek Orthodox Church of America for its isolationism from other churches, the limitations that the Church imposed on women and the Church's other antiquated organizational practices was received with deafening silence by those who could make changes. Sometimes, going against the norms changed the course of the discussion and other times it produced an embarrassing silence.

Sometimes people laughed with me and other times at me; a few times I split the group, and other times I united it. A few times people approached me and told me how much they appreciated what I said or done, and a few times people whispered their disapproval by criticizing my liberal views and there were a couple of times when I was called radical, leftist, Protestantizer, undiplomatic and worse. But, I stood up and was counted. I followed Mazis' appeal to us and was engaged by word and deed on the issues that mattered at the time. In time I was guided to help create a corporate transformative organization and my career was devoted to creating Participative Management systems based on excellence in performance of the work, trust, teamwork and care for one another. Many of the stories in this book show the ways one can respond meaningfully to the events one encounters, if the purpose of one's life is doing some good in the world, or as I would say now, getting closer to God.

12

When I Needed Strength

"For when I am weak, then I am strong." (2 Cor. 12:10b)

Saint Paul

During the summer, when I was on vacation in Eleusis at my grandmother's house, I used to spend the meager allowance my father gave me every month on bike rentals. I would rent the oldest and most beat up bike in the store for half an hour or an hour at most, and go as far as I could go in the allotted time. Having a bike became an obsession. Sometimes, I would hang around the bicycle store and do some chores, so the owner could give me a freebie for an hour or so. I needed a bike to be part of a group that included m friends and some of the good-looking girls who lived near the seashore in mansions. I would have done hard labor to get the money and buy a used bike, but no one had that kind of work.

I was on the lookout for opportunities that might come along. One day, I had been swimming with the entire gang at one of the piers of the main harbor of Eleusis and, as I climbed out after a dive, I saw a beautiful red bike leaning up against one of the nearby bushes. I was dripping seawater as I approached and stared with admiration at that bike. A man appeared from behind the bush and stared at me. "You like my bike?" he asked with a friendly smile.

"It's a great looking bike," I said, my eyes fixed on it. "Is it English?" I asked, recognizing the shield of a Raleigh bicycle.

"Sure is. You want to try it out?"

"My swimsuit is still wet," I said.

"It's fine. Go ahead and go around the harbor."

I climbed up and pedaled away. I felt the wind on my face and the thrill of freedom. I was elated. If I could only get a damn bike, I kept thinking as I passed by all the houses of girls I knew by the seashore.

I returned to the place I had started from and rested the bike back on the bush where I had found it. I told the man that he had a terrific bike, thanked him for letting me try it, and turned to leave.

"I can lend you the bike sometimes, if you want it," the man said.

I stopped dead on my tracks. "You can?"

"Sure! Come to the place I work some afternoon, four o'clock, and I'll let you use it until I leave at midnight. I'm at the Chemical Factory's warehouse. Use the back door from the ruins."

I said that I might take him up on that and thanked him.

I knew the Chemical Factory, at the harbor, because it stunk the whole area with its foul smell. I was delighted that I had finally found someone willing to let me use a bike for a while. It wasn't every day one comes across people willing to share their goods, I thought thankfully. It would have been perfect, but for the stench. "A stinking bike is better than no bike at all," I thought.

A few days later, I walked to the warehouse where the man said he was working. I saw a small door near the big warehouse door at the front of the Factory and I pushed it to see if it was open. I wouldn't have to go around the warehouse to the back door in the burning sun. The door yielded and I went in the cool dark entry. I could see no one around. The back door, some distance away, was slightly open, so I headed that way. The place seemed deserted. The warehouse was much cooler than the burning ground outside. The smell of chemicals was repulsive, but familiar. I took a few steps into the building. Just dark space in all directions, except for the sliver of light trickling in from the slightly open door at the far end of space.

"Anybody here?" I called out, because I didn't know the man's name.

"Over here," I heard a voice respond from the depths of the left side of the warehouse. I walked cautiously toward the source of the voice.

"Where are you?" I called out. Moments later I found myself staring at one of the building's walls only a couple of feet away and stopped.

"How are you, my friend?" the man said and grabbed me from behind, his arm around my chest "The bike is right over here."

I froze. Mute and stunned. And then, every muscle turned to stone. Fear broke and burst to anger and exploded outside of me. Every part I had was at war, pushing, kicking, arms flailing, searching for a hit, a blow, a blast. I slid down through the hold made out of the rapist's arms and his locked hands. I hit something, with my foot, somewhere. He was as ferocious as Vous, but I had fought him before and was not afraid anymore. I hit him and heard a gut howl. I was free and he was down. I run toward the sliver of light at the back door, toward the hill of the ancient ruins of the temple of Persephone and the chapel of Saint Zacharias at the top, next to the clock-tower of Eleusis on the hilltop. The snake hadn't come out. I sat at the stoop of the chapel to catch my breath. The clock bell rung three times and I crossed myself thanking God, joyous that I escaped.

I started going back home. I kept an eye on the back door of the warehouse to make sure the snake didn't slither out. This was my hill. My uncle, the poet Orestes Laskos, had married Stella Greka, a famous singer, on this Chapel a couple of years before. I had been up on that hill many times before, looking for the entrance to the Sanctuary of the "Eleusinian Mysteries", the thousands of years old entrance to the caves. I had searched for tombs, and shards from ancient vessels and small marble chunks of columns with something sculpted on them. I had found nothing – no sanctuary entrance, no bones of initiates or priests and no shards. My cousin Nondas and I found a marble chunk of a small column once without any writing on it, but we could never decide who was the owner, so we left the column in the yard of our grand-mother's house, where it was probably buried again when the house was torn down and a tower for a Healthcare building was erected some years later.

At the time of this experience, I thanked Cod in a traditional way that I used when something good happened in my life. I had no idea that God cared about me. Later, after I knew that God is a real presence I my life, I believed, like Saint Paull, that the Holly Spirit, the Power of God, was also nearby and did what I could have never done alone.

13

Swims and Siestas with Cicadas

S ummers in Eleusis were infused with magic. Many exciting things happened that filled the days with vibrant memories. The salty breeze of the sea at dreamy beaches caressed us after a swim and the perfume of the pine trees filled our hearts as we ate out in the yard under the old pine tree. For many years, whenever I was down, I would think of the hot summer afternoons with the cicadas singing outside in the merciless sun and myself lying down for a siesta in one of the cool, shady bedrooms of my grandmother's house, reading "Gone with the Wind" or the short stories of Karkavitsas' sailors, or some other story of adventure, love or mystery I would borrow from my uncle, doctor Andonis' library. I would sleep for a couple of hours and wake up refreshed and ready for athletic games or for mischievous adventures with my cousin Nondas, Mitsos the "Sheriff," "The Other Nondas," our cousin, who was almost two years older than we were, and anyone else who cared to join us in our improvised madness.

We wasted time pleasantly like the cicadas, with swimming, sports, reading books before siestas and making up games no one had ever played before or would ever play again. We took trips to the farms of relatives and local friends on the back of donkeys, sometimes riding horses and acting like cowboys after that. And every evening, dressed in our summer whites, we strolled in the town square to watch the girls go by and talk about the day's happenings. Most evenings we'd end up going to the outdoor movies to see Alan Ladd rounding cattle and fighting Indians in the West or gawk at Esther Williams diving into the cobalt waters of some exotic island of the Pacific. Sometimes we paid the full price of admission, now and then we mooched off an uncle or an older cousin, like Omeros or "The Other Nondas." More often than not, we climbed up on trees overlooking the wall fence of the theater and watched the movie hanging from the branches like great apes, or made friends who lived next to the movie theater and watched movies hugging the wall fences between the movie theater and the friend's yard. But, none of these alternatives were certain, so we had a final option that was more of an adventure than a means of watching a movie on the cheap: we would sneak into the theater by deception.

One way was to sneak in with a rush of paying customers, hoping that the doorman would be so preoccupied with the collection of tickets that he wouldn't notice us. That approach worked some of the time, but now and then one of us would get caught by the doorman, grabbed by the ear and dragged out of the group of paying customers, where he could be seen by people and shamed as a cheap, sneaky scoundrel. It was a high-risk maneuver and I attempted it only once, out of desperation to see a good movie.

The final but most exciting approach to joining the comfortably seated customers in the theater as they enjoyed the moments before the movie started chewing *passatempo* or peanuts, required planning, cunning and agility. It could work only for one of the two movie theaters, the Rex, because it was located next to a peach orchard. A wall fence separated the peach orchard, from the movie theater and it could be scaled. First, you had to scale a wall fence to get into the orchard from the street; then you had to find your way among the trees to the spot on the wall separating the orchard from the movie theater grounds and climb over that. Scaling this separating wall was tricky, because on top of it rested a barbed wire coil, which had to be stretched out enough to allow a boy's torso to twist through it without the barbs gouging his flesh. If one succeeded doing that, he landed on the waiting area in front of the toilets' stalls. We had done this often enough to know all the moves, but there was always a chance that the muscular doorman who guarded the main entrance to the theater would start nosing around the toilet area and find us slithering through the fence.

One night, a clear, starry, warm night, I was the first to make it through the fence and quickly run into the first open toilet stall to pass as a paying customer doing his business; Nondas was next, but his pants got stuck on a barb of the fence and Mitsos was trying to free him. I watched and waited, unable to reach him and help him from my side. It took a couple of minutes, but he finally made it and jumped down and took the stall next to mine. Last to drop down the wall was Mitsos who was built like a cat and slid through and landed in the anteroom. The three of us now straightened our clothes combed our hair and got ready to leave the toilet area and proceed to blend with the rest of the theatergoers. Mitsos opened the door and stepped out with a cowboy swagger headed for a gunfight. Nondas and I followed close by. We hadn't taken more than ten steps when the fat doorman fell upon Mitsos and Nondas and grabbed them by their shirts. "I got you," I heard the doorman call out and I flew to the side, away from the scuffle. I had no time to look. I run bobbing and weaving through the crowd until I managed to slow down and blend with the people entering the seating areas. Nondas and Mitsos were stunned by the booming command of the doorman but they struggled to get out of the man's grip. Nondas escaped first and found a seat near me. Mitsos tore his shirt but he slipped away. Because he was last to get loose, the doorman took after him and chased him around and around the seats of the theater. We watched the shadows of the muscular doorman chasing the spindly Mitsos on the screen as the Fox Movietonews was playing. Later Mitsos told us that he had to run all the way out of the theater to escape his pursuer. He cussed and shouted and was furious that the fat man deprived him of the pleasure of watching Gary Cooper in Sergeant York. Nondas and I tried to console him, telling him that it wasn't one of Cooper's best movies, anyway. Of course, by the time the movie was shown at Rex in Eleusis, Gary Cooper had already received his first Oscar for Best Actor, as Sergeant York, though none of us knew it yet. That was the last time we dropped into the Rex toilets like parachutists from the Garden of Peaches. We bragged about our risky caper to one another and to friends because we felt the thrill of reaching a desired goal, but no one wanted to risk another attempt that could end up with a public humiliation. I was worried for a while that the doorman might remember my face, but when you pay for a ticket, nobody remembers any previous transgressions.

I still had no wheels, but I was doing my best to have a good time without a bike. The girls were wonderful to look at and yearn for their company as they sat around the benches in the square and talked and laughed at things we could only dream about, but they lived by the sea shore, a couple of miles away, beyond reach of blathering idiots on foot. I wonder whether my fortunes would have been any different if I had managed to get my hands on a bike. I suspect that I might have felt like a blathering idiot on wheels. Without a bike, I could only dream of saying, "I happened to be in the neighborhood and thought it would be nice to stop by and tell you how much I like to listen to you laugh in the Town Square."

But, I would snap out of my pedestrian depression, smile at the stars and thank God for saving me from my bike lust.

C

MY MYSTERIOUS
COLLEGE PLAN

14

Providence or Coincidence?

Going to college in America with almost no knowledge of English, without any money I could count on, and without any connections in America to call upon if I needed help, would be a foolish dream for many people, but it was the plan upon which I applied all my skills and talents and resolved to execute. I knew it was a challenge which may not succeed, so I had a Plan B by preparing to participate in the difficult exams of the Polytechnic School of Greece.

Getting a scholarship would be not only a financial base but also a leverage for finding other sources of support. I started the search for scholarships at an American University, by visiting after class, as frequently as I could, the USIA library in downtown Athens and trying to make sense out of the catalogues and the college books I found there. I had no idea of the application process, the criteria for admission, or how to evaluate different schools. I struggled long and hard with these unknowns, familiarizing myself with the language and the steps of the process. There were no guidebooks for college admissions back then, but I could find clues of what each college wanted as I browsed college catalogues. I went on alert as I searched for people who had relatives in America; people who had travelled by ship on long voyages; what Americans value as a people; the history of the United States of America; how American soldiers lived in Greece; what kind of people studied in America and what professions they practiced in America or in Greece, if they chose to return to the homeland. College books on

Math and Physics seemed very easy to me. I learned about the climate of New York, California, Syracuse and Louisiana; the process of getting a passport; the types of scholarships one can get and everything else that could be of use in achieving my objective.

I heard on the radio that the Massachusetts Institute of Technology, MIT, was the top school in the world for a technical education and the California Institute of Technology was second, so I started composing a letter, one word at a time, requesting admission and a scholarship. I sent both letters without delay. One night I had an inspiration: Why not apply to a school, which had a name I could at least recognize? My mind was working overtime and I was exploring every gulf and bayou I could find. After a couple of evenings of research, I zeroed in on Syracuse University, because Syracuse was a colony of Athens in the Golden Era of Athens, in the fifth century BC, and the people who named their American city after that famed ancient colony couldn't be anything other than generous and welcoming to Athenians, as the Syracusans of old surely must have been, before the corrupt Athenian general, Alcibiades, sacked their city, causing great harm to Athens. There was a chance that the New York branch of Syracusans forgave Athens and forgot that event, so I sent a letter to the Syracusans.

Another evening, at the same American Library and Center of Culture reading room, I came upon a catalogue from Louisiana State University. I kept pronouncing the word, Louis-zee-anna, fascinated by the beautiful sound it made and the romantic connotations I could conjure, looking at pictures of the bayous and the nightlife and the Mardi Gras parades. So, I applied to the University of Louisiana. It felt good to have more "irons in the fire," which, as my English book pointed out, was an "English Expression" I needed to learn. The University of Louisiana offered me admission and a full-tuition scholarship of $200. (Multiplying these College-related numbers by 80, will give a rough estimate of today's $). I got a shot of self-confidence from that admission: I had understood the application process, competed in an alien environment and achieved the objective. It proved that I was on the right track. I was happy that at least one American institution of higher learning had recognized my ability and granted me admission with a scholarship. I went about telling my friends that I had already been admitted to an American college with a scholarship. There was no need for shouting all the details. The school wasn't exactly touted in any kind of media as a model of higher education, and the tuition was a bit on the cheap side, but it was an American College and that was good enough for me to go on exploring.

Next, I received a response from MIT. The letter contained some encouraging words about my excellent performance and concluded with this statement: "I regret to inform you that foreign students are not eligible for scholarship at MIT until they have completed one year of work at the Institute." I stared at the letter as if I was in front of the Great Wall of China and had to get on the other side of it with one leap. The frustration lasted until I got a letter admitting me to Cal Tech with a $600 full tuition scholarship ($48,000.00 in today's dollars). I got the letter as I headed for the bus stop on my way to school and I read it in the bus, going downtown Athens. I got off at my usual stop, and started walking to school. I felt that I had torn down the wall that stood between me and my dreams of being a college student in America, an engineer, an inventor, a philanthropist, an explorer of any field of knowledge that I wanted. But the living expenses for Cal Tech were steep. I had always counted on some help from my parents, but there was no way they could handle all of it. Perhaps, I could work and make up the difference. Somehow, I should be able to make it. Ship fare, scholarship, living expenses, parents' contribution, help from relatives, work during school year, work in the summers – I found myself calculating and exploring every avenue I could imagine for any revenue I could possibly get. I would compete for it; I would work for it; I would ask for it; and, if need be, I would beg for it.

I didn't think to ask Jesus for help. I believed in God, but it didn't feel right to ask and probably get something that improved my standing in the world. That, had to be earned, so that others in need could receive his help. Why would God choose me for such a gift? I hadn't read the bible carefully. I couldn't believe that you could "ask and it will be given to you". That time would come later, much later.

Syracuse University offered me admission, but no scholarship. So much for the ancient ties of a colony to the motherland, I thought. I wasn't interested. There must be other schools to apply to, but which ones? Mrs. Metaxas, an administrator I knew at the American Embassy, told me that it was an honor to be admitted with a scholarship at Cal Tech. I forgot about Louisiana. Everybody seemed to think that Cal Tech was a top school in the country. If one wanted to get the best education possible, that was the school to attend. California, here I come.

With thoughts of connections and calculations bouncing in my head, I was crossing the schoolyard one late afternoon in the spring of my senior year when my eye caught a young man, a little older than me. standing at the entrance of the administration building that housed the principal's office and the offices of a couple of other senior professors. I had seen him before in the schoolyard, but didn't know him.

"How's it going?" he asked in Greek, smiling. He had visited the school with Kalegos, and, after that, Kalegos mentioned that his cousin was studying abroad.

"You must be Kalegos' cousin, studying abroad," I said, a little embarrassed that I couldn't recall his name.

"Tony, that's right, Tony Condaratos," he said in a welcoming tone. "I've seen you around."

He was short, powerfully built, with wavy black hair and a well-trimmed moustache. He seemed to enjoy being there. He said he had stopped by to say hello to some of his old professors. I was so intent on trying to explain my situation that I forgot to introduce myself.

"I'm trying to find a way to go to College in America," I said.

He smiled. "It isn't easy," he said. For a moment I thought he was sharing my predicament.

"It is; if you got the money," I snapped back. Why did I have to be so quick with an argument? I hated it when my impulses slid past my controls and produced the opposite result from what I intended. I didn't want to entertain even for a moment the idea that it was difficult, perhaps, impossible for me to study in America. "I'll need help to make it there," I admitted.

"Have you applied for scholarships? Americans are very generous people," he said. "But you have to have good grades."

He still doesn't remember me, I thought. Everyone knew that I had the grades. "I have a scholarship from Cal Tech, but it's not enough," I blurted out, anxious to show him that I was working on the goals I had set and even getting some results.

"Yeah," he said laughing, as if he just found the answer to a puzzle he had been working on. "Sure. You do have the grades! I remember you getting the prize from the Ministry: Kizilos, right?"

"Tolis Kizilos," I said. "I got the grades, but not the dough." I took a step closer, and we shook hands.

"Cal Tech is good." Then, after a moment's hesitation, he asked, "Have you applied to MIT?" He was staring at me eagerly, still sporting that half silly, half mocking, yet welcoming smile.

"I did, but they turned me down," I said, tired of thinking about applications again. "I asked if they could give me a scholarship, and they said foreign students have to be there for a year before they are eligible to apply for scholarships."

He looked at me for a long moment, as if I wasn't there; his eyes staring at some faraway vision. Then, something happened for which I have no explanation.

"If you send me your grades and your prizes from the Ministry of Education, all of these, officially translated, along with a letter asking for admission to MIT with a scholarship, I'll take them personally to the Advisor of Foreign Students." He stopped, as if to weigh a thought. "Professor Chalmers is always looking for good students. And, I'll put in a good word for you," he said and looked me in the eye waiting for my response as if we were in a dare.

I stared at him, unable to believe what he had just said. Without asking for help or casting spells at him, Tony Condaratos, a total stranger before our chance meeting, had offered to champion my cause. He heard my asking for help and had offered some. Why? People don't just take on another person's burdens and carry them for the distance without some benefit to themselves. Do they? What could he be up to?

"I appreciate any help I can get, and I certainly will get all my papers to you," I said as sincerely as I could. I still couldn't believe that anything would come out of his noble gesture. "Cal Tech gave me $600 for tuition, but it's not enough to cover books and living expenses," I added plaintively, as if he was the man who personally limited the amount of that scholarship.

"MIT is a great school and they may do better."

"You think they can make an exception in my case?" I persisted in my doubts. I barely stopped myself from saying, "I doubt it."

"Write a good letter and have all your papers in order. Paul Chalmers is a man who can move mountains to help foreign students, especially top students; but he wants to have all the facts and papers properly done." He took out a little notepad from his back pocket and jotted something down. He took his eyes off the writing and stared at me. "Chalmers has a heart of gold. He's a very caring person. Don't forget: everything officially done." He finished writing, tore the page and handed it to me. "Send your stuff to me on this address."

I reached out and took the little scrap of paper with the key to my future on it. I shook his hand and thanked him for his goodwill and all that he was willing to do for me.

"I'll be back in America in a couple of weeks, so I'll get your package in person. It'll take you more than a month to get everything translated officially and validated. The bureaucracy is killing this country."

"It took me a month to get my passport, and I had to pull some strings to get it that fast," I said, agreeing with him completely.

I hated the waiting and the sleazy ways government clerks forced you to deal with them, if you needed approval for any kind of papers. Every clerk of the bureaucracy became a plenipotentiary of the realm when he held his seal in his hand and decided if he would convert your paper to an official document of the government or let you dangle in limbo for days or weeks or forever.

"The American government is more efficient. People have a job to do and they do it well without money under the table."

"Are there many Greek students at MIT?" I asked, having regained my emotional balance. He named several students from Varvakeion who were studying there, most of them in graduate school, and a couple of the stars, who had become professors.

"We have a good community," he said, and then, laughing, "Some Greek Americans are always trying to get us to marry their daughters. They believe that MIT graduates are good catches." He glanced at his watch. "I better check and see if any of the wise men of yore are available now. I knew that there was a meeting, but it was supposed to be over almost half an hour ago."

"Was Mazis one of the teachers you wanted to see?" I asked, thinking that, if the teachers' meeting hadn't run over, I wouldn't have met Tony.

"Yeah. We all have been touched by his quirks, his tricks and his brilliance, haven't we?" He had already turned to get back into the building, but he stopped abruptly. "It would also help, if you could get a couple of professors to write letters of recommendation. Some guys say that they help."

"I can do that. I'll have them translated, also."

"Good," he said, waving goodbye. "I hope we'll see each other in Cambridge next fall," he said, as if everything between now and that day was only a matter of time.

"From your mouth to God's ear," I called out to him, using a common Greek wish for success. And, at that moment I had the strange sensation that God had done what I was hoping for through Tony Condaratos. This wasn't just a chance event. God had introduced himself to me and I had taken a step toward him.

15

Prayer or Diligence?

walked toward the bus stop on Lamentation Square, taking in the cool air of that spring evening filled with hope. It was drizzling, tiny drops suspended in space and memory. Riding the bus, I slipped into a reverie and felt the passage of the colored lights from all the marquis wash over the store windows and statues and sparkling cars flowing like a river up ahead of us. I wanted the people hurrying in the wet streets to have something in mind that gave them hope for tomorrow, a purpose for living without anxiety. I was still in my head when we reached Neos Cosmos, now a neighborhood bustling with construction work and life all the way out in the streets. This abode of outsiders with the tantalizing smells of souvlaki and shish-kabob from the tavernas out in the streets had been my home for a long time; but it wouldn't be forever. The air was electric, charged with hints of adventure and the joy of discovery. Nothing had smelled that good for a very long time, and I would have to leave it all behind, perhaps forever.

"Hey, young man," Kyr-Philippas, the grocer, greeted me as I went by. "Tell your mother we just got the tomatoes she was asking for."

"Thanks; I'll tell her," I said and moved on. I passed by the gardenia plant being reborn in Koula's garden. Tony, the chef in white work clothes at "The Taverna Nostimos," standing beside the pit of his revolving gyros smiled and tapped his toque with a couple of fingers a couple of times toward me. The neighborhood was trying to lure me back, and it was good to know it.

I couldn't help but feel buoyed by the other Tony's optimism. But, how could this stranger be at the spot where I found him, at the time that I happened to walk by, because a meeting happened to be delayed? And why did we start talking about scholarships rather than gossip about his cousin who happened to be in the same school with me, or his pending meeting with Mazis and the other old professors he had come by to see? Coincidence, I thought, the remarkable alignment of two or more events or circumstances without obvious causal connection would have been called chance. And what about synchronicity? Two people headed toward different destinations meet, without any intention to do so, at a given place and time and produce a greatly desired outcome. Meeting Tony Condaratos was unpredictable, improbable and potentially life altering. I still didn't dare believe that God Almighty would bother to throw such a good pass my way, even though I had been asking for his help for some time. I didn't really believe that God will do what I asked. He isn't a vending machine that receives your wish in a crumpled little paper and makes things happen. I wouldn't even dare say that I had made such a transaction with God, if I ever had. That would mean that I was good and had God's favor, and no one is good enough in the eyes of God to get freebies like that. Perhaps one doesn't have to be good to ask and get what one asked for. Perhaps, Tony is just a good man and I would have to ask him where that goodness comes from; or God gave Tony the idea to do what he wants done and Tony just decided to do it without knowing anything about the origin of his idea. Such things happen all the time. Yet, keeping God completely out of the event just didn't seem logical. What can we say about all these providential acts that happen with wondrous randomness, so often in this unpredictable world we inhabit? For whom do they happen, and why? That night I told my parents the good news. My mother was knitting a sweater for me and paused and looked at me as if she had been expecting something like that.

"I have been praying to my 'Little Jesus' to give you some help," she said. Why not? She believed that these things were a child's play for the Creator of the universe. I had to work a little harder to convince my father that something good would come out of this encounter with Tony Condaratos.

I worked very hard to write the best letter I was able to write for MIT. The couple of friends who could help me with the English letter were gone on their vacations so I had no one to help me.

I asked Professor Xifaras, my teacher of Modern Greek, and Professor Passas my Algebra teacher, to write letters of recommendation for me. Professor Passas signed the letter I translated as soon as I presented it to him, but professor Xifaras wanted me to read him the translated letter before he could sign it.

"How do I know that the letter says what I wrote?" he asked me. He had a point, and for a moment we stared at each other like strangers struggling to place each other's face in the right context. I couldn't believe that I hadn't thought about that and brought his letter in Greek with me.

"You could take the letter with you, Sir, and have somebody else translate what I wrote," I replied a little hurt.

"Start reading slowly," professor Xifaras suggested.

"Can you understand English, Sir?"

"How far from Latin, Greek and French can it be?" he said with resolve. "Read slowly and I'll stop you and ask you to translate a specific word, if I can't understand it, or if it is not the word I remember writing."

I read the entire letter to him while he stared intently at the ceiling. I had to stop and translate only half a dozen words. "It's not that I don't trust you to translate accurately," he said gently, "or that I don't trust you to be honest when you translate, but it is irresponsible for me to sign something that I don't understand. You must remember that. It could save you a lot of grief later in life."

"Thank you for the advice, Sir," I mumbled. "And for your very kind letter."

"Mr. Kizilos, you earned every word I wrote for you," he said thoughtfully. "When you go to America, don't forget your heritage." And the great Xifaras who had given 40 years of his life to instill the right Greek ideas and values to the most promising high school students of the country shook my hand and left.

I had all my documents officially translated at the appropriate office at the Ministry of Education, got photocopies of my prizes, and all relevant papers, wrote a "thank you" letter to Tony Condaratos, bundled everything together in a brown manila envelope and mailed it to him.

"Regardless of the outcome of your effort," I wrote to Tony Condaratos, "your willingness to help me, a person you hardly knew, is heartwarming and has moved me profoundly. I won't let you down and, I pray, that God will help you in all your goals."

A month or so later, the doorbell rung and my mother run downstairs to answer it. "Tolly-y-y-y-y, a letter from America! "my mother's voice echoed through the house. We hugged each other and I opened the letter. Professor Paul Chalmers, Advisor to foreign students at MIT congratulated me for my admission to MIT with a scholarship of $900! Nothing more joyous than a hoped-for desire becoming real

16

Networking Galore

Somehow, my mother heard from one of her sisters that the daughter of one of their aunts was married to the influential director of the electric power generation station for greater Athens, a man whose name in English, literally translated, means Dragon! My aunt said that her aunt thought it would be a good idea to get in touch with the Dragon's wife and find out if her husband knew anyone who might be able to help me with my plan to go to College in America. My mother contacted the Dragon lady, and got a promise from her that she would indeed talk to the Dragon. The Dragon lady called back and asked that I call her husband in a couple of days. She gave my mother a telephone number where he could be reached.

When I called two days later, Mr. Dragon told me that he had discussed my situation with a ship-owner friend of his, who was willing to see me and discuss my transportation problem. He gave me his name and a phone number to call. The ship owner's name was Pateras, which literally means Father, in Greek. So, a connection was established from me to my mother to my aunt to her aunt to the Dragon's wife, to Mr. Dragon and finally to Mr. 'Father'.

This God of ours has some ways of doing things that can make you drop down on your knees and thank him on the spot. Nothing was the result of planning; everything happening was improbable. Were these events a coincidence of unrelated events, or another set of providential acts? I was beginning to think that God was working some of the levers that made my life run.

A week later, I found myself in Mr. Father's office. He listened to my story and told me that he might be able to help me with the travel expenses, if I was willing to work for them. He told me that he had several ships that go all over the world, including America, and he would arrange for me to travel in one of them as a sailor, if I could get a sailor's work license and passport, in addition to my regular passport, so he could hire me for the duration of the trip. I accepted his generous offer and thanked him. The next day I started working on ways and means on how to get the sailor's papers I needed.

Uncle Gerassimos, my father's brother, was a Commander in the Greek Coast Guard at that time, and immediately offered to help me get my papers in order. To get the process rolling I had to pass a physical exam by the Piraeus Harbor Authorities. I remember standing half-naked in a large hall with a couple of dozen sailors and stevedores and comparing my puny body's musculature to the powerfully built bodies of seasoned sailors and dock workers, who had spent years doing hard physical labor. I was healthy, but I wasn't sure that they would find me fit for duty on a merchant ship. I tried to look tough and cool and even spat on the floor a couple of times, as they were doing, to show everybody that I wasn't that different from them. I passed the exam, and uncle Gerassimos helped me with all the papers I needed to have issued at the Ministry of Commercial Shipping. I got my naval passport and admired it because it would give me the opportunity to do "real" work for the first time in my life.

Then, I spent three weeks in the maze of the Greek bureaucracy, going from government office to government office, filling applications, signing affidavits, licking and affixing dozens of service stamps on them and sweating in front of various cogs of the machinery, to get documents for taking a small amount of foreign exchange out of the country, and documents for postponing my military service, where I was supposed to serve as a naval officer, if I wasn't a college student in good standing at the time I became twenty one years old.

The more I dealt with the government bureaucrats, the less contact

I wanted to have with them. Every official wielding his stamp of approval made me feel powerless, and I hated having to beg for my rights. Dealing with the bossy bureaucrats behind battered desks when barking their directions at my face was painful. I bore the brunt of their gruff ways because a part of me felt sorry for these lifers, occupying their little, cubbyholes without any prospect of change. I was so frustrated with the government bureaucracy that I counted it as one of the reasons I wanted to get out of Greece. They were good people ground up by the system.

I met another Greek student, Tony Hambouris, at the American Embassy, when he was applying for his visa. He had been admitted to MIT and was getting ready to leave for America. We became friends and agreed to stick together when we found ourselves in Cambridge and, perhaps, get rooms in the same dormitory. Tony had already bought his tickets on an ocean liner, and had passed with flying colors the interview with the consular official. His English was near perfect, having studied at the American College of Athens, probably, I thought, with some kind of scholarship, because he wasn't rich.

Living with uncertainty had never been a big problem for me, because I could focus my energies on any issue at hand and usually come up with a solution that was helpful; but, the situation I found myself in required living with many uncertainties for weeks on end, and without anything I could do to end the uncertainty. I wasn't sure whether the government would approve any of my applications, whether I could pass the consular exam, whether Mr. Pateras would find a ship to send me to America in time, whether my father could scrape up enough money to support me partly at MIT for the first year at least, whether I could find enough work at school to supplement my expenses, whether I could find a summer job, whether my visa would permit me to work at any job I found outside the school, whether I could find somebody to stay with for the few days or weeks before the dormitories were open and the school started . . .

When time for my interview with a consular official came, I was very nervous. Mrs. Metaxas told me that all would go just fine because I had worked hard, but I couldn't believe in myself enough to relax. I walked in the official's room like a lamb ready for slaughter. How on earth could I impress this American official with my "Hello" and "How are you" English? I wanted to burry my emotions deep inside myself beneath my soul, where they could never be detected. This however is something I'll ever be able to do in this lifetime. So, I looked scared, and lost, and embarrassed at my inadequate ability to express myself, and everyone could see it. Only God who knows the future would have been chuckling at my predicament, knowing that this is the 9th book I have written.

The official who received me was probably working for the ambassador, but I thought of him as "the Ambassador," and treated him like one. He asked me to sit down, pointing to a chair in front of his desk, and he took his seat behind his desk and started reading my file. He said something, which I understood to be approval of my record in high school performance and something about my interest in poetry and math, the American culture, and in playing chess and belonging to clubs. He chuckled at my enthusiasm when he read my comments I had written about the USIA books. He asked me a question about America and MIT that I didn't understand, but I gave him the answer I had rehearsed with Kostis Gartsos, another friend, and Tony Hambouris, who advised me to say that I wanted to go to America because "America is tops in technology."

At some point in the broken English conversation I was using, guessing and taking chances, he handed me a magazine, which I had seen at the racks of the USIA library and recognized it as the Readers' Digest. Somehow, recognizing the magazine had a calming effect on me. "Can you read the first paragraph, please?" he asked as politely as one could possibly do, pointing to the article where he had opened the magazine. He has decided to put me out of my misery, I thought, as I picked up the magazine and held it like a sharp blade one could use to slash his throat. The first paragraph of the first column was about five lines long. It contained no more than three short sentences and I started reading. I wasn't too bad at reading simple sentences, and my words were recognizable, if there weren't too many curves thrown at me by w's and s-h's and other unsavory letters like u's and various "a" combination like those one finds in "enough" or "aunt." I thought I did all right in reading, and the Ambassador smiled. "And, what does this paragraph say, Mr. Kizilos?" the "ambassador" asked.

I had no idea what I had just read. All my attention had been channeled to the reading, not the understanding of the paragraph. Even I was surprised at my ignorance, but I must have looked sick. He was getting ready to ask me to relax for a bit, or lie down on the couch behind me and rest, but I glanced again at my paragraph of doom and desolation, and the word "soap" jumped up before my eyes, my consciousness, my very soul. "It says something about "soap," I said grasping at "soap" as if it were a lifeline.

"That's right," he said helpfully. "Anything else?"

"Soap fabrication facts," I said throwing the dice on the French word "fabrique," and the Italian word "fabrica" and the Latin "de facto," all of which had something to do, I supposed, with "factory" in the paragraph.

"That's exactly right!" the Ambassador cheered, as if he had managed to read the paragraph all by himself.

"I am poor with my English, but will make better," I mumbled, exhausted by the effort. It sounded worse than anything I had said thus far, and I knew it. I was ashamed and shut up.

He kept talking, and I picked up a few words here and there to piece together his message, more or less. He said that the important thing was that I had demonstrated remarkable "motivation for learning," and my "English would improve" rapidly once I was "in America." He said that they wanted students who had shown their willingness to "work hard and perform with excellence." He was sure that I would "do well in America," gave me the student Visa I wanted and wished me "smooth sailing." This bureaucrat is a pleasure to deal with, I thought, and looked forward to a good stay in America. All I had to do is get there, somehow. And find some survival money.

Mr. Pateras called my father on the phone and asked that I get in touch with him. I went to his office sometime after my interview at the Embassy, and he told me that the ship he was planning to place me in was going first to Antwerp, Belgium, where it was scheduled to stay for a couple of weeks before heading for America. He advised me to go to the Belgian Embassy and obtain a visitor's Visa from them, so I could get out of the ship during my stay there. The Belgians had some difficulty grasping the complications of my roundabout scheme to get from point A to point B, but they accepted my story nevertheless and gave me a Visitor's Visa for two weeks. So, the second entry in my Greek passport was a Visa from the Belgian Embassy! I kept looking at it in disbelief. What other unpredictable things were in store for me? Immediately, my father found a trusted friend he had worked with at the plant, who had a friend that lived in Belgium and gave us a letter of recommendation. The letter was addressed to a Mr. Finkelstein and was asking him to assist me, if I needed help while in Belgium. I have no idea what catastrophe my father imagined might befall me, but he was covering all the bases he could, and I had learned not to object to any help that was given to me, even help that I didn't need. I reported to Mr. Pateras with some pride that I had executed the orders he gave me, trying to demonstrate to him that obstacles would not discourage me. The time of departure was near.

17

More Gifts from Above

"Every good endowment and every perfect gift is from above, coming down from the Father of lights." (James 1:17a)

Saint James

I sensed that my parents had been worried for months about the entire enterprise of my study abroad, but they were very careful to be supportive of my goals. My admission to MIT with a scholarship had given them confidence that my efforts produced results and they wanted to help. One afternoon, I remember, they called me into their bedroom to tell me "something important," as my father put it. He stood up on a chair by the icon-holding cabinet, hanging high up on the wall of their bedroom, and opened a little drawer at the bottom of it. He took out a small bag and untied the string around it. It was a bag full of gold sovereigns. I was dazzled by the glitter of gold and astounded by my father's effort. I had no idea they kept anything but some crosses braided from palm leaves and some dried-up flowers from church ceremonies along with their wedding crowns.

"These will help with your education," my father said, pouring a few sovereigns on the palm of his hand and jiggling them. "It isn't much, but we'll do what we can, and God and your work will help you to make it in college."

"You'll be fine and do great," my mother said and held me close to her.

I was moved to tears. I always knew my parents were good providers, but I never thought that they would go as far as to part with the money they were saving to build the house they had hoped for all their lives. I expected an allowance from his monthly salary to give me a start in life, but not such generosity. "Thank you," I said and hugged them. The three of us stayed hugging each other for a while. When I first broached the subject of going to America, I had been a little worried that my mother might have second thoughts and wouldn't let me go. But I shared my ups and downs with her and she came around. She was a dreamer and an adventurer at heart, like her brothers, The Navy submarine Captain and the Poet-Movie-Maker, and wouldn't oppose me from realizing my dream. My father was a logical man, and I knew he would come along, if dreams turned to results with effort. When he realized that colleges, Mr. Pateras and many others were going out of their way to help me, he decided that the project was good for everyone and was ready to back me up. My mother and I could convey meanings without words, and she knew how thankful I was to her. She smiled blissfully and watched as I hugged my father.

The Bank of Greece issued its preliminary decision on the amount of currency I would be allowed to receive abroad from my parents, and it was meager by any standards, but it was just enough to make attendance at MIT possible. Now that I had the Student Visa and could work, I would find something to do and earn my keep. I had no idea what that might be, but neither did I have any doubt that I would survive – somehow.

Time was getting short and my ship's schedule was still up in the air. Finally, Mr. Pateras' secretary called and asked that I come to his office for another meeting with him. When I got there, she was very busy and I had no chance to get any hints as to what kind of news was awaiting me. I went in to Mr. Pateras' office, but he didn't ask me to sit down, as he had done before.

"I thought that I could send you to America with one of my ships that is going first to Antwerp, Belgium, as I told you, but the plans have changed and I'm not sure that the ship will go to America after Belgium. It may, but it also may turn right back and head for India through the Suez Canal. That wouldn't be good for you." Here he paused and looked at my downcast face. "Here," he said and thrust a sealed envelope toward me. "Take this to the address shown on the envelope; give it to Thomas, who works there, and bring the envelope he will give you back here, to me." I took the envelope from his hand while in a daze, but I felt that, in spite of all these difficulties, Mr. Father wouldn't leave me in a lurch. I thanked him and left.

The address on the envelop wasn't too far away from his office in downtown Athens, so I walked there as fast as I could, short of running. What if Thomas was sick today? What if Mr. Pateras was trying to send me on another ship that might get stranded at some other port that he hadn't counted on? It occurred to me that I should start preparing again for the Polytechnic exams, because I had forgotten about them for a while. But, could Mr. Pateras find a ship that would leave Greece after the exams at the Polytechnic? And if he did that, wouldn't it be too late? Besides, beggars can't be choosers. I would have to commit to go or stay; there was no way I could do both It cannot happen that way, I kept thinking; it cannot go that way. Maybe, I would have to take a chance and go with the ship, and if it turns back and goes to India, I lose; but if it continues on to America, I win. Do they allow students to register late at MIT? A fifty-fifty chance is better than no chance at all. In this shadowy, befuddled state of mind, I got to the address marked on the envelope, entered what seemed to me like a commercial transport business office, found Thomas sitting behind a desk and gave him the envelope.

"Mr. Pateras told me to give you this," I said, hoping that he would know what it was all about.

"Yes; he called me. Please, wait a couple minutes and I'll give you an envelope to take back to him," he said with a smile.

Things were looking up, or I had entered La-La-Land and was playing a stooge. No! Things were going well. Thomas is working, and

Mr. Pateras is at the controls. What more could a person ask? I asked God to help me and I had a strange feeling that he would.

"Take this to Mr. Pateras," Thomas said, and handed me another sealed envelope. "Mr. Pateras is a fine man," he added.

I agreed with him, thanked him and started on the way back, thinking about the meaning of these messages I was carrying back and forth. Could a couple of sealed envelopes and some accidental connections shape my future? Where did this Mr. Pateras come from? Did he know a Mr. Tony Condaratos? What if I hadn't known anything about "soap"? How did it happen that Tony Condaratos was standing outside the administration building of my school in Athens, Greece, at the time that I was passing by, when he hadn't been in the school for a year or more? My recent life started to look like a made-up story. I was walking as fast as I could, thinking of the many coincidences that had brought me to that moment. God was having something to do with all this, or all these events were part and parcel of the random order of the universe.

I gave Mr. Pateras the envelope. He opened it and examined the contents. "As I told you, your arrival in America in time for your studies with my ship cannot be guaranteed. For this reason, I have decided to buy a ticket for you on the regular ocean liner, the "Nea Hellas," that leaves in three weeks from Piraeus for New York. You'll be in America by mid-August. Will you be ready?"

I stood still, moved by grace. I hadn't expected this kind of generosity from a stranger. "Thank you, Sir, I'll be ready," I mumbled and shook Mr. Father's hand. I wanted to add that I had been ready to travel on that ship since the day a stowaway was caught in that ship, but I kept this to myself.

"Well, not yet," he added and sat down. "Hear me out, first." I sat down to steady myself. "I'll pay, as a gift to you, half of your ticket, and your father can pay me the other half in several payments over the course of a year. This is the ticket. Take it. Tell your father what I told you, and let me know if he accepts my terms." I thanked him again and promised to inform him of my father's decision within a day or two.

"I hope he accepts, and you can go to America, soon. I hope you'll do well in school."

"I'll do my best," I said with conviction.

My father accepted the terms of Mr. Pateras' generous offer. He was very impressed by a stranger's generosity to us and, as I found out later, he paid his half of the ticket as he promised. And, I was pretty sure, that Mr. Pateras had a very good day at the office.

D

STUDENT, STEEWORKER, HUSBAND

18

Love and Laplace Transforms

A couple of months before I left for the steel mills to earn some money for the next school year, I was taking a class in advanced Calculus for Engineers. It was neither assigned nor needed for graduation, but it would help me to satisfy some of the course requirements for the Master's Degree, which I was planning to start and finish in one year because the Greek Navy had refused to extend my exemption for an advanced degree and every month I was late in starting my draft duties in Greece after obtaining the Bachelor's degree would add two months to my four years of service as a naval officer. I could be an old man by the time I completed my obligations!

It was April and the snow was finally gone and green was showing up all around the campus. I was absorbing the new knowledge of unlocking the mysteries of nature using Laplace transforms, Bessel functions, Vector analysis and all the mathematical tools with utter delight, as if I were going through a protracted initiation ritual of some secret society.

There was a girl sitting at the front of the class every time I got there. She seemed to mind her own business to the exclusion of any other comings and goings. One day I got to the class feeling really good after working on the assigned problem we had, and when professor Levinson outlined the answer, I raised my hand.

"Professor, I solved the problem another way," I said. The girl turned around, and I caught a glimpse of her face. In that brief moment that our eyes met I felt a desire to know her. Her solitary existence in that classroom gave the momentary turn of her head and her wondering look a special significance. She is curious about my accent, I thought, and went on with my alternative solution to the problem, hoping I was not only right but also profound. I have to meet her, I thought as the class ended. I approached as she was leaving the class.

"I noticed you taking a lot of notes," I said, having no idea what would come after that comment.

"It helps sometimes," she said without asking for explanations.

"What are you taking the course for?" I asked. I couldn't believe what I was saying; yet she wasn't taken aback. Her eyes seemed to welcome me.

"I happened to test out of differential equations."

This wasn't good news. I hadn't tested out of anything at MIT. I didn't even know that one could "test out" of anything. I didn't know what "test out" meant until she used the expression. I had taken that course and it wasn't easy. But, Calculus was a subject I understood well. I was sure I could hold my own, if this coed happened to be one of the much talked about, freakishly smart MIT coeds. But, how would I know? She didn't ask questions; she didn't make any comments; she never spoke to anyone, and I had never seen anything she wrote down. The only data I had was that momentary but meaningful look she cast my way and our brief exchange. Most American male students at MIT were worried about the relational and social weirdness of the MIT coeds, but I had no concerns about that; I was only concerned with girls' looks, and intelligence. If a girl was beautiful, and smart, but not freakishly smart, I was in the game. There was no time to think about all the things running feverishly through my mind. Any moment now we would split up because she was headed for the main exit and I was going to the dreary mechanical engineering labs for testing bubble jet atomizers for spray cans.

"Could I borrow your notes," I heard myself say. She wasn't shocked; she wasn't even surprised. Our eyes met again and I knew she wouldn't judge me. "I haven't taken many notes, and I saw you write a lot in class," I explained, defending my stupid request, even though there was no rejection, not even a question from her.

"Sure; here," she said and handed me her notebook with a smile.

"Thank you." I felt betrayed by my ego. She had several chances to show me off and took advantage of none. Who was she? "What is your name?"

"Betty; Betty Ahola," she said. "And yours?"

"Tolly Kizilos." Her blue-green eyes drew me closer to her.

"I hope you can read my handwriting," I heard her say with the same soft, soothing voice she had said everything else.

Then, I thought about her. How will she brush up for the exam, without her notes? And why couldn't I return the notebook to her and find out where she lives? "I can return it to you, so you can brush up for the exam, also," I said.

"My address is on the first page."

"OK. I'll see you soon."

"Yes."

At the lab, I tried to work on the design of a more focused jet, but my thoughts were dancing on that bright face and the open heart that said "Yes" and wouldn't flinch at my muddled moves and kamikaze requests. She does have a good heart, I thought, and I felt the touch of velvet on my face.

"I met a real great girl," I told Tony when we met later that evening.

"And, if I may ask: what makes her great?" Tony asked in his smartass way.

"She is beautiful, smart and good-hearted," I replied so fast that I surprised even myself.

"This is not the time to meet great girls, man," he warned. "This is the time for fast work with attractive and willing girls."

"This is not that kind of situation," I said and clamped up.

Later that night I skimmed through Betty's notes and tried to figure out what kind of MIT coed I was dealing with. I was like an explorer looking for a buried treasure. But whatever else calculus may be, it is no Rorschach test, so all I could say from perusing her notes was that she was very much up to speed in math, meticulous and rather well organized. I felt a pang of guilt. But, why did I care about her so much as to stoop to such a search? I closed the notebook and set it aside. The exam was coming up and I didn't want to feel that I had done well in the exam because I was helped by that notebook.

Next day I returned the notebook to her. She came to the door with a white towel wrapped around her hair.

"I brought you your notes," I said.

"Oh, thank you."

"No; I thank you." I was anxious. I always dreaded asking a girl for a date. "Would you like to go to the Esplanade for a cup of coffee with me?" I felt stupid and vulnerable.

"I just washed my hair," she said.

"I guess you can't go?"

"Sorry. Not tonight," she said. But, the refusal didn't hurt because I believed her. She wasn't using her hair as an excuse. Not this time. Not with me.

"Some other evening, perhaps," I mumbled already retreating.

"Yes," she said again. I gazed into her face and the eyes and her heart gave me the same welcome warmth as she had given me before.

I sat at my usual place in the back of the room for the exam and solved all the problems without difficulty. I wanted to approach Betty after class and talk with her, but I was hesitant. I wanted now to know as much as I could about her and talking would be the way. When I raised my head at the end of the hour, she had already handed in her exam and was on her way out. There will be plenty of time to talk with her and find out, I consoled myself.

At the next class, I sat behind her, determined to get to know her better, something I had never done with any other coed. She greeted me with a smile.

"You left in a hurry after class the other day," I said.

"I had a meeting with an instructor" she explained.

"I thought you were avoiding me," I managed to joke. She raised her eyebrows, as if the assumption was preposterous. "What course are you in?" If she was in Business or the Humanities, I could breathe easier; but some fields could threaten any male ego, and I was hoping that she wasn't in one of them.

"Physics," she said, and there was a soothing tone in her voice, as if she wanted to put me at ease again. Physics was a field that could scare the crap out of anyone. But, somehow, I wasn't deterred. There wasn't a smidgeon of the smartass in any of her answers.

The class began with professor Levinson distributing the exam papers. I had a ninety-five. It was one of the highest grades I ever got at MIT. I looked at it and felt proud of my work. But, what did she get? I nudged forward a bit and looked at her exam. "You did great," I said, looking at her paper marked with a bold ninety-four in red, at the top of the page.

"What about you?" she asked, but the question was flat. Nothing depended on my grade.

I also had no interest in gloating now. "Ninety-five," I said without enthusiasm. And professor Levinson went on lecturing on Bessel functions the method of Stodola and Vianello for solving differential equations while I thought of Betty's quiet beauty, those blue-green eyes on her cloudless face. Two people brought together from two distant corners of the world by accident or providence. What would have happened, if I had got a ninety? What about an 87?

At the end of the class I walked with her and asked her if she would like to have that cup of coffee I had asked her for the other night. "Sure," she said as if this was something we had done a hundred times before. I thought that she was interested to know me as much as I was in knowing her. She wanted to know about Athens and Greece and I wanted to know about Ely, Minnesota, her hometown in the middle of evergreen forests and crystal-clear lakes. We talked about our parents and our siblings and the high schools we had attended and the courses we were taking at the time. Time was flowing by smoothly and I wanted it to go on forever. I asked her if she would like to have dinner with me at the Omonia, the Greek restaurant I liked. "That would be nice," she said, as if having dinner was exactly what she had in mind as well.

We ordered some lamb dishes and retsina wine and went on talking about our reasons for coming to MIT to be ground up and reformatted into scientists and engineers. I told her how I had fought to excel and come to America, and about my dreams to see the world and do something worthwhile in my life. After a few minutes, I realized that I was doing all the talking and stopped. I felt guilty and short changed at the same time. My goal was to find out what kind of a person she was and all I had found was how easy and pleasant it was to talk to her and receive a sense of kindness instead of facts.

"Here I am laying out all my dreams and you've said so little," I complained.

"But you have so many interesting stories to tell."

"It's because you are such a good listener," I protested. "You are able to pull things out of me without even trying!" And, boy, was she a good listener! She had no urge to show anyone that she was ahead of anyone, or at the top of anything. She was where she wanted to be and that was just fine with her. But, was it possible to get anywhere without ambition? Why was ambition related to talking?

"You said that you were taking a Poetry class for your humanities elective?" I asked remembering that she had mentioned that previously.

"Yes; I like literature." She waited for a long moment, but when I kept silent, she went on. "I write poems sometimes," she offered with reluctance.

"Then why come to MIT?" I pounced, reverting to the investigative mode I was used to. But why? She was no adversary; I wasn't competing against her. Sometimes I hated myself for my antagonistic style. "It must be hard going through the rigors of one discipline, especially Physics, when you want to pursue another," I offered.

"I came to MIT to study Physics for the same reason I write poetry," she said. She raised her glass and took a sip. "I want to understand God."

I raised my glass and she raised hers and I taught her how to wish the best to one's friend. "Stin iyia sou; to your health," I said, and she repeated the words with pronunciation so perfect that everyone who heard her in the small dining room congratulated us by raising their glasses and drinking a little for our health and well-being.

I took her hand and we walked toward my car. It was dark now, and the blue neon lights of the "Jesus Saves" sign across the street cast a tranquil glow on the street. I felt so hopeful that night, and everything I could think seemed possible.

"How about going to the movies?" I asked her, still wanting to go on feeling the warmth of her presence.

"Let's go," she said playfully, as if we were kids determined to play hooky that evening. We were ready to hop and skip to the parking lot. We found a movie and sat in the dark, holding each other's dreams and desires in our embrace. We kissed and were drawn to one another and felt the tender joys of love. It was a matter of the heart first of all, something found in the wispy places where spirits dwell, nurtured by flesh and blood into robust humanity. It was another gift of God, but we didn't recognize it until time revealed it to us. I was in love with Betty, but it would take some trials and tribulations before my sly head could catch up with the truth of my heart. The culture had instilled in me the distorted belief that a man cannot admit he is in love and still command the respect of his beloved. For quite some time I held back a little and didn't show this wonderful girl that I was totally nuts about her.

We went out a few times and got to know each other better. Then the school year was over and I had to go looking for work in the steel mills again. We were in love, but it took many years before we knew the heart and mind of the other. One evening I was thinking how wonderful our life together would be. I felt I had fought for her and had won her in some grand contest. I had worked hard to do well in high school; I managed to overcome obstacles and come to America; I came to MIT believing that God was with me. She was typing one of her papers and I was stretched out in the sofa when my voice rung out: "I got you girl; you are mine!" I said, but she didn't stir.

She stopped typing, turned her chair toward me and said with conviction made of strength and steel: "You had no chance. You were mine when I heard your first words in class, Professah!" Her shiny eyes claiming victory slowly gave way to the softness of a dream. "I knew when I was a little girl that I would be with a boy from across the sea." Her eyes held on to love: "You couldn't escape; it was all in my dream."

"I love you," I said and my mind signed this with: "I'm yours."

We were married a couple of years after that.

19

MIT for Dummies

I have just landed in America, and started my student life. I am alone in my dorm room at MIT studying as hard as I can and keeping an eye on the night that hugs my window. Four floors down, a streetlight breaks up the darkness. I am sitting on a regulation chair, before a green-topped regulation desk, staring and despairing at the assigned books. Across the football field, cheers and jeers have been chilled by the November frost, but the giant ketchup bottle peddling Heinz 57 still spills its river of red neon sauce. The city spreads its edges out and up, leaving only faint lights behind. Cambridge has gathered ambitions from all over the globe. My goal is to take in all the knowhow I can from this mother lode of expertise, enjoy practicing my profession and do some good in the world. The people I left behind are limping back, demanding to be recognized. I know them, but they don't know me anymore. I am a stranger here too. I am surrounded by Americans, foreigners from every land of the globe that I know nothing about, strange Greeks bragging about their ships and factories and sports cars, or wannabes like me, pinching pennies to make it. Everyone speaks English, but I understand close to nothing. Classes have just started and I am already behind. I would give a lot even for misunderstanding the English language. I feel lost. I am plagued by doubts and climb out of my window to the fire escape ledge. Soon, I'll have to write an essay on Shakespeare's "King Lear" and the thought terrifies me.

These four-square feet of the fire escape's ironworks belong to me and to the night. Here I can sit alone and shrink the miles of ocean to my home in beloved Athens. The couple of months I have been away from home weigh their heavy days inside me. I depart from Piraeus by boat over and over again, as mother, father and sister wave their last goodbyes. It was done – why must it be undone so many times to be forgotten? Thousands of arms are moving up and down waiving goodbyes, like a multitude of upended beetles kicking the air in despair. I feel a tear of regret, and the red sauce across the way turns muddy. I hold on to the memory of the Attic sky, as it was burnt in my heart the day I knew I would be leaving home. "You'll be going on a long voyage," a gypsy up on Philopappou Hill of Athens had told me. I kept my eyes on the blue of the sky, smiled and gave her a good tip. There is no escape from this room. Did I forfeit my claim to happiness when I left behind my people and all the futures rooted there? I will always wonder. I have pawned all pliant dreams to pay for a stake on this uncharted voyage. I have to make it work.

I wipe the tear off and study carefully solutions to the math problems for tomorrow's exam. Calculus is not a problem, if you know algebra and can pick up the scent of the unknowns. I do know algebra and can sniff what needs to be found in Greek or in English, but philosophy . . . that's another matter. I take Plato's Republic and give it a glance. The English book feels ten times heavier than it did in Greek. There is no way that I can read fifty pages in English by tomorrow, but I remember that justice is a quality of the soul, not a social convention and a few other bits and pieces of wisdom from my high school class, when Professor Xifaras was delivering his lectures on Plato. They'll have to do.

I have met up with Tony Hambouris at MIT, as we had planned in Athens. We are trying to orient ourselves and avoid talking about home. Tony looks dapper and is looking for girls in his desirous but disinterested way. He believes that if you show you are interested in a girl, you've lost her. "Stay cool and look bored," he advises. But isn't that disingenuous? He recoils at the use of the word. "What do you expect me to do – tell a girl I just met that I want to make love to her right now? Right here? You have to act indifferently, or she'll think you are a sex maniac out of some asylum." That's not what I meant, not what I meant at all. I'll have to learn from experience or by accident, somehow. "We should go to one of the acquaintances dances they have every weekend," he tells me. I have no money, no language and no time for dates. Not yet. Then he comes up with a bit of wisdom that gives me food for thought. "Girls are human beings and want the same things that we do," he says and turns my ethical applecart upside down. I had thought girls had different interests, but now I see his point: we are all made of flesh and blood, and, therefore, similar desires. And boundaries? Better go slow here and think more about such weighty matters.

We usually find some diversion, like the TV at the lobby of the upscale Baker House dorm, to stave off remembering. Rene from San Salvador is slouched on an armchair eating his paper napkin, his "after dinner dessert," he tells us. "Clean, white paper is good, no?" He really means it, and we realize we've come across another head case inhabiting the realm.

I found out that Tony Condaratos was staying at Baker House and paid him a visit soon after school started. We hugged each other and I thanked him and got all the details about the way he got Professor Chalmers to reevaluate my application. He said it was all due to my hard work and the "strong package" I had put together. I thanked him again for his interest and his efforts.

Somebody knocked at the door and asked if his desk lamp had arrived. Tony assured him that it would arrive within the week and the guy left. Tony smiled and pointed at the neon lamp on his desk. "I sell these lamps and make a few bucks for some spending money," he said. It had never occurred to me that one could go into business from his dorm room, and I congratulated him for his ingenuity. I thought the idea was wonderful and wished I could do it too. Tony asked how I was getting along and I said "fine," not wanting to pile any more cares on him.

"Listen," he said holding me by the shoulder as I was leaving his room, "This is America and everything will be fine." He laughed in such a gregarious way that I couldn't help but feel uplifted. "Let me know if you need any help, OK?" I was so moved by his interest in me and I didn't want to talk. I shook my head. We agreed to get together sometime soon for coffee, and I left.

He was a year older and we didn't get together for a long time. I saw him a few times when he joined the Greek crowd. We had some good times together, visiting the Greek Church in Boston and dancing with the girls. Many years later, I visited him and his wife, at his home in Washington DC, when he was working for the United States government and I was on a business trip for Honeywell, Inc.. We got to renew our friendship and discussed the experiences we had after leaving MIT, and our plans for the future. After graduation, Tony went to Greece to practice as an engineer in a power plant. He wanted to "live like a Greek," he said. He had found out that the people around him were acting irresponsibly and had no interest in teamwork. "It's a dog-eat-dog world in our homeland," he said bitterly.

He had returned to America disappointed by his Greek work experience. "They don't want our help," he said, sadness clouding his face. I mentioned that another Greek from MIT had gone to Greece only to return to his MIT professorship, disappointed by the intrusion of politics into his research projects. The news didn't help Tony. The man cared about the homeland. Tony said that he was enjoying his government job very much. But, it was clear to me that he was a restless man and was always looking for other things to do. He told me that he had written a book on Santorini, his family's homeland, with archaeological evidence proving the island's links to the ancient continent of Atlantis. He said that he was thinking about going back to Greece and teach engineering at the newly established University of Patras. When I visited Greece some years later, I found out that Tony had become a well-known OD consultant in Athens and, later, an executive at a major hospital in Athens and was as always hopeful, helpful and forceful. Tony Condaratos was a great friend to all the people who knew him – "all heart," as the Greeks say, and filled with dreams and dynamism. When my father was dying after an accident at the nursing home he was in and there was no room to give him, I called Tony and he somehow arranged to find a place for him. I heard from fellow students at Varvakeion that he was greatly esteemed for his organization of the hospital system of Greece. I didn't see him on that trip, but a couple of years after that I heard that he died. I'm looking forward to thanking him for all his help to others. He was the kind of guy who fought to win for others.

Many of the foreign students hang out at Walton's cafeteria across the Mass Avenue entrance of MIT. It is an easy way to forget the grind of schoolwork for a while. We are getting to know each other here. I have met some Greeks and wait for them to show up, as I watch faces of strangers get muzzled by coffee mugs, mugs staining the dappled white Formica tabletops, breaths and voices breaking up the lingering cigarette smoke – all rituals of pagan cultists praying for empowerment through various notions of success. The din of foreignness in accents, languages, colors, dress and manners is soothing. I realize that I have to work hard to become a foreigner and I get ready to laugh at myself when I see Miltos and George coming. I wish more Americans would bother to bother me.

Tony and I were surprised to find so many foreign students at MIT. Walton's cafeteria was like a junior chamber of the UN assembly. Here the world comes together to commiserate and make comparisons between the old country and this strange country we have flocked into but cannot put in a bin and label, yet. There is a thinly veiled affinity among foreign students, and we get to know many of them. Some kind of weird brotherhood is being established here. We can share thoughts and feelings without much prep.

We just join the discussions that go on at the tables and proceed to debate any issue that is on the table. First encounters feel like reunions. It seems that the foreign accents make us more comfortable. Raj is as forlorn as any Greek I know, so he's always present wherever we clump together. I think he meditates a lot because I've seen him stare into the night without moving for long stretches of time. I don't know if it does him any good. We asked him in what caste does he belong and he said he was a Brahmin. His father is a judge in India's supreme court, but I have never seen him put on airs toward anyone around us, including some other Indians who admitted to us that they are "untouchables." We thought they were a bit haughty. I suppose, if you are a Brahmin and make it to MIT is not a big deal; but if you can do that from the untouchable caste, you've got to have moxie. Raj refuses to pay attention to these things.

Nobody knows what George Zetas will bring up for discussion, and everyone knows that Miltos will talk about the rich Greek students at MIT. "The rich have pockets but no hearts," says Miltos, puffing on a cigarette.

"Not all of them," I protest, thinking of Mr. Father.

"It's not right to assume that every ship-owner is a horse's ass like Kartos, or as weird as George Zeta."

"You think I'm weird?" George asks with genuine surprise, even though we have told him countless times.

"Yes, George, my friend," says Tony and smiles at him. "But, you are also very nice."

"And, let's not forget that you're crazy and angry – a bad combination, if you ask me," Miltos chuckles as he teases him.

"He's had a hard life, right Milt?" I pile on Miltos' affectionate sarcasm.

"Everyone is something he wishes he wasn't," Raj says, as if the thought had reminded him of something forgotten long ago.

"What are we?" I ask, probing his wisdom.

"Insecure, insensitive, moochers, girl-crazy dogs, tech tools . . . take your pick," Tony offers a response that includes all of our sins.

"If we knew that, we wouldn't be here," Raj says, but doesn't explain. No one asks him to explain because the answer might be obvious and the interlocutor would look stupid.

"Hell, everyone must also find something to be proud of. What is our thing? Not money or a famous family, that's for sure," Miltos says in earnest.

"I thought it was intellectual superiority," I say, "but that was before we came to this hellhole of intelligence freaks with monstrous IQs and scads of accomplishments. Where the hell do they find the time to learn about Fermat's last theorem and Veblen's Theory of the Leisure

Class, and work in hospitals, teach the poor, start businesses, or hook oscilloscopes to radios? I have no idea," I protested, dropping a couple of the new names I had learnt from Howard, another dorm resident with knowledge to spare.

"Everybody is in the middle of some heap or other," Tony lamented. "I'm going to use engineering to go into business. That's where I'll end up. Something that involves taking a risk and puts luck in play."

And we filled the cracks of the day with idle conversation and hard work, with problem solving, emotions, memories and dreams. We had few answers – they were always hard to come by when we were learning more about the world every day. But we made every day count for something, as if it was a sin to let it slip by without learning.

"So, can you spare twenty bucks for your poor old buddy over here?" Miltos asks George, continuing a conversation that had probably began hours ago.

George opens his billfold and looks inside. "No cash," he says, "Only checks." He looks at Miltos searching for a response. "Alright, I'll buy you dinner, if that's what you want."

"Thank you. That, and some cigarettes, if your budget allows," Miltos says.

It is dark when I go to Tony' room, to see how he is doing. No. I want to make sure that he hasn't discovered some way to do a lot better than I'm doing without letting me know of it. He understands what is going on around him. Donald, his roommate, is a Korean War veteran on the GI Bill, and they are having long discussions about the Truman Plan that saved Greece and the existence of God that will save the world.

I find out that Bud, the guy who is in the single room across the balcony from Tony's room, is an heir of the Heinz family fortune. "The ketchup bottle people," says Tony, who already knows a lot about the American culture and translates a few words for me now and then.

"He drinks all night and sleeps all day," Don, the veteran, says, voicing his disapproval.

"Pattel, the nephew of a billionaire from Mumbai, is three doors down from your room," says Mitko, another resident of the dorm.

Mitko is a Bulgarian, with a knack for math. "Very sharp mind," he says. "He doesn't belong here. He should be kicked out to Harvard." When Mitko makes a judgement, I've learned to pay attention. I ask why. "This Pattel is a genius in politics, history, society's structure and can't even breath when he opens the book of "Descriptive Geometry." He stops, looks up with closed eyes, and says, "Somebody who hates him must have driven him to Mechanical Engineering.

And then the conversations turn to the careers we plan to pursue. I understand a little better what is going on. Donald is in electrical engineering and he already knows a lot about radios and telephones. He has made electrical devices that open doors, attached solenoids that operate water valves, knows how to connect oscilloscopes to amplifiers and how to hook up an alarm bell to a photoelectric eye to detect intruders. All I know about electronics is that, if you look behind a radio through the peepholes of the cover, you can see vacuum tubes glowing with little faint, reddish lights. I have to rethink my career plans.

A few months later I will conclude that I can understand mechanical engineering better than my major in Electrical Engineering, because I have touched machines and breathed machine oil and I'll have a better chance to compete there. I will switch my major to mechanical engineering and be content for a while. I will find out later, that in spite of having done well as a research engineer, received many patents and advanced in the ranks, inventing products and building various devices, I wasn't cut out to be an engineer. I never cared that much about how things work. I would bet on a strong bent toward human relations and succeed in organization development both as practitioner and a thinker, then as a teacher, a novelist, a poet of sorts and an amateur theologian. I knew from those early days, listening to Mitko and some of the other guys, that there would be changes. I never knew how many or how great they would be to make me believe that what I was doing always had meaning and made me happy.

But for now, I'm having trouble connecting nouns to verbs, adjectives to nouns, and I yawn to hide my ignorance. "Exam tomorrow," I announce and leave the gathering. I go to bed and fall asleep trying to convince myself that I belong here. I heard Jerry my roommate through clouds of dreams when he returned from his excursion to downtown Boston with a bunch of other guys. In the morning, like my father, I thought of all the money I made by staying home rather than carousing. If you have only a couple of dollars to your name, necessity, not free will, guides your morals. I grabbed a handful of cornflakes in the dining room and run to the classroom.

The days are measured by the learning I get and the grades I collect. Christmas came and everyone who could get out of Burton House did so. They were in a hurry to leave and shouted their goodbyes and their Merry Christmases on the run. There were jokes and laughter in the hallways and bags, lots of bags everywhere, and the stairs were ringing with yells and triumphant cries reminiscent of the jubilation at the end of the war. After that, silence rushed in like a mountain of water to fill the hull of a sinking ship.

But we are still here – those of us who have no plans to go anywhere any time soon. Tony, Mitko the Bulgarian, Raj, Miltos, Tariq, an Iraqi chemical engineering student Tony has befriended and Howard, the Brooklyn Jew and fellow explorer of the mind and the world, all shipwrecked sailors stranded on this barren shore, people of faith and agnostics, singing strange songs of longing and return in the showers, looking for rescue. Emptiness heightens the expectation of a hopeful echo. We'll argue and agree and play cards and drink and laugh at happy people and brag about achievements and success, and what does it all mean, anyway. But we'll never reminisce. Not in public, anyway. Not on this joyous season!

A few of these fellow-foreigners will be there as usual dealing and wheeling with facts and fictions, chasing dreams, and making deals, building nest eggs and college funds and working their day and night so they can belong. Immigration is the blood transfusion America gets from the world to keep itself invigorated.

In the meantime, I got a job cleaning rooms, making beds and emptying wastebaskets at the dorm. I am a little worried because I may have to spend the entire Christmas vacation just reading Shakespeare's

King Lear and writing a six-page paper on it. I have to do it, come hell or high water. Every day I devote at least three hours to reading with a dictionary by my side, keeping notes and sounding out the words that I've never heard before in my life. Every now and then I flip the pages I have read and count them with a certain pride. The paper – how am I going to write a paper with only one year of study in the English language? God help me. Keep working.

Evenings, I argue with Howard about the existence of God as far as my English will permit. He says that my cosmological argument will not stand the onslaught of science much longer, and tries to tear it down. I find out that trying to prove God's existence based on the existence of a finely tuned universe out of nothing constitutes "the cosmological argument." I have no doubt that Howard is wrong. He says he doubts everything, and I learn that everyone is entitled to his or her opinion. Not that I don't have my moments of doubt, but God exists and doesn't give a hoot about anyone's doubts. He may even like to watch me struggle with my doubts.

"I got a job, and earn some money to pay for my many needs," I write proudly home. "I miss you all, and send you many kisses and special hugs for my little sister, Vasso." My mother says that Vasso and dad are doing fine and will be sending letters soon. The Muslim student ten doors from my room squats on his little carpet and prays every noon when I go by to clean rooms.

Mitko is nowhere to be found. Tony says that he found a girlfriend and has a good time. We are both silent for a while, trying to imagine the tryst of the lucky Bulgarian. Jerry, my Jewish roommate told me that he planned to ask a girl he has known since fifth grade for a date. I wished him good luck and Merry Christmas. He smiled and wished me Happy Hanukah. I didn't know enough to get either his joke or my mistake. I had no idea what "Hanukah" meant but I never suspected that he would call me names.

On Christmas Day, I went to the Botsis' home for dinner. Mrs. Botsis took me aside and said that they had invited Mike and his wife to come for dinner, since he and I had worked well with each other at the

Danbury Room, when I was a busboy and he was a waiter. Mike arrived soon after that and proceeded to tell all of them how I had managed to survive in the jungle of Danbury Room under his protective guidance. I told a few Greek jokes and had everybody in stitches. All these Greeks were my only friends when I first came to Boston. Mike and some other Greeks got together back then and found a month's work for me, showed me how to get a Social Security Card, taught me the elements of serving the restaurant's clients and made me useful. I had so many mentors among these humble and wonderful people that I stopped counting. As they say, "it takes a village."

They were all happy to see me doing well and wanted to know how I was progressing in school. When I told them that school was hard but I was doing OK, they urged me to keep at it and take the pain. "There's no free lunch in this country," everyone agreed. Tom Botsis came out of his splendid isolation, leaned forward on his recliner and said, "Ain't that the truth! Nobody gives a damn about you . . . only they want something . . . You pay, is all." He was a happy, hard-working man, the best barber in his little barber store.

We took our seats and waited. Mrs. Botsis and a couple of other women brought the food to the table. We must have been about a dozen adults all in all and about as many children in an adjacent room. I stared at the variety, the quality and the amount of food that was prepared. Was I one of the people Tom Botsis was talking about? This was a barber's home, and the food was fit for a king. The atmosphere in the room was festive. We forgot the daily cares and troubles and gave every moment a chance to flourish.

"Isn't that a great country?" someone said. Everyone raised his glass of retsina wine.

"Merry Christmas to you all!" Tom Botsis said.

"Stin iyia sas, everybody," I said along with the others.

Ever so slowly, I'm getting used to the deprivation of contact with the people I love. The school's demands pushed me away from all other needs and landed me in the middle of a battlefield to defend my intellectual survival with all the skills and talents I had. I think that Calculus is going to give me an A or B. Physics is hard, but Mazis did a good job of teaching us the fundamentals, so I should do well. Chemistry will always be a problem for me, and I will only try for an average grade. I did well in Plato's Republic with some help from Jerry, my roommate, in the paper I wrote on the allegory of the cave, and if I can manage a fair grade in the Lear paper, I could end up with a B in Humanities. Wouldn't that be a joke on the Institute? I have no idea how I'll be able to read a play by the master of the English language and write a paper that makes any sense. Tony and Jerry have promised to give me a hand with grammar, syntax and spelling, if I provide the ideas and the rough draft of the paper. I thank them for their help and go to work, trying to grasp some meanings from the text. My job was tedious and boring, but the few extra dollars I made working allowed me to have dinner at the Omonia Greek restaurant once in a while with my friends. After Christmas, I got a job doing data reduction with a Marchant calculator at a Civil Engineering lab along with a couple of other guys. We were never told what we were calculating, but we figured that we were doing stress analysis calculations to assess the damage various structures sustained after a nuclear bomb blast. Having learned the routine and the rewards of work, I began searching for a more challenging position.

I finished my essay on King Lear, managed to get enough down on the exam papers on the pre- and post-Socratic, Greek philosophers, did just fine in calculus, physics and chemistry exams and did what I had to do in projective geometry. When the first semester grades came in the mail, I found out that I had made the Low Dean's list that first semester, getting a B in my Shakespearean essay and A,'s and B's in all the other courses. I felt totally happy, performing better than I expected with the impoverished English language I had. That was one hell of a meaningful first semester. Howard made the high end of the High Dean's list and the intellectual average of that part of the world was adequately restored. My roommate Jerry was also on the High Dean's list. I don't know how happy or how meaningful their first semester was, but I hoped it was as good as mine.

20

Salt of the Earth: My Fellow-Steel-Workers

As soon as the exams ended, the Greek students with the big bank accounts left town for their summer homes on the Aegean islands and trips to Paris or Rome, or safaris in Africa. Zaharias and George and Paul Mercier were going to New York and to points around the globe after that. Tony was going to tough it out in Cambridge with a part time job. I envied the guys who were going back home and would have a chance to see their families again and travel to these magical places. I couldn't afford to do any of that. I didn't manage to get back home until twelve long, interminable years had gone by. The link with my birthplace was broken and would never be restored. I became a stranger to my home because that was the only way I could survive. And every summer I saw all the rich foreign students return home, I felt a deep longing for my people. I learned to cut off this feeling of wanting to return home before it had a chance to grow and choke me. I had a goal and I would achieve it.

I was ready to leave Boston with a bus ticket and five dollars in my pocket, borrowed from Tony. There was a distant great uncle of my mother in the Chicago area, and I was planning to go there and ask for his help in getting a job. I wanted to earn enough money, not only to survive for the summer without remittances from Greece, but also to have some left over when I got back to school in the fall. Tony asked me what I would do if I couldn't find a job and I told him it wouldn't happen. I was afraid of being stranded, but I believed that, somehow, I would achieve my goal.

The truth is that my worries were dwarfed by the excitement I felt, striking out by myself into the unknown all over again. I was broke and alone in a strange land, but I was healthy, street-smart, highly motivated with a "can-do" attitude that wouldn't quit; I had principles tested by experience and believed in God, who helps when you cannot help yourself. I was ready and willing to face the challenges that no doubt would arrive. I was headed for the steel mills of East Chicago. I should have been more worried than I was.

"Gary and East Chicago are the armpits of America's labor body," somebody said to me. People told me that these places need laborers and pay good wages. They pay double for overtime, and I'm ready to go after any job like a dog goes after meat.

Night creeps in. The bus plows on the highway with a relentless drone. "Clearfield! Half hour stop," the bus driver announces and pulls the handbrake in front of The Crystal-Clear Cafe. Bodies rise from the shadows around me. The stench from the men's room sneaks outside and assaults us. We wait for our turn taking shallow breaths. We next take to the counters in the diner and wait for the waitress to get to us. One hamburger and a cup of coffee at the Clearfield Café will have to last for the rest of the day. I'm left with three dollars in my pocket.

"You going far?" a man on the stool next to me asks.

"East Chicago," I say.

"Got a job, yet?'

"No. I will get one, as soon as I get there."

"Don't count your chickens before they hatch."

"I will find something in the steel mills, or restaurants; construction also."

"Good luck," he sneers and leaves.

I should have saved a few dollars to see me through this transition period. "Save." I remember telling my father how I would save some money, so I wouldn't need help for the summers. I thought he would be comforted by that "Save."

The people crawl back into their shadows and the bus rolls again.

No one has taken a seat near me. The ride lasts forever. The steady hum of engine and rubber on the road isolates and lulls the mind into reveries. I'm a great Greek poet composing the Ode to Clearfield, my magnum opus, while sunbathing in Tahiti with my bikini-clad girlfriend frolicking in the sand.

I'm looking for an answer to what makes millions of workers go to work every day without rebelling against the lousy lot life and circumstances dealt them. Are there any bus drivers whose childhood dream was to drive a bus when they grow up? Society entrusts them with dozens of lives, but pays them very little, compared to used car salesmen or bureaucrats wielding rubber stamps. Bus drivers are not looking for adventure; they are not doing their job as a way to a life of learning; and they don't get their jollies confined for hours on sweaty driver seats. What do they know that I don't? I make up answers, but I cannot fit the pieces of the puzzle together. In the humanities classes we talked a lot about Truth and Beauty and the Virtues of Aristotle. Now, I want to know if I'll find a job anywhere and warn others about counting their chickens before they hatch.

Night has settled down. Some passengers get off and new ones come aboard. A woman with a baby takes the seat in front of me. The baby cries, and she offers her breast to it. The baby is hungry because I can hear its lusty sucking, cooing noises over the steady hum of the bus. I think again about the knowledge I need to draw from this expedition to the sweat-lands of America. The mother and her baby are in the mix of answers, or questions, but I am too drowsy and cramped to think clearly about anything. How long before we get to the Promised Land? Night creeps everywhere now. I'm hungry, but I still have only three dollars in my pocket.

The air rushes in from the open window. Through holes of dreams I see the outskirts of hopelessness. It is only a summer. Fires burn unchecked from smokestacks like tongues of mythical beasts struggling to articulate a hopeless message. Uncle Orestes was a poet and lived in the moment when he was young, but ended up living in the past when he was old. He thought Africa had the answers, but all he found there was more questions.

How much of what is can be allotted to futility? Smog and fog blur the outlines of factories that crouch in the dark. All lights are yellow, like halos of bowing saints. The Steel Town lies comatose on the shore of Lake Michigan. The smell of industry, a blend of fumes from oil on steel and the debris of coal and lime and sulfur engulf me. I take it all in as if it could have a hidden meaning for me. Those who haven't shed sweat and suffered pain from work can afford a romantic view of labor. The rest of us know what Saint Paul knew: "we know that our sufferings produce perseverance, perseverance character, and character hope." I caught myself in the romantic babble and touched my face. I should quit imagining reality. I was looking out of the window, absorbing what I thought was a town made of nightmares. The deceptive tranquility, the silence of desolation, clouds of steam glowing red near the ground, cranes perched above mountains of coal and limestone. The entire complex was overwhelming.

"East Chicago! East Chicago!" the bus driver called out and stopped at the Greyhound depot, next to a "Speedy Laundromat" and the "Fill It Gas Station." Across the street there was a hamburger joint and a red neon sign with Liquors writ large next to a yellow sign of a pedestal glass. I knew that this city had a lot to teach me, but I didn't know what, yet. The visual scene was recorded deep in my memory resisting any future efforts to erase it.

I got off the bus and walked toward the blue neon lights of "Summit and Rooms for Rent." The streets were littered with crumpled paper cups, newspapers, cigarette butts, spilled liquids and rubbish that moved at every puff of a breeze. I passed a doorway with a small sign that read "Bingo." The lights were turned off and I had no idea what Bingo was. I signed for a room, paid the clerk and picked up a key with a wooden tag. He gave me the room number and pointed to a corridor. The chairs the bedspread the walls, everything in the room had large, reddish flowers and greenish leaves. A mad decorator with intent to obliterate beauty once and for all had been let loose in that room. I took off my pants, drew back the sheets and left the world.

Early next day, I appeared at the house of my mother's distant uncle and was welcomed into their home. Uncle Vangelis was a big man, loud and volatile, with the temperament of most of the people on my mother's family. He was a hard-working owner of a diner, who had immigrated to America in the early part of the century to work and raise a family. He had a very quiet and welcoming wife and two daughters, a little older than me, who were curious and kept probing me with questions about everything Greek and everything related to college life. They offered me a room at their home until I was settled, and my uncle told me where to go and get a job.

"'Inland Steel'," he bragged, "the biggest employer in the East Chicago area."

Years later, after I had worked in the steel mills of East Chicago, my view of working people changed radically from politely ignoring their presence or hiding my elitist attitude, to embracing them warmly. I saw why people who never got much education and didn't pursue academic work are often, rightly called "the salt of the earth," and why so much of what makes life worthwhile comes through the work of blue-collar workers. I experienced this reordering of my values when I started laughing at the jokes they told to pass the time, the crude but creative ways they invented to make sense out of the grind of work and the meaningless foul words that welcomed friendship when they spiced their speech. It took me a couple of weeks after I got back to school to clean up my language from the four-letter words I used all summer long at the steel mills. These words were spoken at the mills among people bound together by trust and a sense of brotherhood, not competitiveness, jealousy and disdain. The "fuck" of the steel mills had none of the poison it carries in other venues. I couldn't understand why they were generally cheerful, helpful to each other and never daunted by their life-long routine.

Though a greenhorn, I started offering suggestions on work improvements and found out that my coworkers listened and used some of the solutions I came up with. Of course, they would tease me and call me smartass and even be defensive sometimes, but they were not too proud to follow some of my suggestions.

I came to admire Jake, the steel worker with the eighth-grade education, who headed the crew of one of the pickling lines for cold rolled steel, where I worked that first summer, after my freshman year. He could do the job with the most motivated crew in the mill, faster than any other crew, and with the least scrap waste. When Jake sat at the operator's seat, high above the 300-foot long Mesta Machine and the rest of us were at our posts, that monster of a machine obeyed like a hundred yoked oxen. Jake worked the controls with levers and buttons of many shapes and colors, and we fed hot steel coils through the behemoth's mouth, to press them down with its massive steel rollers into thinner gauge and harden them and drive them screeching and steaming into the belly of the beast, which was a two hundred-and-fifty-foot long tank like a sewer tunnel, only filled with acid to temper the steel and coat it and make it into the sheet metal needed for making cars, refrigerators and every other little monster our society uses.

Jake had been a steel worker for thirty-eight years and had a thriving family life. He was not an average man. He was a member of the elite, as far as I was concerned. He had the respect of his peers and deserved it. The bosses consulted him every time they had a difficult order to deliver to a customer, or when they wanted to make a change in the process and the equipment. He was a stickler for quality work, but he was also flexible when it came to helping any one of us do the work our way.

At first, I was the only laborer pulling scrap, but halfway through the summer, they hired another man to work with me and take over after I left for school. Calvin told me he was thrilled to get his job and planned to make a career working at the mill, advancing to better and better positions and making more and more money as the years went by. He wanted to have a family and he thought he could afford it after a few years in the mill. He was black and, at first, cautious with a foreigner like me. Getting to know Calvin made me think that my foreign accent and his skin color were somehow equivalent. Calvin was strong and smart, but he couldn't afford to take chances when it came to following the bosses' directions. He liked his job and didn't want some crazy foreigner messing it up. He was a little older than me and from another world, but talking about our different experiences we found that we had a lot in common and got along very well and became friends.

When Calvin showed up, we took turns doing our job at the pickling line. Several workers were busy lining up coils for the machine, checking the orders to set the parameters, get the coil into the feeder rollers, check the oil bearings, the strength of the acid after a few runs and so on. Calvin and I removed the scrap from the beginnings and the ends of the steel coils after a huge blade cut them off. Then the "joiner" would join the pieces together and, if the joint was good, he would signal Jake to start the coil rolling. The newly spliced coil would plunge into the acid tank and travel at thirty miles an hour with deafening noise. If the joint was bad, Jake would curse the coil and the "joiner" and everybody else responsible until his fury was exhausted and he was ready to begin the grind again. There would be no letup until the joint was "good" and the coil rolling.

It normally took three minutes working and three minutes watching the other guy work. I thought that it was a wasteful way of doing the job, so I started reading "The Cane Mutiny", three minutes at the time. Calvin watched me horrified. He was afraid of what the bosses would say if I was caught reading a book. Jake didn't mind, as long as the work was done right and, I thought, if Jake is happy no boss would care either. Then, Calvin and I had the night shift, and the boss-traffic was very rare, and it seemed to me that this routine of three minutes on and three minutes off was too wasteful to continue it. Calvin had nothing to do for his three minutes off. So, I proposed that he work for four hours straight, while I found a spot behind some stacked machinery parts to read or sleep, and then we would switch. Calvin freaked out at this. He wanted no part of such radical departure from the routine. But, the inefficiency was gnawing at me, and I went on reasoning with him quietly, until he agreed to try it. He could work his four hours and then stand nearby and watch me, if he didn't want to go somewhere and relax. To put his mind at rest, I told him that if any question came up while he was on the job, he could say truthfully that it was my idea. That, convinced him to go along. So, Calvin and I, without any official sanction, changed the workflow and no one was ever troubled by it. Calvin couldn't believe that he was free to sleep for four hours while he was getting paid. I should have understood his caution to take risks, but I didn't know the history of African-Americans at that time.

But some days at the steel mill weren't always, so quiet and peaceful as I have described thus far. Our life always has some suffering saved for us. When the machine went down and the whole crew was struggling to check and fix the malfunction of the Mesta Monster, Calvin and I were, working in the rat-infested underbelly of the machine pits. On one of these midnight breakdowns, I was told to go down a pit, under the steel drum rollers, to find out if there were any fluids leaking from the countless hydraulic lines crowding the space. The pit was like a tomb, dripping with moisture and the floor was wet with pools of dark oil mixed with water. The smell of grease was overwhelming and I thought I would choke. A rat was caught in my flashlight beam and scampered, sloshing on the muddy floor past my boots as I advanced. I was repulsed by the disorder of tubes and hoses and debris. I heard no telltale dripping and saw no ripples on the pool of oil on the floor, so I concluded that there was no leak and got out. Jake's crew had found a gear with broken teeth close to the other end of the beast. "At the but of the beast," Jake told a boss.

Sometimes I would be taken off the line and assigned for a few days at some other job. Once, I was in a labor gang sweeping the floor of a warehouse. I was given an area by the pusher and told to work as fast as I could and clean it. When I got done, I sat down admiring the sparkling clean floor and reading a piece of a newspaper I picked off the floor. Sometime later, the pusher showed up and came straight at me huffing and puffing.

"What the hell you trying to do to me, boy? You want to get me fired?" he shouted at me.

"What did I do bad?" I protested.

"You think we pay people to read newspapers here?"

"You told me to clean floor good, and I did it. Look! Clean!" I defended myself.

"You get back there and work that broom nonstop or you go home and play with yourself, boy. Hear?" Then, by way of an explanation, he added, "If one of the bosses sees you reading rather than working your butt off, he'll have my ass. Get it?"

"Yes sir!" I said without hesitation. And I went back to work, moving that broom as if my life depended on its perpetual motion. When the floor was sparkling clean and all the dirt dumped in the garbage can, I would tilt the can down and empty whatever I had put in there, and spread it all around, so I could keep working hard, cleaning the newly dirtied floor. I changed my goal from cleaning the floor as fast and as well as possible, to filling the garbage can as fast and as full of dirt as possible, and end up with a floor as clean as possible that way.

"Good work, boy," the pusher congratulated me when he stopped by next time. "You're sure a good learner. "I just smiled and went on sweeping. "Hey man" the pusher stopped and turned toward me. "Someday, when my boss is not on my tail, I'll let you do things your way," he said.

I smiled and shook my head.

"OK, man," he said and walked away.

21

Stupid Is . . .

When I wasn't working I would be at my uncle's home watching wrestling on TV, or hanging out with some Greeks I had met at work or at my uncle's diner. On a couple of occasions, I went to the nightclubs of Chicago and Cicero with these friends and caught a glimpse of the seedy side of America. One evening, that first summer I was there, I went to a Greek wedding in town and was encouraged by my cousins to eat the Greek delicacies and have some fun. I had bought an old car by that time and I drove it to the parking lot of the reception hall. I had no insurance, no registration and no license – just a permit -- but I was sure I could handle the short distance to the wedding. There was a lot of food and plenty of drinking. I had a glass of wine and a full plate of roast lamb and decided to leave. There were some young people staggering drunk out of the hall and I was avoided them. Getting drunk was a repulsive behavior for me and my friends in Greece, because it revealed lack of self-control. I got back to my car in the parking lot and backed up to maneuver out of my stall. Unfortunately, I hooked the front bumper of the car behind me. I was about to come out and check the damage when a guy opened the passenger door of my car.

"Don't try to get away, friend," he shouted at me holding the door open. "You're stuck, and I got you." An ugly, defiant, mean rush of energy overwhelmed my thinking. Some other entity got control of my body and was executing movements I never even thought I had. Instead of getting out and checking, or negotiating, or arguing, or fighting with that obnoxious drunkard, I shifted the car into gear and started rocking the car to unhook my bumper from his and get out of there.

"You cannot get away, buddy!" the man insisted.

And I saw myself banging his car back and dragging it forward with force, while he still held on to the door of my car risking a blow to his body, or worse. On the third or fourth try, I disengaged my car from his and he let go of the door to avoid getting hurt. I stepped on the pedal down to the metal for the first time and sped at screeching speed through the parking lot out into the street and then the highway. I was racing at high speed, totally given to the road ahead, and didn't hear the police sirens behind me. I just couldn't afford an encounter with the police without a license, insurance and registration any more than a man could afford going to his wedding naked. I paid no attention to the red lights I passed. The sirens got louder and I became afraid. I stopped the car when I caught the flashing lights at the rear-view mirror. I must have been in a chase without knowing it, because the cops approached my car with guns drawn and when I got out they manhandled me and loaded me in a paddy wagon and took me to the police station.

It was quiet now. I felt calm and safe there. The horrid thing I was afraid would swallow me begun to show its tail. They asked me to give them my belt and whatever was in my clothes and put me in a jail cell. I was the only prisoner there. When I realized that I was arrested, that I was in fact a prisoner, I became anxious again and started thinking very fast of all the monstrous things that could happen to me. I asked why they had brought me to the police station and was told that my offense was "reckless driving," which I took to mean driving without acknowledging the presence of the police. They asked me if I wanted to call anyone and I gave them my uncle's name. I had no idea how smart that move was because I didn't want my relatives to know what an idiot I had been. But I didn't have many options. The policeman behind the desk smiled when he found out that I was a nephew of Vangelis Laskos and a foreign student in Cambridge, working at Inland Steel for the summer. I imagined being taken to court and accused of a crime and found to be guilty and rotting in jail before being deported. How much time would I have to spend in jail?

I asked when they would take me to court, but the policeman said that he wasn't sure how long it would take. I felt that because of that one streak of madness that had taken me over, I had flushed my education, probably my career and my life in America down the drain. The hours went by, as I waited for a word from someone who could tell me what would happen to me. I was numb and dozed off on the only chair in the cell. I heard the heavy footsteps of the policeman from the desk approaching.

"It's all over now," he said in a pleasant tone of voice. "You can go home." I thought he was part of my nightmare. A joker, sent to torment me. I looked at him in disbelief. He opened the door and we walked back to his desk where he returned my stuff to me.

"Did you contact my uncle, Mr. Laskos?" I asked. It was like asking a magician how he performed his trick.

"Oh, we don't want to put our college boys in jail, now; do we?" he said and looked at me with a relaxed smile, as if he was welcoming his wayward son back home.

"Thank you," I said and meant it more than at any other time I had uttered these words to another stranger.

I thanked my uncle for straightening things out with the police and assured him that I would never embarrass him again.

I had been a guest for about a month at my uncle's house and I felt that I should do something to help and express my gratitude. My uncle's diner attracted a lot of workers from the steel mills and the surrounding businesses and he was very busy on weekday evenings. I would stop there sometimes for a good steak after work and I knew he was shorthanded. It remembered that many policemen knew my uncle's restaurant and some of them dropped by for a cup of coffee and donuts, or a "small steak" now and them. I thought that I should give him a hand and do some good in the world.

One afternoon, after I had just finished my day shift, I stopped at the diner and offered to help him that evening. He was a little surprised and welcomed the offer.

"Sure," he said, "You can start right now. I show you what you do."

He reached under the counter and gave me an apron to wear. My uncle was a big man with a big belly and the apron looked a little too big for me, but I took it and wrapped it around my body like a robe with a belt. I felt like a butcher about to enter some bizarre rink. I started to pick up some empty dishes that lay on the counter, but my uncle stopped me. "You've got to put on the hat!" he said, as if that was something anyone should have known. I laid down the dishes and stared at him as he approached me holding a huge, white, chef's hat in his beefy hands.

"I don't need that," I said, shocked by the image of a short little guy my size, weighted down by that massive topper.

My uncle smiled. "You can't work without the hat," he said, as if he wanted to let me into the secrets of a cherished profession. And he took a step closer and offered me the hat like it was a crown on a silk pillow for a prince.

I looked at that monstrous hat and saw an unbending will reflected in his eyes, the Laskos' stubborn determination, and I took a step back. "I want to help, but I cannot wear that hat," I protested. I just didn't want to obey. "Let me put on some other hat," I tried to negotiate.

My uncle turned his back to me and moved away with the hat, shaking his head. It was clear that we were done.

"I'm sorry," I said, and got out of the store.

Later that evening I told my aunt and my cousins that I would be moving out in a day or two, at most. I don't remember if my aunt and my cousins tried to get me to change my decision. They probably did, but I couldn't do that at the time. I cannot remember talking to my uncle, or even if I tried to talk to him. I know that I thought of the many times my uncle had helped me, but I couldn't abandon the stand I had taken. I don't know what deep, lurking emotions blocked my reason again and produced such an outlandish decision at that time, but they did. I knew I didn't like the laughable figure I would cut and told myself that this was the reason. The fact that this man had given me shelter for months, that he saved my freedom, my college life and probably my right to stay in America, seemed to have been wiped out of my mind. I won a prideful and hatless head with no brain or gratitude inside. I hated being who I had become, but couldn't change my mind.

Later, much later, I realized that fear, not just vanity nailed me to such obstinacy. I was afraid that if I obeyed my uncle's demand, I would be subservient to him. I felt that I would never be myself again. I was the little boy who disobeyed his father's direction to hold on to his hand in crossing streets in downtown Athens and ran through deadly speeding cars and streetcars and getting nearly killed. I was the grade school student who accepted daily punishment, rather than obey the teacher's orders. I was the worker who was told to shave when I showed up for work at the snack bar of the graduate house at MIT and refused to obey. I needed the money from that job, but I told the short order cook he could keep his job and walked out.

After I left my uncle's home, I was depressed. I owed him a lot and now there was no way to pay back my debt to him. It took time and many other events to find out who I was and learn to hold on to my humanity.

The next day, I found an efficiency apartment next to a couple of Puerto Rican workers at the steel mill, who became my friends.

As I said, I had a car, but I had not been able to get a license and registration yet. I needed both, so I could drive back to Boston. One of my Puerto-Rican friends said that he had some old registration plates he didn't need, and we could put them on and use the car, rather than let it go to waste. I was uneasy about doing that, but I needed the experience of driving, if I was to pass the driving test and I didn't think that it would be a serious offense if, by chance, the discrepancy of invalid plates was discovered. And so, one of my amigos mounted the plates and he and I drove the car around town.

I was taking a course in Economics at Indiana University that summer, to fulfill the Economics requirement of MIT. I was going to class one afternoon, when I ran a stoplight. I got flustered and tried to get away from that corner, so I paid no attention to any other stoplights that I might have passed. I heard a police siren, but I couldn't see a police car, so I figured it might be wise to keep going and avoid any encounter with a policeman. I convinced myself quickly that the policeman was dealing with someone else's problems and kept going. Then the flashing red light of a cruiser appeared behind me and I knew that I was the culprit the cop was after. I instantly froze on the side of the road.

The state trooper approached me and asked me where I was going.

"I'm taking a class in Economics at the University extension," I said, staying calm and academic.

"Do you know that you ran three red lights?"

I did and I didn't, so I said, "Three?"

"You most certainly did. And, you were speeding – twenty miles over the speed limit. Did you know that?" I said nothing. I prayed very hard that the Lord would divert this cop's attention and he would not ask me for my license, which I didn't have, or my registration, which would compound my crime, because that plate had been around for a long time and might have been used for crimes I didn't know about. And, since I had only a permit and no license to drive, I prayed for protection against that evil, as well. There would be no uncle to lean upon this time, but there would be jail time. My mind was racing to construct a story to get myself out of the mess I was in. He thinks I'm guilty of all these driving violations, but oh boy, is he going to be surprised when he finds out that I am a thoroughgoing criminal. Should I pretend that I am a stupid foreigner, who didn't know any better? I didn't think it would stick; and it just wasn't right. Then, my scheming work stopped. I was doing bad things deliberately. I decided to withdraw and count on God to get me out of this mess.

"How would you like to appear in court on Monday morning?" the policeman asked in a conversational tone.

"I would prefer not to," I said in all honesty and in total confusion.

"You would not prefer!" he repeated mockingly. "How much money have you got with you?" he asked, staring at me intensely. I took my wallet out of my back pocket and pulled out my cash.

"Two dollars, Sir," I said, and showed him the two bills and my wallet, embarrassed at my lack of resources. I prayed that he would not take my wallet and see the yellow permit and discover what else I was lacking. He took the two dollars and looked at me with the sympathy of an older, wiser man.

"Buddy, you are in ba-a-a-ad shape!" he said and pocketed the money.

"I am sorry," I said sheepishly.

"OK. You can go, now. But drive carefully, will you?"

"Thank you," I said, and looking up at the clear bright sky, I added, "Lord!"

I drove off slowly and prayed for wisdom. Why was I doing wrong, when I intended right? Was I trying to excuse myself and had no idea that I had to obey to do right? I was an engineer and had no license to rampant philosophizing, but philosophizing was what I loved to do when I was away from the rolling mill and roamed free in my dreamscapes. It takes time to get to where one is going.

Time to leave Steel-Town and head out east to Academia approached fast. I got the car registered and scheduled an appointment for the driving test. A kind man, calm and easy-going was my instructor. He was patient and pointed out errors I made without rancor. The test ended in a friendly way.

"I would like to approve your application for driving, but you made a few more errors than is allowed. I'm sorry, I can't give you a license," he said, and I knew that he was troubled.

"I know I made a few mistakes, but there was nothing real serious, was there?" I was shocked. What should I do? Drive illegally, or forget the car and take the bus again? I made the only decision I could make at that time. I looked at my tolerant instructor and ruefully I said: "I'm leaving tomorrow to go back to school in Boston. You can give me a license, trusting that I would do my best to practice all that you taught me, or let me drive illegally." I was done, but kept looking hopefully at him. Waiting for his verdict.

"I hope you remember the errors you made and don't repeat them. And, by the way, remember that the road doesn't belong to you." He went to the office and came out holding my Indiana driver's license He smiled. "Have a good trip," he said and waved.

"I'll drive to stay alive," I said and added, "Thanks for the trust."

Why is God being so lenient to me? I kept thinking on and off on my way to Boston. I felt that I was protected and helped, a rare thing for me. There was much work that needed to be done, but I had started paying attention to my experiences in life, and I had the sense that I wasn't alone in the world.

22

On the Road to Augusta

"You shall love your neighbor as yourself."
Mark 12:31a

For Easter vacation, the year after the summer I recounted above, Tony, Miltos, Demos and I decided to head north into the forests and seashores of New England. We packed into Tony' car, an old 47 Ford he had bought with some money a relative of his had sent him as a gift that first summer, and were off toward New Hampshire, Maine and beyond. We were jubilant to have made it as far as we had for a year and a summer and all we wanted to do was enjoy the ride going north into the evergreens and the sea. Demos had found a brochure that promised a good time to any able-bodied youth who made it to the Festival of Friendship in Augusta Maine, so our default destination became the Festival and we all talked about the girls waiting for us up there and the fun we would have dancing, drinking, eating and cavorting with them. We had enough money for gas and food on highway diners, but not much more than that. We entered New Hampshire and passed by Lawrence, where America's textile production had reached its peak and the working class had felt its union power decades ago, and we headed up past Haverhill where Greek immigrants had set roots since the beginning of the century and from where many Greek American college students hailed. We stopped at Portsmouth, New Hampshire, and stood on a bluff and gazed at the astounding complex of islets and bridges and cranes and ships all painted on a mural of gigantic proportions and hung from the sky for our benefit in memory of those who labored and sweated to make it a great harbor once.

"Human beings can build wonders!" said Demos, puffing on a cigarette.

"When they are not killing each other," came Miltos' obligatory opposition.

"Lots of blood and sweat out there," I said.

"Enough chit-chat, guys," Tony intervened. "We better hit the road, if we are going to make the Festival."

And off we were, going north on highway 218 and then on 27, further up toward Augusta, toward the pole, toward some kind of Eldorado. It started to rain and we became quiet, as if the opaqueness that descended all around us required contemplation and respect. The lull of the engine was hypnotic, but Miltos was in charge of keeping Tony awake, shouting insults to all of us, or cursing all capitalists, or imperialists, or cannibals every few minutes. We travelled for one maybe two hours in this mode of limited awareness until the rain stopped and the sun came out and we started singing Greek songs about girls with green eyes and long flowing hair on their shoulders, or black olive eyes and long black braids down to their waists. We were dreaming again.

The forests hugged the road and everybody wanted to stop at a clearing and relax for a while. Tony pulled the old black beetle of a Ford car on a little rest area by the side of the road and we got out. We went some distance into the trees, found a clearing in the woods and sat down on the grass under the sun that God had sent us to enjoy. We were happy frolicking and shouting in Greek and teasing each other about the girls we would meet and how we would behave and laughing merrily along.

Suddenly, a big man with a red hat burst out from a nearby thicket holding a riffle and pointing it at us.

"Get the hell out of my land you goddamn foreign bastards, or I'll blow your brains out," he shouted. He was trembling with anger without any cause from us. We were stunned. No one moved. We just stared at the man. We had no thoughts, no words, no motion left in us. His howling anger wiped out all the life we had.

"Get!" the man shouted waving his riffle from us toward the exit of the clearing.

We looked at each other and, without words, agreed that there was no way to reason with that man. We picked up our thermos with coffee and the paper bag with a couple of sandwiches we had planned to enjoy eating in the woods and beat it out of there. We had seen the ugly face of America and wanted no part of it. We got in the car and sped away.

I think that Tony was as shaken by the encounter with the bigot as the rest of us, but didn't want to show it. His attention wasn't on the driving. We hadn't gone more than ten miles when he cut the wheel to the left to avoid a pothole, overcorrected, veered to the right and the car skidded past the soft shoulder and came to rest on a muddy ditch just below the shoulder. He tried to rock the car, but only managed to get it deeper in the black muck. We got out and tried to push while he revved up the engine, but we only managed to get mud all over us.

"Bad luck," mumbled Demos.

"Sorry, guys," Tony said in contrition, "I was trying to avoid a pothole. Stupid maneuver!"

"We have to get to some gas station and get help," I said looking around at the interminable, deserted highway.

"If they don't chase us away with bazookas . . ." Miltos mumbled to himself.

A truck was passing by at that moment and it slowed down. The truck stopped, and we all held our breaths. The driver got out and sauntered to the edge of the shoulder as if he wanted to get a better look at the car. "She's pretty deep in the mud, isn't she," he said.

"We didn't realize the shoulder was so soft," Tony said.

"It's been raining for days on and off," the man said as if he wanted to exonerate our driver from guilt. "I'm gone to have to get a chain to pull you out," the man said, looking at each one of us in succession. "I'll be back before you know it. We'll pull her out of that mess." And he got back in his truck and was gone.

We looked at each other asking each other without words what to make of this. Was he coming back? Would he come back with help, or with another rifle? Demos was the first to venture an opinion.

"He seems like a do-gooder," he said without much conviction.

"This is America, guys," Miltos weighed in. "He'll come back alright and will pull us out, and charge us an arm and a leg. We are in need and he provides a service without competition." He paused. "Capitalism in its ugliest form of a market," he delivered his prognostication with aplomb.

"I don't think he's coming back," I said, feeling the gloom of abandonment. Back then, I used to start with gloom rather than wait for a lousy outcome to hit me. I could have saved myself a lot of premature sadness had I been able to reason better. And this, after so many people had helped me, just because I was in need and asked them.

We waited for the truck with anticipation. We gathered our money and decided that we could pay him or someone else $50 with enough left over for gas to get back. Fifteen minutes later, we saw the truck coming toward us. Our spirits lifted. I was very happy to have been so wrong, once again. The driver was alone. He dragged a chain out of his truck with some help from Tony and Demos and hooked it to our car. He made sure the chain was tight and got back in his truck and slowly started inching forward with our mud-mired Ford behind. The chain held. We watched the car creep up the side of the shoulder like a reluctant beast yoked to the chain and dragged to safety. We held our breaths as the driver did his job with expertise. It seemed that he had done this a thousand times before. The car was back on the road, dripping muck, but otherwise intact. Not a bad way to drum up some business, I thought.

The man got out and we helped him pull the chain and store it in his truck. We thanked him for rescuing us.

Tony approached him. "What do we owe you, Sir, for your work?" he asked with as humble a tone of voice as anyone could have produced. And, I knew, he meant it.

"Oh, nothing," the man said. "I just wanted to help you all."

Miltos stepped forward, closer to the man. "We appreciate your help, but we would like to pay you for your labor," he said with a businesslike efficiency of a man who wants to pay his bill as a matter of pride.

The man glanced at him. "If I was stuck in your neighborhood, wouldn't you give me a hand?" he asked. Miltos stepped back.

"We really want to thank you, sir," Tony repeated.

"It's OK, guys. I like to help strangers in trouble." He climbed up to his truck and before shutting the door, he said, "Where do you guys come from, anyway."

"Greece," we said with one voice. "We're going to the Festival, in Augusta."

He was troubled. "Sorry, boys, but they called it off yesterday," he said, his face showing sadness. "The field was all mud." He shut his door and lowered the window. "Greece is far away," he said as if talking to himself. Then he smiled. "You guys are young and we want you to have fun, anyway. Augusta is a nice town. Go to 'Lorna's Bar and Grill' and have some fun there. She's also got the best hamburgers in town." He made a U-turn and stepped on the gas. His arm was out of the window, waiving at us.

"What a guy!" I said with admiration.

"Weird!" said Miltos.

We started arguing as we did on anything that had room for alternative explanations. In the end we came to the consensus that we had seen two sides of the American psyche, and the more I have thought about the man with the gun and the man with the heart of gold the more I have found that consensus made sense. That's America, the best and the worst there is. America is the world, after all, how could it be anything other than that? But, America, sometimes, lifts itself above the normal state of existence and surprises the world. When that happens, it is a moment of wonder and a great privilege to be a U.S. citizen. The rest of the time, it makes no difference which flag you salute.

We never got to the Festival, but we did visit Augusta briefly. It was a nice city with welcoming people, but we were tired and couldn't afford to stay in a motel. We had a good dinner at "Lorna's" and headed back to our base. We were thoughtful all the way back, as if we were trying to assemble pieces of a puzzle that didn't fit exactly. Miltos was working on a revised theory of Capitalism, which includes altruism. We had begun working on the puzzle everyone works on sooner or later after living in America or anywhere else for that matter. What is America like?

23

The Loan

Sometimes, Tony and I would visit one of our Greek friends working at the Graduate House cafeteria and he would serve us an extra-generous meal, which was good for a couple of days, counting what we stuffed in our pockets. On Thanksgiving and Christmas, when most students had left for home, there was extra food left over and less supervision, so we would carry it in trays from the kitchen back to the apartment and have enough food for a few days. When my money from Greece came, I paid the money I had borrowed from George and Tony and anyone else who had a few extra bucks to lend me for a month and I was left with enough for aa few groceries. I would buy some rice, spaghetti and a pound or two of sirloin steak from "Stop and Shop". I would flatten the steak with a light bulb unscrewed from the kitchen ceiling fixture– I had no hammer – until it was about a quarter of an inch thick; then, I would cut it into four pieces and store it in the refrigerator to provide myself with meals for four days. I felt great having created a system that secured four meals, gave me some peace of mind for a while and I could relax and solve some problems for a couple of days. Moreover, having converted a light bulb to a hammer was consolation enough for me during those days of blatant poverty and absence of ingenuity.

It was about that time that the ceiling in my bedroom started to leak drop by drop in a steady drip by my bed. I placed a wastebasket to collect the rainwater and waited for the super to come and fix it. The steady echo of the drops felt like hammer blows inside my head. I would close my eyes and dream of driving on long straight country roads in Louisiana or Alabama with windows open and the radio blasting triumphant songs. The illusion of independence persisted, even as I started missing classes, sleeping during classes and slipping into the dark labyrinths of lassitude. When my grades for the first semester of that year arrived, they told a story of declining performance. I was on a trajectory for failure and I became afraid. My only consolation was that I hadn't flunked a course, yet.

George was usually unaware of the emotional state of anyone around him, but he did think fast and blurted out whatever came to his mind when you nudged him into reality. Sometimes he made unexpectedly helpful remarks and never knew it. One day, as I was discussing the perennially lousy state of my finances, he turned to me and, in his characteristic impetuousness said, "You should stop bitching about being broke, swallow your pride and get a damn loan from the school." He fired his words at me without hiding his disgust.

I wasn't used to him talking like that to anybody. "What the hell are you talking about, Georgie?" I countered, ready for a showdown. "I'm starved, close to being homeless, hoping for a C in a couple of courses and you're telling me that I'm bitching?"

"They give loans to students like you. Go get one." He said as if what he said was a trite bit of information provided to a client by some accounting firm.

"They give loans to people who have no way to pay them back? Are they nuts?"

George looked at me and saw an ignoramus from the hill country of Greece. "This is the American way! When are you going to figure out that this is the New World? You borrow now and you pay it back with a little interest later. Everybody wins."

"I'm not a citizen," I protested. "I don't know that they'll let me be around to earn a living and pay back a loan. They know that."

"What have you got to lose?" Tony said, appearing from behind the newspaper he was reading. The eccentric and the pragmatic advice I got made me pause. I said that I would think about it.

A couple of days later, I got a letter from Professor Chalmers, the Advisor to Foreign Students who was instrumental in my coming to MIT, asking me to go and see him at his office. I was very concerned that they had already taken my scholarship away and he was just going to inform me of that fact. "Mr. Kizilos, you're done here. Good luck to you. Sorry, but you didn't make it." I couldn't stop thinking of the worst that could happen: expulsion and return to Greece humiliated. So? I'll buckle down, pass the exam at some Greek school and go on.

    I went to Professor Chalmers' office the next day. I met his secretary in the waiting room and she informed him that I wanted to see him in response to his letter. He told her to send me in. I knocked at his door and entered his office hesitantly.

    "Come in, young man," he welcomed me with a joyous smile. I responded with a meek greeting, confused by his attitude. I thought I was going to a funeral, but instead I walked into some kind of reception. What is he up to? Is he letting me down gently? "Sit down, sit down," he said and picked up a file from his desk and studied it. "I see that your grades weren't so good this last semester. Is there some problem?" He waited for me to answer. "We are here to help you deal with problems. It's what we do."

    "I'm hungry, Sir," I blurted out without any introduction. "I don't have enough money to live on. I made some mistakes. . ."

    "You're hungry?" he burst out loudly and leaned forward as if someone had stabbed him in the back. "You should have come to me sooner. No reason to be hungry, Mr. Kizilos. We can help you. The School is on your side. Lean on us."

    I couldn't believe how hurt he was. It seemed that he was feeling my hunger.

    He opened a side drawer in his great desk and taking out an envelope said, "A great lady in Boston has established an emergency fund for foreign students." He counted some bills and returned the envelope to his desk drawer. "Here are a hundred and fifty dollars for you to spend getting some good food right away and covering any other needs you have now," he said and handed me the money. "I don't want to hear that you are hungry again. I want you to go to the bursar's office tomorrow and take out a loan to cover your needs. I will call and arrange for it."

"I cannot pay it back, Sir."

"You will, when you earn money after you graduate and find a professional position. But, till that time comes, you will have the funds you need to function well. Your job is to do the best you can in your classes."

"I will," I said and shook his hand, thanking him for coming to my rescue again. That evening I went to the Omonia Greek restaurant and had a rack of lamb with red sauce and rice with a glass of retsina wine, toasting the generosity of professor Chalmers, MIT and America. I thanked God for another providential assist.

Next day I took out a loan and managed to continue with better performance till the end of the school year. I paid the small loan I received from MIT in the first six months after I got my Master's degree and started my first job as a professional engineer, a year and a half later. The loan was small because I managed to land a research assistant's job and pay for my expenses that way, instead of borrowing more. I didn't like loans and lived my life with no loans except for a car and home mortgages.

When Betty and I were done with our MIT education, we decided to get married in Cambridge and then head to Ohio for my first job in Heat Transfer with a small company. It was a time of learning how to live together and plan for the future. Betty found out that she was a very good programmer and worked in the same area in the early days of computing, building the math infrastructure for the solution of real problems. After I paid my MIT loan out of my first paycheck I learned how to invest in the stock market with my subsequent paychecks. And, forever looking for what else was there to do, I taught a Physics class in a nearby Canton College at night. The nights I was free, Betty and I would go to a drive-in theater to see a couple of movies and have Betty's favorite popcorn with real butter.

After a year in Ohio, I was offered a job by Honeywell and we piled our bags in the new Ford, we received as a wedding gift from Betty's father and headed for Minneapolis, Minnesota.

E

STEERING IN AND OUT
OF ENGINEERING

24

Mysteries of the Draft Board

I had been working in the Department of Machine Controls of Honeywell Inc. and was designing a complex control device full of transistors and electro-mechanical components to allow a milling machine to cut metal automatically in predetermined two-dimensional designs. I had learned enough about circuit design to advance beyond expectations on the project and the company was planning to exhibit a milling machine operating with my device at the Chicago Control Conference that was taking place that fall.

I was worn out from the effort and felt guilty for spending a lot of time testing the system by cutting half-inch-deep letter H designs on aluminum plates for the Honeywell demonstration at the show, while my wife, Betty was pregnant and alone at home. The situation was more stressful because I had received my 1A notice for my army draft obligation, five years from the start of the Vietnam war. Our baby was due in December and I was asking the Draft Board through its Clerk to postpone my induction in the Army, for three months after the baby was born. We had no relatives in the area and couldn't think how Betty and the baby would make it all alone.

The Clerk, a very callous, older woman, who never looked at me when I was talking to her, told me that the Army made no exceptions. I felt the obligation to serve, not only because it was the law, but also because the country had done so many good things for me and I felt an obligation to pay some of it back. But the Clerk had no intention to even sympathize with me.

When I asked for an appeal to the entire board, she stared at me as if I had done some shameful deed and then gave me a date and told me to be there, because the board won't wait more than five minutes.

I presented myself as directed and appealed to them for reasonableness, then for compassion. I was a foreigner with a green card and very willing to serve in my new country's army, but not before my child was born. I said I wanted, at least one-month delay after my son's birth. I might have done better talking to a stone wall. No questions, no comments, no emotions of any kind. "Request for postponement denied," I think they said, but I can't really remember the exact wording of the rejection, because I was furious for their patent disinterest in my agonizing problem. I was determined to do something to counter their ignorance of my presence in the world of human beings. To hell with your board and your war with little struggling Vietnam. I thanked them for giving me three days to get to a recruiter and register in the army. I would be drafted within the month. If I had stayed in Greece, I would be an officer in the navy, but I left for a better life in the world. I went to MIT and I'll end up dead in some Jungle of Vietnam.

I went home and let my wife console me. "We'll manage," she said, but I didn't push her to tell me how. We spent a couple of hours searching for alternatives, none of which was a good solution, but all of them solved the problem when we discussed them holding each other with love. I'm sure we both prayed to Christ for a solution, but it seemed to me, anyway, that this was an action that didn't require a miracle. Just a little compassion would do. We should be able to handle it alone. Yet, I prayed and I'm sure Betty did also.

It was Friday afternoon when I made it to the recruiter's office. I told the only soldier around that I was ordered to report and register with him. He cast a quick glance at the clock on the wall and asked me If I could come next Monday. I wasn't sure that this extension of the deadline was going to get me in trouble, but the soldier reassured me that it would be just fine. A couple of days extra meant more days of anxiety about what was happening, what was going to happen; where would I pop up in the vast expanse of the United States Army, and so on and on. I agreed to show up on Monday afternoon. The soldier smiled and said "Monday, then."

As I was walking back to my car, in the same corridor I had used to get to the Draft Board, I noticed the office for the recruiting of naval officers and the thought of joining this group as I would have done had I stayed in Greece struck my mind with force. The draft Board aura had soured me and I wanted to get away from them. I barged in the office as if I had prepared this move years ago: Tolly Kizilos, naval officer in the United States Navy! The image of my uncle, Captain Laskos, a hero with a bronze statue to his name and poems to boot, came to my mind. I explained to the three people gathered around a desk that I was asked to register with the army recruiter, but I wanted to know if I could join the navy, instead. I told them that I was near-sighted and they said that they could check my eligibility right away. I passed the vision exam. I then said that I wasn't a citizen yet, but I had a green card, so I might not be eligible yet. They said that they could check this also, but they were pretty sure it wouldn't be a problem with a green card. I flashed my green card. They knew other naval officers who had joined with a green card and a commitment to proceed to citizenship. I stopped and realized that I wouldn't have to see the army recruiter again. Was that true? "Once you join with us the Army is out of luck," one of the two men around the desk said. He was a muscular six-footer making sure that no army half pint could possibly argue and win anything from him and his people. We chatted for a few minutes about being allowed to join after my wife gave birth in three months. The woman naval officer blew it off with a spontaneous "I see no problem with that," she said almost proudly defending my rightful request.

I counted my blessings and sat down to enjoy the victory that had come my way. Thank you, Lord, again. The woman who was the lead officer with a couple of gold stripes on her sleeve lined some papers before me on the desk. "If you sign now, we can go to work on all the issues," she said. I picked up the pen, ready to sign and get out of the recruitment ordeal and the anxiety piled up on me by life's unpredictable events. Then I glanced at the form I was given. The words "four years commitment" popped up before me.

"Four years?" I heard myself gulp. I was almost out of breath.

"That's standard," the muscular man said casually. I noticed that he was a petty officer. I could talk to him.

"You mean that I have to serve for four years?" The words came out like a burp. And then, recovering, I offered the most inane reason for my defense: "It's two years with the army," I said.

"Officers serve for four years, Sir," the lady officer responded more officiously than I expected. The switch that sets the mood of a group's affection had been suddenly turned down. I stood up, looked around and promised to think about the situation.

"Monday afternoon," I said and then added, expressing my anxiety with a pain-driven smile: "I'll be either here, or down the corridor," I said at no one in particular, perhaps to myself, and left and went home. I didn't know it at the time but the story hadn't ended yet. The best part of a true-life story always comes slowly and then explodes and there is nothing left of the narrative at all. So, I wouldn't stop before that explosion was delivered hastily and unadorned.

Monday morning I'm at work and count the minutes till noon comes. I can't concentrate enough to do a dollar's worth of electronic design, but I keep checking what I have already done to make sure there are no errors when the device makes its debut in Chicago. And then the phone rings. A man wants to talk to Apostolos Kizilos. I tell him that I am that person. Then, calmly, with a clear, authoritative tone of voice the man identifies himself and gives me an order: "I am Captain McNeil" he says. "I am working on your case for induction in the Army. I will take care of it, and I want you to stay where you are and do what you have been doing." I interrupted him in protest.

"I cannot do that sir. I have been ordered to enlist today at the Army recruiter's office." Captain McNeil was unperturbed.

"Don't go to any recruiters' office; don't visit any Draft Board offices; don't contact any armed forces personnel. There is no need for you to do anything other than what you are doing now, O.K.?" I uttered an O.K. still in a trance and before I could muster a cohesive thought, before I could formulate a question asking who Captain McNeil was, Captain McNeil terminated the connection and I haven't heard for him in the intervening half a century or so. I don't know if there ever was a Captain McNeil in real life, but that's how I wasn't drafted. I figured if Captain McNeil was a figment of my imagination or a prankster, the Draft Board would find me and punish me in a hurry. I have wandered about my 1A classification and all the things that used to surround the draft and I have come up with a plausible explanation. The work I was doing for the company at the time wasn't concerned with defense, but it was of value to industry and the company had needs I knew nothing about. As it turned out I ended up doing a lot of defense work for the government a couple of years later. Was Captain McNeil or some company sharpie in HR blessed with the gift of prophesy? Was he human or an angelic being? There are always things that happen in the real world that have no explanation. I couldn't imagine that God had any interest in my draft board status, but he is known to do things we didn't expect him to even consider. Regardless of what answer one wants to give to this life event of mine, my subsequent career shows that in this case the right thing was done. I felt refreshed.

25

Engineer, Inventor, Project Leader, Done

worked for thirty years at Honeywell Inc., a Fortune 500 Corporation in Minneapolis, assigned to various types of work. My engineering career flourished for twelve years, and then, I ended it. I loved what I was doing at the time I did it, and said to one of the divisional vice presidents, high up on the ladder of power, that I would pay money to do the work I was doing. He asked "Why" and I told him that creating something new was meaningful and made me happy. "Does anybody else feel the same way?" he asked. "Everybody in our group," I said, but I don't think he believed me. I had a Bachelor's and Master's degrees from MIT, but I never thought that I was an exceptional engineer, perhaps because I had been around the best professors and students of engineering in the country for too long. I was never sure why I studied Mechanical Engineering rather than Philosophy or Theology, for example. When I sked my wife why she came to MIT to study Physics, she had an answer that made sense to me: "I wanted to understand God's work," she said. And she was serious, because she was taking Quantum Mechanics at the time, while I was testing vacuum cleaners.

I suppose, I had to study something that the Greek government determined was valuable enough to the country, to allow some currency to leave the country. If I had said that I wanted to study philosophy, theology or literature, they would have laughed and told me I couldn't do better than head for the University of Athens down the street. But, I wanted to explore the world and do something big for others and for me, just as I had said and written during the exams for my High School exam, and Mechanical Engineering could become, I thought, a nice vehicle for my dream's realization. Besides, I was pretty good in math and was happy solving problems.

But, that was before I experienced MIT. I no longer had the childhood belief I grew up with, that I could rise to the top of any group of people I was in, if I really wanted to. I had matured enough to know that I had strengths and weaknesses like everybody else and could be just a good engineer. I reasoned that I should find jobs that allowed me to use the skills and talents I had to do my job as well as I could. I knew, for example the math for all the thermodynamic cycles that convert heat to power, but I had no idea what was under the hood of a car, so I stayed away from applications work. And, I was a very formidable competitor, when I committed to a subject.

It hadn't taken long for me to learn that I could make up for my deficits using my imagination to solve problems in new ways, create new devices, innovate, call it exploring new territory. It is what makes one pursue problems that become dreams before they yield solutions. It is the urge to make good and beautiful new things that improve the world somehow. I had already proved to myself that I was diligent and resilient in whatever goal I pursued. I didn't give up, until the job was done. It took some time before I learned that there were times that I failed, and times that I succeeded because I got help that I hadn't expected to get.

For me, engineering was a journey of discovery and invention, a risky but enjoyable game, and I did it not only on the job but almost all the time, to make things for use at home, in the steel mills, on vacation, and a few times for things that got me six U.S. patents at work and funding from the government to develop some of them. It took me a few moves and a couple of years to land a position at the Research Department of the company for which I cared enough to give it all I had. The advanced research we were all doing in machine controls, lasers, aerodynamics, computers and other fields was both fun to do and good for the defense of the country, especially during the Cold War era.

After doing development work in machine controls for a couple of years, I had a chance to apply for the ideal research work at our company's Research Department for Aerospace and Defense. I worked hard on my interview and was pleased with my presentation, but I didn't get the job. I interpreted my unsuccessful effort to get the job I wanted, not as a failure, but as a setback to overcome. I vowed to try again when an opportunity came up. I got a job in the Defense Production Division of the company and kept looking for an assignment to the Research Department. When an opportunity arose for temporary work at the Research Department, I went after it and this time, after I had worked there for a few months, I was accepted in the fold.

Years later, when I had succeeded in a variety of projects at the Research Department and had advanced several times to become a senior research engineer and my interviewer and supervisor for a while, Dr. William T. Sacket, had been promoted to the position of Director of Research, and had become a wise advisor for me and many others, I asked him why he had turned me down after my first interview, back when I first joined the company, causing me to hop skip and jump until I finally managed to get transferred to the Research Department. Bill stared at me, knowing that I wouldn't like the answer to the question I was asking.

"When I asked you, 'what salary would you accept,' you gave me a very low figure," he said, and kept his eyes on me, watching for my response.

I was angry, but I kept my composure. "I was trying to make it easy for you to hire me," I managed to say, battling against my fury and my stupidity. "I would have paid to get that job," I said and paused. "I wasn't even a citizen at the time, and I was trying to get a job that requires a Secret Security Clearance, in a military Research group," I said, getting the words out fast, struggling to turn anger into sadness and failing to do so. I managed to contain myself and listen to what this wise friend had to say.

"I hired the other guy, who believed he was worth a lot more money than you," Bill said, showing no guilt at all for his decision. It took me a few years, but I found out the managing, interacting and mentoring way of Dr. Bill Sackett: truth, trust and openness. And, that was the beginning of a long-lasting relationship that progressed from mentoring to friendship over many years. Confronting the unpleasantness of reality is the first step into maturity.

Another time, when somebody at headquarters had imposed a very harsh rule on the company facilities, I went to Bill and protested. "It isn't fair to leave only one entrance to the building after 5:30," I told him. That "fairness issue" was my favorite way of defending righteousness and Bill must have had enough of it when he said: "Who told you that everything has to be fair?" he grinned and agreed to look into the issue.

Eventually Bill, and I, supported by the corporate leadership, formed a legendary team with the distinct goal of empowering people with specific actions that changed the organization. I'll tell that story as it happened later on because everyone has the responsibility to empower others and demand -- yes, demand -- that they be treated by everyone as fully mature human beings, or the project of the corporation will not fare well, and won't be done well even with AI, Big Data or cyborgs prancing up and down the stairways.

So, I entered the Research Department of Honeywell and found a home in, Fluidics, a new area of work that was just beginning to grow. We were trying to find out how to make switches and amplifiers which worked by controlling airflow in small, carefully designed and machined channels in aluminum or any light but sturdy material, rather than relying on Electronics. Working with airflow is much better than working with electricity, if the environment is explosive; or, because working with airflow can do some things that electricity wasn't meant to do, like control the airstream on aircraft surfaces with small streams of airflow rather than ailerons and other moving metal parts. I won't bother to explain the physics of the work we did – it takes equations, data from dozens of manometers and other instruments, with graphs, drawings and models – but it would be instructive to see how new things happen sometimes. The story of one of our more interesting inventions will help you catch a glimpse of the mystery of inspiration.

One afternoon, I was drinking coffee in my office while thinking about laminar fluid flow on curved surfaces. As I tipped the coffee cup slowly, my mind was into airflow swirls around aircraft wings, the coffee wrapped around the edge of the cup and spilled on my chin and on, down to my shirt collar. I went to the lab across the hall from my office to clean the cup and myself and started moving a loose water hose around the cup's outside surface. Imagining aircraft flow on wings, I focused on the water doing the strange things we all know it does sometimes when you pour tea slowly from a teapot to a teacup and the tea turns back and wets your sleeve. That's the Coanda effect, named after the Romanian scientist Henri Coanda, born in 1886, who discovered it, and described the tendency of a fluid jet to remain attached to a convex surface. The difference, I think, between Coanda and me was that I immediately started thinking that the fluid wasn't tea, not coffee, and definitely not liqueur. I thought right away of air and flow around curved surfaces. That was our medium. We were working mostly with airflows! We were into aircraft not teacups.

Dick Reilly, my supervisor at that time, came around and we started turning the water pressure higher, getting two hoses, pushing water against each hose's outflow to change its direction, wrapping it around cups and pots and getting wet in the process. We thought then that we would have something to talk about, if the phenomenon could take place with air jets. Dick was a pilot and knew much better than I did, the fluid flow around an airplane's wings and I was enthused by the possibilities of using fluid flow equations to explain the Coanda-kind of flow on aircraft surfaces. How long would an air jet follow the surface of a cylinder, as its air pressure increased? How do the two air jets interact to set the combined jet's direction when the pressures change? How does the diameter of the attachment surface affect the point of detachment? What should be the dimensions of the rectangular channels that would supply air around the device? We knew right there and then that we had invented a device that could produce an aerodynamic force of variable deflection, by changing the pressures of the jets and change the shape of the airflow around a wing. We imagined an aileron without moving any metal on the surface of a wing.

But, we needed answers to a lot of questions. We knew that asking the right questions was the way to the solutions – the way of research!

My imagination was a thoroughbred galloping on new domains. Think green plains out West with wild horses running. I called the device "Variable Deflection Thruster", VDT for short, and started the analysis and necessary experiments, of air flow around the curved surface of the VDT. And that surface would be a small cylinder (or an ovoid) at the trailing edge of an aircraft wing, thus replacing a moving aileron. It would produce a force up or down, just like an aileron does, but nothing would move on the wing. The air pressure would determine the magnitude of the force. That's much better way to get lift than moving clanging aluminum surfaces. That's what an invention does: makes things easier, or faster, or lasting longer, or better in some way. That's what it does, if it "works".

Dick and I filed for a patent through the company received it with enthusiasm because, in addition to the achievement of an invention, the U.S. Defense Department was interested in the devices we had in mind for research and development. We found the appropriate people in the Navy, who were interested enough in our invention to fund the development of our ideas for their aircraft.

To lower the cost of doing the research, we hired, as it was often done, more than half a dozen college students, mostly from the University of Minnesota, some of them Americans and some foreign students, and all of us in the VDT team had the satisfaction of teaching the young engineers the way one has to think to tackle problems in any field of science and technology. It was an enhancing experience to form lasting relationships with the young people and keep in touch with the concerns and goals of the next generation.

Every noon many of us gathered in a lunch room of our own, unpacked our sandwiches and separated in groups to play Krieg-Spiel a much more difficult form of chess, because it requires you to play without looking at the opponent's pieces. The people who were not playing at the time would gather around the opposing players and kibitz and debate and argue quietly, secretly and sometimes raucously about the positions and the good moves, and the counterfactuals, creating a festive atmosphere of intellectual pleasure. We formed teams and worked together or had one-on-one discussions. We were so often in touch with one another that we became brothers united in the VDT Team and were interested in each other's work, well-being and family. We learned from each other's suggestions and taught each other what we thought we knew and asked for the help we needed.

And it wasn't always a matter of work. We talked about our worldviews and morality and faith. I remember spending some time with Jake, an engineer who was a Christian and believed that he should not read any book other than the bible, because such breadth was bound to corrupt the reader. I had to work hard to get him to consider some classic books. Some years later, having become stronger in his faith he was thankful that he had gained a broader perspective of the faith and the world reading books by other Christians and non-Christians. "The mind is a gift of God and can help us use it for Kingdom Work," he said quoting Doctor Gregory Boyd a preacher of renown. I had expressed my wholehearted agreement and told him that I had become interested in the Problem of Evil, that had tested human minds for more than two thousand years. Our friendship grew and our faith was strengthened. We worked hard on the government projects and talked literature at lunch

We were able to secure government funding for our research and employed more than a dozen people who enjoyed the work they were doing. We tested the device in our labs and in a wind tunnel and became confident that the device would produce powerful aerodynamic forces in a controllable way. Based on the data we had, we decided to test the VDT on a Beechcraft aircraft airplane. We built a new rudder with the device on its rear end, and planned how to attach it to a, exactly where the conventional rudder was. We teamed with a crew of aircraft technicians and pilots and started working at the airport, moving engines, connecting pipes, tightening pipe-connections with some guys who knew what they were doing and some of us who were mere cheerleaders. Finally, we bought a Volkswagen motor and loaded it on the Beechcraft aircraft, hooked it to a blower we also bought, and bolted the system inside the plane. We connected the retrofitted VDT-rudder we had on the plane's tail and supplied it with pressurized air from a blower system we installed. I sat down far from our project and cast a long curious stare at the plane with the silver-glazed rudder. We did it, I thought, and thanked God for what he helped us accomplish. Then, I prayed for a safe and successful end of our goal.

We decided that we would fly two planes: one with the retrofitted VDT-rudder and a regular plane with the evaluation and photography team aboard. The Beechcraft would be piloted by an expert pilot and there would be some engineers and technicians, who knew what to do in case something went wrong inside the test plane with the Volkswagen motor and the blower or the aircraft. If anything went wrong with this machinery, if the VDT air was cut off or a pipe sprung a leak, the rudder would not work, and the plane would be hard to control. I had worked for years on the device and the building of the rudder of the plane and I wanted to observe how it really worked, but others knew much more about flight and I deferred to them. So, I planned to be at the observer plane because I could make a quick evaluation of the operation of the device, and I had nothing to offer with the flying of airplanes or the fixing of motors, blowers and the other equipment. Also, I had met Glen Merrill, a jovial and self-confident man, who joined the project as a crew member in the test group. Glen, I understood, was a pilot and had been in the Army with some relevant experience to the work we were doing. I felt confident that he could handle any adverse situation better than anybody else.

I hadn't thought about the VDT for several days, but when everything was ready and we set the test date, I started to think about the ways the VDT or the plane could fail, and I started worrying. I was the leader of this operation and I felt the responsibility for it. Should I ride the Beechcraft and let my colleague, Glen, who was in charge of the machinery in the Beechcraft, ride the observation plane? I thought about changing places with him, but I became afraid of coming up with a situation with more risk for everybody, since I didn't know what to do if trouble with the motor, or the blower or some pipe or wire broke out, or the pilot needed help. But, the more I thought about the flight the more I realized that I was also afraid to place myself into the test plane. My head was telling me that I had made the right decision, but I knew my heart would pile guilt upon guilt on me, if anything went wrong and Glen was hurt while I was fine. Was I putting a friend at risk? I lost some sleep thinking about my situation and I decided to talk with Glen the next day.

I asked Glen how it was with him, being in the test airplane. Was he OK taking the risk? Glen is a soft-spoken but steely man, who, seemed to know his mind and would never be pushed to a job he didn't want to do. I was sure he would speak up and I would change positions with him. He smiled at me, as if I was on the wrong track and assured me that he was doing fine. I had the feeling that I would offend him, if I was to go further. I wasn't involved in hiring. I was satisfied that he knew what he was doing and liked his calm and certain way he did things. I assured him that all was going well and left him to pack his stuff in a backpack he had. So, I left him, thinking that things were as good as they could be.

A few minutes later, however, I happened to pass by the room where Glen was getting ready. The door was open and I glanced at him. He was taking some pills from the white bottle. I was stared far away as Glen was shoving stuff into his backpack. "Getting ready," he said with conviction. I didn't believe him, but I didn't say anything. He could say "No", feel a little humbled, and go on. But I was fearful also, and didn't reveal that at the time. And I didn't forget. I thought of all the work we had done and felt sure that everything would work smoothly. No need to fret. But the risk was there, and I couldn't deny it. I had taken many risks in my life, everybody has. Life without risks is not worth living, I thought I heard a Greek ancestor mumble on his way to the agora. I imposed silence on myself and went on.

A few minutes later we were up in the air flying our work with our fears, our dreams and our never-resting imagination. It seemed strange to see the aircraft turn left, then right, left, then right, without anything moving on its surface. I mean, the rudder was solid but the plane was turning as we wanted it to do. The dream had become reality. It was the only such thing in the world!

The project work would go on for a few more years, but it would not become the new way of flying aircraft any time soon. The amount of air required to produce the forces needed for aircraft control using the VDT was more than today's aircraft designers were willing to divert from propulsion to control. But the experience we had working in teams for a common goal was very meaningful because we became friends and cared for each other and learned from each other and became better human beings.

Some forty-eight years later, meeting a few guys from the VDT team over pizza and pop, I told everybody that I was afraid the day of the flight, and I felt guilty for letting Glen fly on the test plane. Then, I asked Glen sitting among us, to tell us whether his expertise made him unafraid, or he was afraid, also, but kept it to himself. Glen broke out laughing.

"I was terrified, not afraid, man," Glen admitted and went on to explain how his stomach gave him trouble and had survived by gulping tablets of Pepto-Bismol. I apologized to him for not being more direct and discussing the way he felt more openly. I think that someone in the Beechcraft group had assigned him to fly there. Glen was as afraid as I was, but did his job and I did mine. I was sure that he wouldn't have changed his post, if the offer was made; and if I was in his place, I wouldn't have changed it either.

Some strange force, deep in our mind and soul, arises at the appointed time and commits us to do what we know we must do. Sometimes we are right, and sometimes we are wrong, but the world doesn't always know it. We both felt good with the memory dump we had. There are some things we do that bother us and we cannot forget. They remind us that we are flawed and need God's mercy and grace to stand up again, humbled, but wiser and stronger, and carry on.

26

Bushwhacked

There are times when everything seems to be out of place, breaking into an alien domain. The mind is unable to connect the experience one should have to the one he is having. What am I doing here, so far away from the home I knew well in my early years? This is my home now. Sometime ago, somewhere along the way I took a turn and I found a new home. What was a thought, became a fact. Drop the dreams of the drive and connect to the present moment. It is my home now. And there is nothing more real than this now. I had just entered the house and hugged my wife in the kitchen just before my three sons gathered around demanding attention for a variety of experiences from things they did to things I was supposed to do. My oldest son was puffing on his toy pipe and carried a replica of my briefcase. The other two boys wanted to know if I could set up the recorder so they could listen to singers and storytellers I recorded for them from the radio and the TV. Don't they know that it's a hot summer afternoon and the sun is pouring numbing fluids in the mind? What will they ask me for next? My oldest son has learned the entire collection of Dr. Seuss I think and is ready to recite it. He has a better memory than I have and I admire him for that. Admire? I was proud of him. The youngest one wants to recite Chaucer and the middle one can speak like Duffy Duck, walk like him and drive me to tears laughing. I love to play and teach and tease and hug and squeeze and wrestle and compete and surprise all of them with something they hadn't thought or expected. They don't like the limits I urge them to have on TV watching, the reports they have to give for the TV shows they watch, or the checking up of the friends they have, or the charts of their school grades I keep. This won't last for long. A day will come when they will confront me, telling me to leave them alone, refuse to abide with the more stringent limits I will try to impose on them. They will hate me for a while and I'll have to grin and growl and accept it all. Who knows – they may even love me.

Now they want to hung out with me, laugh and play. But not today boys; not with the air-conditioner so close to its last legs covering only half the house, the other half having been isolated from the barely breath-supporting air by two bed sheets hanging from the ceiling in the hallway after a laborious nail-tacking on the wall a couple of days ago. Do I want to hear the new recording from the radio? I have to listen to Chaucer recited by the youngest brother or plead with the storyteller to begin his latest story.

I ask for a few moments of relief. They don't know I have reached the end of my rope at work. I am fed up with the job I used to love once. The Vietnam war has worn me down. It is the government contracts and my inability to convince anybody near me that the war is fought for no good reason, without any gain and plenty of loss. Betty knows my soul and her eyes show that she understands how I feel. I have told her that I feel ground up writing contracts for weapons, objecting to schemes that can kill civilians as well as soldiers. What are we doing here? Are the Russians going to stay put and admire our Star Wars feats without acting before they are helpless? When will the efficiency of slaughter stop? Betty's sorrow for my predicament is tangible. I can tell by the way her mixing of the sauce for our dinner slows down. I don't want to explain the day's bitter moments, so I hit the couch and seek refuge under imaginary clouds.

I hadn't counted on the job being so gut wrenching. Is there some thread of meaning hidden under the carpet? I feel guilty for robbing fatherhood-time from my sons and the only person that has loved me without any preconditions. I got to rest now and wait for the evening to make it up to Betty and the kids. Perhaps at dinner; maybe watching a good Monty Python episode on TV. I need some help to get out of this hole I dug for myself. A friendly coworker told me that I should be more careful on what I say because he heard people wondering if I am loyal. Protesting against the leaders of a pointless war? Be careful. That's how it was when I was in Athens, Greece and the Nazis were occupying the country. It was no different when the Communists and the Fascists were carrying out fratricides as Greeks had done in times past.

I had been on the couch long enough when Betty called us for dinner and the kids had to turn off the TV and scamper to the dining room table. I stretched my arms and my hand felt the newspaper lying on the floor. I picked it up and cast a quick look on the front page. Nothing but news of the war. It was 1969 and the killing was going on and on without news of an end. I turned to page two. I was ready to drop the paper and go to the table for dinner, but my eyes caught a small box announcing a competition for The Bush Foundation Leadership Fellowship in August. I felt a sudden rush of excitement, perhaps joy. I read carefully the few words announcing the award amount and the timing for the competition. I folded the newspaper and approached my wife. "I'm going to give this a try," I said and showed her the announcement. "It may be my way out of the gloom I'm in at work." She read the announcement and smiled. "Why not?"

There would be four fellowships awarded, each worth eighteen thousand dollars over a period of eighteen months. I snapped out and read on. One could use the money to do just about anything one wanted to do, provided he had a plan that offered something meaningful to the person, had value in the world and was approved by the organizers of the Fellowship. In addition, there would be intelligence and other tests and group discussions of participants facilitated by educators, and professionals from various fields. Finally, one would be asked to face a panel of judges alone and respond to their questions.

I was excited by the chance to compete and do my best. After all, I had been competing, one way or another, all my life and had usually done well, whether the prize was worth anything or not. This battle was mine. The prize was freedom to do something that had meaning for me and could do something good in the world. I had a strange sense that I had already won the contest. It seemed to me that this fellowship was mine already. It was my way out of the prison I had put myself in. I discussed the project with Betty. She had always trusted me to do things responsibly and effectively, so she smiled approvingly. We hugged and kissed. We were so much more than two when we were tackling together life's problems.

I had never heard about this Foundation before. It hadn't occurred to me that there were bundles of fellowship money to be given on merit to anyone willing to compete and do well enough to win. That night I remembered how I had managed to come to America. Competition was one of my strengths. But how was it that I found out at the time when I needed help the most? Was it a coincidence or was God offering me a precious gift again? It seemed that he word "coincidence" wasn't useful anymore.

The Interviewer was a man I had met at some political meeting. I was surprised to see him there. Perhaps we had the same political values. He was a friendly person and I did my best to answer all his questions with honesty and conviction. It seemed to me that his worldview wasn't too different than mine. If it had been different I might have tried to change his view and would have been kept out of the cohort, proclaiming the worth of my character. I was spared the trial.

I did well in the written tests and entered the group discussion part of the competition. They brought politicians, philosophers, scientists and other luminaries to talk about the plight of the world and wanted suggestions on how to save it. They asked us to offer some answers. No hand was raised. I felt the need to speak and raised my hand. It was time to offer my best idea. "None of us can save the world," I said. "We are not God. But we can do something that helps some people in the world. I bet that each one of us has something like that in mind." I wanted to know if anyone else would come up with a better answer. I would have to give answers that were not only true, but also effective. If one of the other people gave answers that got the group's support, eloquent answers wouldn't do much good. An older African American man with gray hair raised his hand. "Whatever we do we need to do it not only for others but also with others. We cannot change much of the world working alone. We can do miracles when we band together. Besides, that's the way of the Lord Almighty," he said and folded his hands. I heard "Right on!" and "Amen" and a couple of other approving comments. There was no doubt in my mind that he had a better answer than I did. "The race is on," I thought and reminded myself that I had to do better to stay in the competition.

We had coffee breaks and lunch breaks and bar discussions. I was satisfied with the way things were going, but I wasn't sure I was among the top four candidates, judging by their responses. If I wasn't competing with anybody, or discussing something, or debating or somehow having an opponent, I was lost. It was never easy to start a friendly chat. I didn't know how to enjoy a person's presence, and my clumsiness was hurting me. I was sipping a glass of wine and feeling totally alone. Then an older man sat next to me and got a good discussion going about the great things previous Bush winners had achieved. "Did you know that Arnie, our governor, won a leadership fellowship four years ago?" I engaged in the discussion and time went by.

Next day, one of the lecturers presented a survey of the most pressing issues society was facing: discrimination, pointless wars, gun violence in our country, women's rights, and other things that plague our society. Then, he stopped abruptly and asked us to decide by consensus what we believed to be the worst problem society faced at the time. He gave us half an hour to work on the problem and we went to work listing the problems anyone wanted to place on the board. I got up and placed the War in Vietnam, as one problem with serious consequences. The war in Vietnam was horrible, but it didn't seem to be as important to the group as it was to me and to three or four others. I thought that whatever we agreed upon should be applicable to several problems of society. Our selfishness is the cause of most evil, I thought, but I knew that I couldn't say it that way. Others kept adding issues of concern to them. Then, it came to me that "money is the source of all evil" and I called out "Wealth Inequality". The list was finished in less than ten minutes and by the end of the hour "Wealth Inequality" had become the most pervasive societal issue we had. I felt that I had done a good thing and didn't care much whether the judges liked it or not. It was the thing that was important even in the issue of the war in Vietnam.

That afternoon I was called for a discussion with the judges of the Fellowship. I don't remember the order in which I was called, but I was among the first. I went in the room with all my senses on alert. The Judges offered me a choice of making a tea from an elaborate teapot and I accepted it to show I wasn't afraid of messing things up and spilling tea all over, or looking for a teaspoon under their luxurious table. I wanted all my hands free to handle the tea, so I didn't reach for a cookie. I sat down across the array of finely tailored group of judges and gave them an overview of the meeting thus far. Yes, "Wealth Inequality" is the worst problem facing us. "But, don't you think that the news would be in the newspapers sometimes?" I said that it would be in time, after people dug into the Industrial- Military Complex, the puny rise in wages of the working class, the unjust tax code. The death of the poor versus that of the rich, the existence of diseases that kill millions of poor children in Africa and so on. I was going full speed and it occurred to me that there was a wall I was to hit very soon. I stopped. "Mr. Kizilos," the man at the center of the table of the judges said, "do you want to abolish the capitalist system?"

"No, Sir," I protested. I want to abolish a system which allows a thousand people to own half the country. "Capitalism works fine if it becomes enlightened by a sense of compassion."

Most judges joined the discussion, some doubling down, others rushing to help me, all with thoughtful questions and meaningful answers. They were impressed by my daring position and straight answers. Then they asked me what I was planning to do, if I won a fellowship. I told them that I would do something worthwhile for me and for others. Two hours later they announced the four fellowships.

I was one of the four leadership winners; the African American man with the gray hair was another. I had never been in competition with the other two winners, so I don't remember them. No one of the four of us ever became governor of the state, or a known political figure, as far as I can tell.

The organizers of the Bush Fellowship thought that I may want to branch into politics and suggested that I take a trip to the Kennedy Institute at Harvard. I told them that I wanted to write a book, probably a novel about the inner workings of a dysfunctional social system, but I would like to find out if politics could be something I could do and bring about some good to others and myself. After I spent a couple of days at the Institute I was sure it wasn't something I could do, or wanted to do. The discussions were too remote from the problems they were supposedly exploring and trying to solve. I tried to inject some new ways of looking at things and I got nowhere. People wanted to discuss issues, didn't seem ready to solve problems, like "Why are we in Vietnam?" And "How are we going to get out of there?" So, I got back home and told the organizers that I wanted to get an MFA and do some writing at the Creative Writers Workshop of the University of Iowa.

27

Trumpeting for Angels

In 1976 the whole family stormed Europe and Greece. It was a time for exploration and discovery of Greece and the rest of Europe, time to jostle and joke, visit the dreams we had stored for a long time and be stunned by the wonders of the past. We were there to admire and applaud things and ways that lifted us from the ground to the clouds, break out of our suburban singularity and enjoy the world's cultural plurality. Our three sons, Betty and I were going to have fun, free and fair, watching the boys, now 12 to 16 years old, grow in experience, judgement and view of the world. We visited gardens, fountains, museums, towers and graves we had only in mind, and happened to discover and were stunned to see and wonder. We met tight schedules and missed some critical connections here and there, so we could become patient and invent games to pass the time knowing each other's ways better than before.

We all had favorite things to see and do and tried to please each other. Peter had to visit Foyle's famous bookstore and a flea-market with antiques and gadgets and maps of land from hundreds of years ago to mark property rights of the landowners and keep the peasants locked to their serfdom.

Some of us wanted to travel on the underground, speeding in the dark and getting nowhere. Paul, Betty and I admired the novelty of the shapes of the towers and the majesty of the Cathedrals with real graves built on the walls, like Isaak Newton in Westminster Cathedral and John Donne in Saint Paul Cathedral. Mark was a kind of guide, pointing at things out of the way with stoops and steps to structures that we may want to see, like Madam Tussaud's Museum with real and unforgettable fiction and history good and bad greats no one dares to forget or ignore, like Dracula and Darth Vader, Hitler, Churchill and Mary Queen of Scotts who had her head chopped off. They all finished their tour and came back with a conclusion: "Dad," Mark said with some sadness, "there are bad guys and heroes in there, but we didn't see any saints." I was surprised. No one had seen a saint, so I said, "Some people are really good and are doing good work, so we can think of them as saints." Silence. "Not if they don't believe in God," Peter, our oldest objected. And we moved on to the Tower of London to debate the issue as we had been doing all along about so many issues. In Paris, at the tomb of Napoleon, I was approached by a man who told me to act respectfully and not wear a multicolored hat. I responded by saying that I wore the same hat throughout my trip to Europe, and I laughed because I didn't think it was proper for a nation to honor a dictator with such a magnificent tomb.

He was about to call the tomb guards and I started moving out with the family. The boys want to know the story and I gave a snapshot of Napoleon's history, which wasn't much. "Your hat is fine," Paul tried to console me, as Betty shook her head disapprovingly. We were ready for some food at a good restaurant.

In Greece, my parents were happy to see their grandchildren again and the boys were happy to submit to hugs and kisses and stroking of their heads for it is there that all the unexpected future events can live hidden till they blossom and some good things are added to the world. Peter and Paul were a little older, already in their mid-teens, but Mark was still a boy, still in grade school and all my relatives had to pinch his chubby, rosy cheeks, admiring his good looks and wishing him good luck and protect him from the evil eye that always wants to take down the goodness of human beings. If they knew that he was already playing the trumpet and reciting poems from the school stage, that he could do magic tricks and play football in his school team, they might have done some harm to his cheeks from excessive admiration. I explained all this to the boys, though they knew that the pinchers were expressing their love and admiration. My father was particularly impressed when I told him that Mark wanted to skip the sixth grade because he was a very good student and he thought he would be bored if he stayed in his regular class. I didn't tell them that I had not wanted him to do that. I didn't think it would do any good being less experienced when the world started throwing curved balls at him and he would have to be as experienced as possible to handle them and stay in the game. I had explained all this to Mark, but he persisted. "I won't help you," I told him, "but, if you want to go ahead with your plan and do whatever is required by the school to achieve your goal, I won't prevent you." I didn't feel good. "If you do manage to skip," I went on, "I'll be a very happy man, admire your guts and support you all the way." Mark had understood, but it wouldn't do any good explaining this to my father. He would have thought that I was wrong, perhaps, stupid or cruel. I guess, I remembered wondering if his herculean work efforts to provide me with the best possible help he could muster were rooted in love or had something to do with my being a very good student, a substitute for the dream that his harsh world had never allowed him to fulfill.

Later, I found out that Peter, his older brother had been secretly encouraging him to skip a grade because he had been bored in that grade and wanted to help Mark do better. So, Mark had taken control of his life and faced the Principal of the school alone. He had filled the forms, submitted to tests, responded to interviews and passed the required IQ test in flying colors. I was proud of his innate ability and his thoughtful solo execution of a complex plan. He had put a stamp of excellence on his character, as Peter had done and Paul was doing in his own self-directed way. We were ready for a new year with school, full of stories to tell our friends and make new connections. Peter was involved in the debate club and Paul was the stage manager in a theatrical play.

Entering the seventh grade required a physical examination for all students. Mark wouldn't have to do that, but his skipping the grade made it absolutely necessary. So, Betty took him to our family doctor for this routine examination. This was the beginning of a period in life that none of us had imagined as a follow-up to the wonders and the fun of our trip abroad. "Doctor Bloom said Mark's blood pressure is too high," my wife said when she called me at work. "He is concerned, because young children don't get a high blood pressure without a 'problem'," she said. "He said that we must take Mark to the hospital right away". Mark had been watching his brothers play football out in the yard when I came from work to take him to the hospital. He had planned to play Center in the school team and wanted to practice. But there would be no football right now.

Mark officially skipped his grade and we all waited for results of further tests and results for the diagnosis of the "problem" he had. Dr. Bloom called the "problem" a disease and tried to diagnose it. He saw Mark in the hospital and started testing, but after a couple of days he admitted straight out that a specialist was needed, and he was looking for one.

This was the beginning of the battle we all would have to fight at the hospital in the weeks ahead. Mark got ready for his hospital stay, and we started bringing him some of his magic tricks to practice, comic books, and Ulysses, one of the classics he had received as a bonus from me, with his promise that he could read it before the year's end. He started by exploring the vicinity to his room and getting situated in his room. Betty and I waited in his room for the specialist to arrive and every now and then met another nurse and asked if she knew when the doctor would arrive.

Compared to Mark, I was a wreck, unable to cope well with the space of unknowing that enclosed me. And then, a six-foot-two, thin man with long black hair comes out of the elevator and asks a nurse at the nurses' station where is Mark Kizilos. I knew who he was but he didn't look like the old professor from Harvard that I had imagined and desperately expected "the specialist" would be. He looked more like a topnotch, thirty-five-year-old basketball player, though his walk was slow and deliberate. I calmed myself down. Dr. Bloom is a wise old owl and would pick a topnotch 'specialist''. Besides, all I wanted to know more than anything else was what did this "specialist" know about mysterious childhood diseases. I suppressed my urge to interview him right there and then, and went up to him and introduced myself as Mark's father. "Dave Brown," he said to me and shook my hand. I told him that we had been anxiously waiting for his arrival and followed the nurse and him to Mark's room. "Doctor Dave Brown," he introduced himself to Betty and Mark and assured us that whatever the problem was he, Dr. Bloom and the staff would stay with us until the problem was solved. He was friendly, interested in Mark's plan for his pastime in the hospital and watched him do a couple of magic tricks, applauding his expertise. "You are quite a wizard, young man," he praised Mark, and started examining him right away. When he finished he came out and announced that Mark had Cushing's Syndrome which produces too much cortisol in various ways that can harm the body, if untreated. He explained to us that the disease was detected early and there are many things to do to make sure which of the many possible problems Mark was having.

"Something in Mark's body is causing him to produce more cortisol than he needs. You've noticed the rounded face, I suppose. It's called 'Moon Face' in the trade and along with his high blood pressure, the red color of his face and so on he has the symptoms of the disease." We asked questions and tried to get answers from him, got worried and expressed it with irritation when he said that there will be several days before we know where exactly the source of the extra cortisol was and how it should be handled. "With care!" I said trying to hide my consternation with a lame joke.

By the time we got home, it was clear to me that the disease was complex and required a better understanding from us. I couldn't believe that Dr. Brown had the expertise to diagnose and cure the disease, so I started familiarizing myself with the tests and procedures involved in the disease. Next day I went to the Honeywell Library and asked the Manager, Maro Thologides to find some relevant books on the topic. Maro was the Librarian and best Information Scientist Honeywell had in its workforce. She could unearth information on any topic one could ask of her. So, in a couple of days, Maro found several books for me to read and offered to provide more specific information, if it was needed.

Cushing's Syndrome refers to excess cortisol for any reason and is different than Cushing's Disease. One of the causes is a cortisol-secreting little tumor in the cortex of the adrenal gland. The tumor, (adenoma) pushes high levels of cortisol to the blood and by negative feedback this causes the pituitary gland in the head, on top of the nose, to reduce substantially the ACTH levels. If one finds that this little adrenal gland tumor is the source of the high cholesterol, one can remove the adrenal gland or glands surgically or otherwise.

But, that's not all that could be wrong. Cushing's Disease (not Syndrome) refers to high cortisol which came from an excess production of ACTH from a pituitary tumor (adenoma). There were many other sources, and if tumors were lodged somewhere else in the body one would have to search and hope to find them without the modern MRI or CAT scan.

"Exactly how?" I asked Dave Brown back then.

"We'll cross that bridge when we get there, he said. "We may get lucky and find the source right away." I could imagine the tumor in the shape of a good size Indian arrowhead, lodged in a lung, the abdomen, the liver, you name it. But I couldn't imagine it inside my boy's head lodged in his pituitary gland. Who would help us extract the devil's nail from his head? A lot of crippling things were possible and I didn't want to go there. I prayed at night that God would give us a hand. I don't know how much I believed that God would bother with us and our problems, but I believed that God could do anything he wanted and might choose to do something good for us now. I never thought that God was a vending machine, where you put in your coins and he delivers the proper miracle. Why us and not the people next door with a boy dying of cancer? I should have prayed for both of us – it wouldn't have been too much.

I studied Cushing's stuff all day long at work and every now and then I'd walk the corridors with a couple of hardcover medical books and, if I could find a scientist that needed a break, I would open a book and ask some more questions. They had no training in biological sciences, they were computer experts, laser experts, experimental psychologists, but they were always willing to tackle a problem and it wasn't hard to get them to think well on my problems and explain what they could. I just couldn't think of anything else to do. Betty had thrown herself into computer programming and didn't want to think about any tumors -- just Mark and coding. I admired her ability to put a lock in various paths of thinking that led to nowhere but anxiety. I had no such lock. I was stuck, and I would stop by the hospital to see how Mark was doing. He was fine and busy with his leather work, making belts pouches and learning to pound signs on leather.

One afternoon I arrived early at the hospital and found Mark ready to take the 24-hour urinary measurement for cortisol. I had studied this test and had the procedure outlined on a chart. When I discovered Dr. Brown having a cup of coffee in the cafeteria, I joined him at his table and went through the steps of the test with him. I was impressed by his total awareness of the process and the measurements. I thanked him for answering all my questions, and he was pleased that I went to him for what was bothering me. He said we'll know something about the source of the disease by tomorrow.

When I went there next day, the measurements had been scrapped because one of the technicians had not followed the time procedure prescribed and the results had to be repeated. I wanted to throw a coffee table against the window wall at the entrance of the hospital, but I restrained myself and contemplated about our flawed human nature instead. I wanted to console Mark for the delay, but I couldn't find him. I asked a nurse and she said she didn't know where he was. I started going around the hospital, but he had disappeared. So, these people, not only couldn't heal my son, but they may have made him worse or even lost him.

I went to the nurses' station and demanded to see my son. The nurse smiled.

"You don't know where he is?" This is no time for jokes and games, I thought, but only said,

"I've been looking for him and I can't find him anywhere. Lisa grabbed my arm.

"Come with me, Mr. Kizilos," Lisa said, like a sergeant giving an order. "Your son is an exceptional child and you should know it." I was ready to tell her to mind her own business, which is to keep an eye on my son, but she looked at me as if I owed her an apology.

"I know, but he is a little boy and I want him to live and be an exceptional man." We walked to the end of that hospital wing to a new huge section in construction. I heard a trumpet playing, faint short bursts of music that grew louder as we got closer to the new hospital wing. We stopped before a huge wooden door and Linda opened it. Mark was near a large window pane facing the sky and playing his trumpet. There was a workbench near him with pieces of leather and tools on it.

"Hi Dad," he said, still holding on to his trumpet. I hugged and kissed him.

"We found this area for Mark to play his music when other people sleep," Lisa said. "And, he not only can play music here, but he can do some fine things with leather." I went closer and saw some of his work.

"Mom brought me the trumpet and my stuff from home," he explained. The nurse looked at me forgivingly.

"Show your dad what you are making. I thought it was special."

"I'll show it to him when it's finished," he said and wrapped up the leather pieces on the bench.

"You fellows have fun. You have a little time till dinner time, Mr. Kizilos," the nurse said and started for the door.

"Thank you, Lisa, "I called out to her. Thanks for taking good care of him."

The next day I found a vaguely familiar person in Mark's room. How did he get in there? Who was watching Mark that day? The man introduced himself and reminded me that we knew each other from the church. He had been talking to Mark about his school athletics and his hobby and was delighted to get to know him. A few minutes later he said goodbye and went out of the room. He wanted to know the size of the cancer in Mark's body. I told him that there was no cancer here. George was his name and said he was so happy that Mark wasn't that sick. Them his face lost all of life's color and he looked stiff, still, dead. "My son died a few days ago," he said, his voice soft coming from afar. A car was backing up and wasn't seen. Struck down dead," he said, and shook my hand and left. Then stopped and asked, "Can I visit Mark again some time?" I nodded and watched him walk away in what must have been a horribly lonely world.

Dr. Brown, Betty and I had a meeting and he said that he wanted to do an angiogram in the adrenal gland area, to find out whether he could prove that the source of the problem was in the adrenal glands. He said the angiogram for a child was a very difficult procedure and would require a specialist. Before I could scream for the tough luck of having difficult problems that require the finding of specialists, he stopped me and declared that fortunately, Dr. Katkov, one of the experts in the procedure was near us and had already talked to him about the case. We had no alternatives. A hard wire-like instrument digging dep into the narrow tube going in and up to a child's body was a nightmare of pain and fear.

We went to see Mark in his room. I held him as if there was no way I could let him go. Betty explained to him that there was another procedure Doctor Brown wanted to do, to make sure we have located the right place for the source of the excess cortisol. She could calm things down better than I could. We were ready to leave when Mark called me back. I went by his bed and waited. He reached under his pillow and pulled a leather wallet with "Tolly Kizilos" pounded on it. He handed it to me and said

"Special for you, dad."

And for that I said "Thank you, Mark. It's the best gift I've ever got." I wiped the tears and knew. "God, thank you," I thought. It was a prayer that came to me from deep in my being. Betty gave him a hug and a kiss and he whispered something in her ear.

The angiogram was scheduled for a couple of days ahead, after Doctor Katkov had a chance to meet and examine Mark. I had no doubt that if the procedure could be done, Doctor Katcov was the person to do it. He inspired confidence and explained to Mark that he could control the discomfort if he was as still as possible. "It will pass and you will be fine again." Then he held his hand and asked, "Will you be my partner in doing this thing?" Mark nodded his agreement and the good doctor gave him a thump up.

I wanted to do something extra for Mark and I stopped at a magic store the next day and bought some tricks for him to learn and have fun. I went to the hospital and laid them out on his bed to examine and practice. Our nurse Lisa came after noon and told us that they were ready for the procedure. Mark held his ground. He asked the man who came to carry him to the procedure room to choose a card from the new deck he had just received as a gift, promising that he could guess the card without looking at it. The man played the game and started rolling the hospital bed. From a distant corridor I hear a surprised cry: "How did you do that?" I imagined Mark smiling and his caregiver laughing his head off.

The procedure revealed that the source of the problem was an adrenal gland. A couple of days later the gland was removed by surgery and his health returned to normal. While recovering, we had the magician Smolen Bergen perform his joyful gig in Mark's room. Mark polished his trumpeting and played the Battle Hymn of the Republic after reciting Lincoln's Gettysburg Address for his school's Lincoln Day celebration. Betty and I listened thankfully to Hummel's Trumpet Concerto in E. We knew God was with us.

F

INTO WRITING AND O.D.

Gratitude for Three Remarkable Organization Builders

I am grateful to Doctor Bill Sackett, who gave me a chance to help him create a transformational corporate organization, Honeywell's Systems and Research Center (SRC) in 1971, based on trust and compassion, teamwork, participative management and outstanding achievement of technical and business goals. The eighteen years I spent working with Bill and other colleagues were the culmination of my work life as a born change agent. I never stopped trying to change myself and the world I could reach and make things a little better for all of us.

Doctor James J. Renier, President of Honeywell Control Systems, deserves the credit for starting Honeywell's process of change with the publication of "People in the 80's" report, commonly referred to as the "Self-Esteem Report", committed to a sustained process of change to increase the employees' participation in the affairs of their organizations and strengthen their self-esteem

I would also like to credit Dr. Roger Heinisch, one of the most enthusiastic and open-minded leaders, who supported and extended the SRC management way in the late 1980s. He was opposed to autocrats and, when asked to give his view on participative management for the Management Guidelines Team Report, he said, "First, I feel it gets the job done. Second, I personally enjoy it. And third I believe the people I work with, also enjoy it."

28

At the Fork, I Chose Right, and Took Along What Was Left

The Road not Taken
Two roads diverged in a yellow wood
And sorry I could not travel both
Robert Frost

We spent an eventful year of learning and growing at the Creative Writing Workshop of the University of Iowa, using the Bush Fellowship money to write, take courses, and get an MFA degree. Betty took courses in psychology, wrote poetry and spent some time cooking fantastic dishes we had never tasted before.

The poet Paul Engle had started the International Writers Workshop as an adjunct to the Iowa Workshop, and I got to meet writers from all over the world. The Cold War was still going on and writers from the Soviet Union and its allies were suspicious of anyone who tried to befriend them. It took me some time to convince them that I wasn't a C.I.A. agent, gathering intel on them.

We came back to Minneapolis with new dreams and ready to face new challenges and learn from new experiences. I started looking for a job teaching English Rhetoric and working on my novel, the book that could decide my future writing prospects. Looking back, I admire my risk-taking ability but I am appalled at my poor judgement. The Bush Fellowship continued for another six months of practice for whatever the recipient had studied or practiced. I raced to complete my novel, a dystopia in the form of black humor, that was born out of my pointless experiences with the happy hippy culture, beat poets and young leftist dreamers, who couldn't focus on a goal and do the work needed to make it happen. I expressed my nostalgia for knowledge and logic by including more than a couple of hundred quotations from the legacy of Western Culture and my disappointment from the dawn of the new age. I thought the book would sell well enough to give me time to write the book I really wanted to write. I wrote eight books before the book you are reading, but I would be a beggar, if our income was based on these books.

Betty, became the bread-winner for the family while the fellowship continued and I continued writing. She was an excellent computer programmer and became a much sought-after Systems Analyst later when she participated in the work done by Honeywell for the Space Shuttle. I had no idea what I was going to do for the rest of my life, if my novel wasn't published, or didn't sell well enough to give us some additional income. I had no intention to return to my engineering career, but I would, if that was needed to provide an adequate income for our family. I wouldn't be happy, but the work would have meaning because my family would survive, in case Betty, who had some serious backpain and breathing problems, couldn't continue to work. Many people find no meaning in their work, and haven't found a way to make their work meaningful.

The dawning of the new age hadn't made a good impression on me because the war drums were still beating fiercely in Vietnam and the system was adding anxiety and dissatisfaction to life. We were drifting toward some hazy happy existence that didn't mean a thing. I thought that the discontented youth would want to continue their opposition to the war and end the violence, but my thinking was wrong. I read the Bardot Thorold, known as the Tibetan Book of the Dead, the Egyptian Book of the Dead, the literature of Zen by Suzuki and Allan Watts, and the Kamasutra, all the books of the rebels of the time starting with Ken Kasey, Allen Ginsberg Richard Brautigan, Norman Mailer and the books of my MFA thesis advisor Seymour Krim at the University of

Iowa, all of them with the goal of discovering the Way of the new era of peace, freedom and happiness. But, the young people and their teachers wanted freedom without any purpose, pot and sex and LSD backed by Timothy Leary's Harvard intellectualizing and theologized by Ram Dass, instead of inner transformation and action for a better world.

The dystopia was all around them, but they couldn't see it. It would take several decades and several wars before the young people came to their senses and started thinking seriously about changing the system with the titanium belly that could digest anything you shoved in its mouth. The writers and publishers and marketers were all after money. I wanted an unrelenting protest for injustices and corruptions, not a high on marihuana. I smoked no pot, because I didn't want any chemical boost on my happiness, if there was any, and didn't want to be a hypocrite when I told my sons to stay away from all dope. Yes, I usually took account of the long-term consequences of a moral way of living. The thought of keeping track of truths and tales for a long time, so I could be morally impeccable, was difficult, but necessary for me.

The future was uncertain, and the recession was getting ugly, but I remained hopeful. I didn't know why. I even went to a hippy festival once, to find out if there was some secret joy to be found in the gathering and the music. I got close to the drums, felt the vibrations on my skin and I couldn't hear much for days, but I didn't feel any joy. I was sad because I couldn't get anybody to discuss what might be done to make people have fun while doing some life-enhancing actions. Nothing much would happen as long as minds and souls followed their selfish motives, floating purposelessly in the crowd. I hadn't found yet any of the truths that guided my life later on, but I knew that, as long as I had a goal to reach, I would be content and continue my pilgrimage.

It didn't even occur to me that my crisis, working as an engineer, was due to my feeling that the work I was doing didn't help me achieve any enduring goal. I had not made the world a little better. Survival wasn't enough. Those who have more gifts, are required to do more, said Christ. I wanted to make a change in the world around me and I was looking for a worthy goal to pursue. I wanted more people to listen to what I said and what I did, but they had their own values and it was hard to change them.

I was becoming aware that we had to stop our aloofness and start caring for others. I hadn't realized that anger, pride, impatience and judgment weren't effective, if one wants to change people's reluctance to commit, or move them out of the crowd's beaten path, or change the mindset of the day's business.

I had yet to grasp the value of small graces and their power of changing the world. Why was the little old woman, who dropped a penny to the collection plate, going to receive the blessings of heaven and the big shots who drop bundles to the plate get zilch? What makes the difference? I wasn't close to anything yet. I hoped that someday somebody would listen to what I or somebody else had to say, or notice some good action somebody took, and choose to do something better than before because of these examples. I was trying to get people to own, not only their actions, but also their emotions and their spiritual motives. I was searching for ways to push people, make them go deeper, no matter what they were doing. If I became a college instructor this would be my goal in teaching. Here is an example of my twisted attempts at move people that way.

When I was a child, I always had some ear problems. The pain was daunting and I had become afraid of otolaryngologists. A couple of times they had to puncture my eardrum without any anesthetic to drain the fluid and that had hurt a lot. It took time for the pain to abate.

Our next-door neighbor, Chuck, in the College town we had been living in, was an otolaryngologist, and I had come to like him. We had some conversations in depth on the inability of people to show compassion to others and the life people were intent on living, using only their brains, and how the hippies at the school were using scrambled thoughts and feelings when writing for fun and fantasy.

Then one of our boys developed a nasty earache and we took him to Chuck on a weekend evening next door for relief of his sudden earache. This wasn't Chuck's clinic, it was his house, so he didn't have any anesthetic and our son had my nightmare experience before the pain stopped. I thought that Chuck did his best for us and told him so.

A couple of days later in another deep discussion with Chuck, I brought up the subject of pain again.

"You were working on my son's ear calmly, without any apparent sign of compassion," I said. "You were bent on relieving his pain - that much was obvious - but how could you stay so distant from him and his agony? Were you able to feel anything?"

Chuck smiled, but let a few seconds pass in silence. "Did you want another mother or a problem solver?" He said, and I saw a muscle of his face relax.

"Both," I said and felt that I had made a mistake. "I wish that all of us could do both and more," I said and added, "I'm sorry, but my dystopia is interfering with my life."

"I'm going to try feeling when I'm operating, but I'll pull my heart out of the procedure, at the slightest error, if somebody else doesn't do it first," he said to slow down my ambush. We smiled and talked about the hippies again, so full of life and so inert. I didn't leave. I stood my ground on the circle and passed the joint around and around, hoping for an entry in the discussion to give them the right way to change things.

I was reading a letter from Bemidji State College in Northern Minnesota, telling me that I was in the top ten percent of all the candidates who had applied for the position of Assistant Professor in Rhetoric at the school, and the results of the selection process would be communicated to me at the end of the month. I was trying to calm down from this latest humbling, one of many I had received by mail, or a phone call, or face to face meetings, when the phone rung and punctured my gloom. I didn't answer. Then the phone started ringing again. Somebody is after me, I thought. The world is trying to run me down. I answered the phone, pushing myself to a more hopeful mindset.

Bill Sackett, my old boss at Honeywell Inc. wanted to know why I hadn't found time to stop by and say hello to a good friend? I protested. I was very much willing to pay him a visit and find out how everyone was doing.

"How are you doing these days? Are you writing?"

"I'm working on a book for disheartened idealists," I said. "I got another six months before the Fellowship runs out."

"Come next Wednesday at two; come over and we'll talk," Bill said in an upbeat tone of voice.

"I'm not going back to engineering," I said and chuckled loudly enough to remind him of my objections, if none were left in his mind. The last time I had talked to him, I happened to express my anxiety as I was leaving my job, and said, "I don't know what I'm going to do, if writing doesn't work." I had felt that his reply was abrupt and harsh: "You can always be a design engineer," he had said back then and I could still feel the chill.

I would meet him, but I had no intention to crawl back to my old job before I found out if I could make a living as a writer or a college teacher. I had six months before the fellowship run out and ended the discussion.

"Done," I said emphatically, but I wasn't pleased with myself. My ego was getting in the way. There were times when I was afraid of my ego; afraid of making an offensive move that would chase a friend away, or accept, or reject an offer to do something that I would regret later. How many years before I moved against it and gained the upper hand? Would I ever get rid of it? It came out of the dark depths of my soul and spoiled some precious moments of love I had built with my wife. A good friend of mine used to remind me that I was bragging shamefully sometimes by sounding loudly a rooster's self-admiration for his dominance in the chickencoop, "Coco – re-e – c-o-o-o!" I may have been happy and proud for my achievements when I was riding high in high school or at work, but I never wanted to burden myself with a bloated ego's self-admiration. I felt the sorrow of impotence like a mosquito you try to squash but have no luck in it, and stopped the introspection. I steadied myself and laughed. It is comical for a person to be afraid that his ego will drive him to be a horse's ass. I thought that the idea might fit my novel better than my life and made a note of it on my calendar, next to the mark of the meeting with Bill next Wednesday.

Bill had secured permission for me to enter the building with a note to meet him at his office. I got a temporary confidential clearance badge at the guard desk and headed for his office where his secretary, Kate, welcomed me with a warm embrace and ushered me in. Bill got up from his chair behind his desk and came to the door to greet me. There was another man in his office and Bill introduced him as the well-known management consultant Dr. Raymond Brant. I was surprised, but since I wasn't asking for anything, I just sat down and relaxed. I had heard that top management used Raymond Brant in some of their gatherings, but I hadn't met him. There had been a time in the past when these leaders had spent a few days on the purpose of our Corporation and had come up with "Profit and Perpetuity." There was a rumor that Dr. Brant had tried to facilitate the discussion between the group that wanted to add the word "People" to the purpose and have it read "People, Profit and Perpetuity" and those who were happy with the way things had always been. The word "People" apparently was left out. All that was a rumor, but the people weren't informed, so they filled the vacuum of information with their hopes and made it a fact.

"I've asked Ray to help me with the human climate issues we have here," Bill said with enthusiasm, as if the three of us were going to have a party. That was his way of problem solving. "I think people are not happy with their work. They come and tell me what bothers them, why Harry is leaving, or Jake doesn't talk to George anymore, but they don't go out there and fix things. I asked Ray to find out what's going on."

It seemed to me that Bill was about to start a plan he had in mind, and I had no idea why I was there. Yet, his enthusiasm was contagious. "I thought that you may be interested in our problems here. You were always interested in teamwork; you wanted to create new ways for conflict resolution; work out an evaluation system."

"And don't forget empowerment of people," I said joking.

He paused, as if he needed a moment to complete his thought, and then said, "You'll be needed here," he said and his face was pale. We are going to grow the organization by combining with the Systems groups. We are going to become the Systems and Research Center with responsibilities much bigger than we've had so far. Broader market, bigger contracts, more interaction with our divisions." He stopped suddenly and looking straight at me, said, "I'll need help from you and many others to make this a successful organization."

"There is something interesting for me to do, Bill, but I don't know yet what it is." I wanted to say something nasty like "Do you mean that you want me to drop my writing project and start working on creating a happy and productive behemoth that you have dreamed up?" but, I had managed to control my sarcastic ego and let Bill continue with his project, whatever it was.

"Good," Bill moved into the opening I provided. "Ray was getting ready to give me a summary of his findings on our troubled organization."

Then he gave the floor to Raymond Brant, who started to explain what he had found in his interviews with the personnel of the Research Department. I followed carefully as he presented the details of his work. I followed what Ray was saying, but I couldn't engage with his report because it was flat and analytical when it needed to be poignant and deeply felt. Then he leaned forward toward Bill and said with a forceful tone of his voice: "The number one problem for this organization is that there is no credibility here."

He had hardly finished uttering his last word when I sprang into action. "Why do you say 'Credibility' Ray, when you mean 'Trust'? I think you are trying to say that people don't trust each other; they don't trust the management and the organization. Words like 'Credibility' are used to gut out the expression of feelings from the work environment. When people don't trust each other or the management they won't express their feelings to each other or anybody else. I can see that!" I said and stopped. I felt good with the stand I had taken.

Dr. Brant was an exceptional consultant and handled the discussion wisely, rather than defend his words and cause a wreck. Bill was thrilled with my intervention and asked me to stay and chat for a while after Raymond left. I got up and was ready to go and wait outside his office, but he asked me to stay where I was. I felt there might still be a chance to work on some project there. My faith in God at that time wasn't strong enough to even think of praying about getting a job. "Hope to see you again," Raymond Brant said and left.

"I'm trying to change the environment of this place and I want you to work with me on that," Bill said, searching for a favorable response. But, Bill was always serious when he talked about the Research Department and its affairs. No leisurely activities; no jokes; no clever comments; no slack; just problem-solving by brain-storming and relationships with people to be improved and people to mentor. We were already working a problem of great interest to a man who could be trusted to make serious commitments to those who worked with him.

Some years ago, he had declared that no one had a chance of getting his approval unless both sides of every issue were openly discussed. I knew that he would want me to tell him that he was right in some things and all wet in others, so I decided to listen and keep my doubts about any work I might want to do in check for a while. "You got it right when you said 'there's got to be more trust here.' Also, more teamwork, more openness, and more expression of feelings. The work we'll have to do at the Center cannot be done by people who are afraid to open up and tell each other what they really think," he said and his frustration was evident.

"Are you sure that our people are afraid?" I asked.

"Some manager wants his engineers to bid on a ridiculous idea that somebody in the Defense Department likes, or something they could care less about, and they get busy working on it rather than call a team together and think how to respond, or have nothing to do with it . . ."

"Some people are reluctant to stand up and speak their mind, Bill; you can't expect everyone to be like you," I protested. "And, that's the way I see it," I added.

"We have to trust and empower people so they can do the work their way, not ours," Bill went on. "We are not building brick walls, which are easy to measure and find out how well a worker is doing. We'll never know what engineers can imagine. create, invent, produce, until we convince them that we support them in every way we can. You know something about telling it like it is, questioning your bosses, because you've been there with your VDT. They'd still be working on the same project, if nobody stood up and stopped the project direction. People must know that they have a choice to express themselves and offer us the ideas that pop up in their minds, not just do what we tell them."

"You have a point there," I said, thinking of my early days at a small company I worked for, before joining Honeywell. One of my supervisors there, congratulated me for the work I was doing, but asked me to be a little more "diplomatic." I breathed in and breathed out and told him that "diplomacy" is used for hiding truths, and I wasn't interested in doing engineering that way. I had the feeling that he liked me even if he couldn't relax with me buzzing around that place.

"People expect a lot from their work and it's not just money. We have to help them achieve what they want to achieve," Bill said and turned his chair and faced out of his window at the sky. "Come and spend some time with the people you know and find out why some people leave and others stay, why people are not excited about what they do. We lost three top performers the last two months and I think they left because they didn't give a damn about what they were doing."

I could feel his passion, but I wasn't sure we could do anything to spread it around. Yet, I knew from my early years that I wanted to be free to work for big ideas, impossible dreams, make lasting improvements for as many people as we could reach. "Innovation happens when people are free," I said, spitting out words I was sure I read somewhere. "You cannot innovate because management orders it." I said, expressing a conviction I always had.

Bill believed that technology would make the world a better place, if people were enjoying their work and created things that mattered to them. I thought he liked me because I stood up and said what I thought could be done and what couldn't. I didn't feel I had achieved much yet. Perhaps, someday, somebody would find the right place to use some of my inventions and ideas, I consoled myself. I wasn't sure why I lost the zeal for my engineering work. Perhaps, I wanted to do what Bill was talking about and work with people, or I wanted to be free and write stories of peace and hope. A professor I knew from a writing class I had attended was leaving the University of Minnesota with a new job to be head of the Adult Education Department at the University of Kansas and he wanted me to go with him and get a PhD in Adult Education. I could have gone there for my Fellowship, rather than be attracted by the magic of fame, influence and honor that some writers attain. Writing made me travel to the Soul and the Universe. But, I was also moved by solving relational tangles, organizational problems, empowering people so we could create a better world. I would never be shy about my dreams.

"I've always wanted to be an engineer-missionary," I said, and the image of the khaki clad engineer with a topee working at some clean water installation in the Nubian Desert of Sudan appeared in my mind again.

"Come and look over the place," Bill said. "It's your home, anyway. You will have an office nearby and you can use my secretary. Log in as many hours as you want and you'll get the salary rate you had before you left. I'll tell the Administration guys you'll be coming back, on part-time, and all will be fine."

"You're asking me to do a professional's job in a field I have no professional experience or credentials," I said. I didn't know why I brought this up, but I regretted that I had done it. Perhaps, I was testing his belief in my competence. "It's a generous offer," I mumbled.

"I am sure you can help the people here. You got something others don't have," he said with conviction.

"What are you going to call me? Missionary to the Corporation?" I laughed, but the thought came to me suddenly and took a seat in my heart. I must say that I did like the honors part of temptation.

"Let's start with Assistant to the Director of Research for now and think of a better title later. I'm sure you'll think of something," he said and tapped me on the shoulder. His belief in my unique abilities made me feel confident enough to stop thinking of what was hard to do and I imagined the helpful services I could perform.

The more I thought about Bill's offer the more it made sense. There were no obvious answers to the problems I could think of, and that was intriguing to me. What did I know about diagnosing and changing people's and organizations' behavior? There were too many questions coming at me, and I had no answers. But, my desire to free people from their false selves and their learned limitations so they could find the truth in themselves and do their own good things, for all of us was strong enough to give me hope and courage for anything I decided to do. When I got home and told Betty about Bill Sackett's generous offer she was excited. "You are a preacher at heart, aren't you?" she said in her playfully approving tone.

"I have to finish my nightmare-novel, first," I reminded her. She never really cared much about the crippled world I had fashioned, even if it was meant to upend the readers and drive them to desire and do whatever it takes to bring about a better world. "It'll be hard to turn Bill down," I said, showing my interest in the offer and steering away from another debate that even I felt I should loose.

She turned and looked at me with a fading smile and one eye lifted up ever so slightly by irony, signifying disbelief. "You wouldn't do that," she said and started serving diner from the platter she was holding. It was Spaghetti with Greek Marinara Lamb Shanks, one of her cooking specialties that the boys and I were crazy about.

I never managed to get a job as an assistant professor at Bemidji State College. It was a bit humbling, but I was too busy with my magnus opus, the dystopian novel that revealed what makes society so mean, violent and unpredictable and makes us helpless to slow down its painful decline. And there was plenty to think about the humanistic organization we were thinking of building at Honeywell's SRC.

I finished the book after several years, writing whenever I could find time from my new profession of Organization Development at Honeywell.

I gave a copy of the book to Bill and a few days later I asked him what he thought of it. "There is an error on page 247," he said and my mind went blank as I stared at him. But that's all he said and went back to his office. I found the error on page 247 and stared at it for a long time trying to understand Bill's mind, without ever coming up with an explanation. Perhaps, I was an eleven-dimensional human being, but he could only see one, maybe two of these dimensions.

My dreams of fame and wealth based on fantastic sales of my magnum opus died without damage to my soul. I was happy presenting my book in the three or four TV and radio stations in the area and explaining how reading a book about a horrible society might motivate readers to see the evils of our society and yearn for a fundamental change. I had to answer a lot of audience questions about travel to Greece and the best islands for a tourist to visit, so I had just a few minutes to explain that my intent was to help readers see the harm that evil leaders can unleash on people, and cause them to demand a better world than the one they are inhabiting. It would take a lot of marketing to find out if I could make it as a successful novelist, and I had no patience, desire, money or aspiration to try it. I wanted to be with Betty and the children, work for the worthy goal of creating a good work life for as many people as I could and write books without expecting much money, fame or admiration coming my way.

Gradually the work became more meaningful than I had imagined, because as a member of the Center Management Team I had many opportunities to help the team create management systems emphasizing openness, excellence, teamwork freedom and participative management. Moreover, I gradually developed the interpersonal skills needed to help individuals create satisfying and productive work relations and rely on support from their team members.

Sometime had gone by since I started working at the Research Department when I remembered that helping a small group develop teamwork skills wasn't much different than what I had done in one of the psychology courses I had taken at MIT. I had started taking courses in group dynamics and organization behavior. I always thought of myself as an engineer, who also likes to write. I was astonished that my memory had blanked out the most relevant knowledge I needed for the job I was doing at SRC. Group Dynamics was the heart of Organization

Development and I had forgotten totally that I had what would amount to a Minor in Organizational Psychology at MIT, the very subject I needed for the job I was doing. Why had I forgotten about that? Betty reminded me that we took one of the courses on the Levittown studies in the Homans book together.

"We had an agreement that I would write the required paper and you would make the required presentation. Remember? The class started at 10 o'clock and you were not there. I was terrified that I may have to make the oral presentation without any preparation, all by myself." The anxiety she had felt back then had come back, heavy and hurting even now.

"I came through; didn't I?" I said and went beside her and asked for her forgiveness. She laid the embroidery she was working on by her other side and smiled at me.

"You should never leave me stranded," she said, her voice coming from her heart.

A couple of years after I started working for Bill, I was at a conference of training professionals, listening to an ad hoc group discussion on Career Development. I was preparing to create a work life experience that would motivate people to look for meaningful goals and find happiness achieving them. Excellence in technology would come not only from the work done, but also from the way the work made the world a better place.

It was then that one of the women leading the discussion of the group recalled the way professor Edgar Schein had talked about group behavior in a class at MIT. "He is still the Father of OD," she said proudly and went on to praise the teaching of a great man.

I had done well in that class -- why didn't I remember him? Had the fear of failure wiped out my memory with all the strengths I had acquired with work? I remembered that when I was Edgar Schein's student, I had dreamed of a career in helping people at work. Was a mysterious guide leading me back to that dream? I had the knowledge back then but not the motivation to work with people and build better organizations. I came to America to become a Mechanical Engineer and I became that. I had allowed other factors to define myself. Now, I knew I was headed to the abandoned dream. I would have to teach that, for sure.

29

Upside Down

"Suffering produces perseverance; perseverance, character; and character, hope." (Rom.5:3b, 4)

Sant Paul,

Not everybody sails lazily on a raft downriver on sleepy summer afternoons. People up north make the days cool on parks in airconditioned towers on city streets, parties on pools and lakes, finding friends and festive atmospheres. We know the summer lightheadedness won't last long. Now is the time to travel and take trips and visit the families of our sons to listen to the stories of the younger grandchildren or enter the fray with the older ones and be worn out playing games with them. I kicked the soccer ball a few times and then sat down by the barbecue and watched them run and kick and block and weave the plays that gave them precious moments to rejoice and remember, perhaps to keep for good and for a long time. Winter seemed far away.

Betty was showing the younger children the pictures she had created for every story she had written in her recently published book, "Jesus is Real", and they were looking and touching the colored images wonder on their fingertips. She started to read one of the stories and they listened. That was Nana and they loved her wholeheartedly. It was the love you see in the eyes of children and their smiles of the whole face and their touch. I could see joy light up her face as the little ones listened and interrupted. "Here is a story that shows how some children were good examples of loving their ailing friend. When Jesus was teaching in a house that became very crowded, four friends carried their paralyzed friend on a stretcher. They wanted Jesus to heal him. . ." there were screeches, enthused voices and questions, but Nana gathered them close and handled the excitement with ease. . . "but there was no room in the house, so they brought him up on the roof, made an opening in the roof and lowered the stretcher down in front of Jesus. When Jesus saw their faith, he said 'Friend your sins are forgiven'. This upset some of the temple keepers of the law, so Jesus said, 'Get up, pick up your stretcher, and walk.' The paralyzed man got up and everyone was amazed." The children got hold of the book and she joined them in their liturgy of wonders and crackling noises.

We stayed until we heard reminders of homework needing to be done and chores still left undone and the necessity for sleep and school and the routines of daily work. We hugged and kissed everyone and they did the same and said "I love you" a hundred times as if the essence of connection was somehow woven in the repetition, as if meaning would go deeper in the heart and stay longer with us. We took off with arms waving goodbye like kite tails flying in the breeze. We were happy to see those we love, those our love had created and the fruits of their love. And we talked about their relationships and their jobs and their progress in whatever they had set their goals to pursue. When Betty saw the "Snow-Queen" sign, the huge parka bundled woman of the North, she said that this was a good day for a "Snow-Queen" cone with caramel and pecans. I was already done with eating, but I knew she wanted this familiar taste to end the outing on a high note, so I stopped outside the store and waited in the car. It had been a day of happy moments and my thoughts were drifting toward the thin clouds over the plains out West.

Betty came out holding the cone. The car door was open just a little and I leaned to open it all the way for her to enter and sit without effort. She came closer and I leaned back. She was ready to enter and sit down. I tried to make sure the car was positioned right. My foot pushed down. The gas pedal roared and the car jumped back and a wall of terror struck my Betty and slammed her down to the ground and oblivion.

I run out and called her, but she wasn't there. "Oh, God, help!" Some people rushed to help her while I run inside the store and screamed at the store people to call the police, the ambulance, my son, anyone. She cannot be dead, just like that. She was so relaxed, so beyond the small spot her body occupied. "Where are they?" The whole world will be gone, if she is gone. The police came and wanted to know why did I do this? My mind, my leg, my foot – they are the guilty. "I made a mistake, and killed her." The ambulance came and they carried her in a stretcher. They asked me if I wanted to come along and I climbed up. Why don't they accuse me openly of my crime? The driver says in fifteen minutes we'll know how things are. A medical technician sits by her side and checks her vital signs. "She's doing O.K.," he says as he glances at me. I pray that all the suffering that's coming be mine, "She is innocent!"

At the hospital they asked her some questions and slowly she gained consciousness and answered them. We all cheered and applauded when she told them where she lives. They did some tests and examined her for all the damages she could have suffered. I waited nearby; talked to my sons and took thankfully their consolation and the blame; I could see sadness and anger and frustration in their eyes their hands and stares. Good and bad -- they were all mine. Don't take her away from us, Lord! And, if she goes, take me out too. I kept a prayer going. It occurred to me that this was something the devil might have had something to do. It was too easy – it was me alone. Don't duck, man!

Two days later we were allowed to go home, and then, in our bedroom kept in the dark, as the doctor recommended, Betty recovered from the concussion she had suffered. I sked her to forgive me, but she said there was nothing to forgive, since, she was certain that I had no intention of doing any harm to her. "What is there to forgive?" I pushed her. "I don't know. . . Perhaps subconsciously I wanted to harm you". She blew it off and warned me to stop inventing causes for guilt. I've been good at that.

Then, she stared at the far-out wall and told me that after she passed out she heard the voice of Christ giving her encouragement and hope. She said that she felt a life-giving warmth like a blanked over her body. I listened carefully to her description of the otherworldly voice and how it affected her will to recover. There was no question in my mind that she had no doubt about the presence of Christ during her ordeal. I cut short the drift to my search for miracles when I was a young boy. Perhaps, I got some time on this planet yet, and I'll encounter a miracle with no doubts. Or, I just did and I'm too stupid to acknowledge it. "I'm going downstairs and make some food you like," I said and kissed her on the side of her forehead, where her face wasn't blemished by the fall. "I believe that he was with you," I said as I left her. She smiled and waved a slight goodbye.

30

Building a Transformative Organization

The following week, after my meeting with Bill Sackett I started working part-time at Honeywell's Research Department where I had worked before. This time, however, my goal wasn't to be recognized as a good researcher, and gain the respect of my peers and advance. A wind had blown and swept away all my past ambitions and accomplishments, giving me a sense of independence and competence in the pursuit of goals that build a better life for all. I had the sense that whatever I was able to do for this humanistic work environment would be for all of us. I had a sense that whatever I was able to do for this organization would be among the defining contributions of my work life.

I wanted to help Bill Sackett transform the good research department he had assembled after years of effort, to an unrivaled research organization which empowered people to choose work that was meaningful to them and resulted in a happier life for all. The management would be responsible for caring and developing people, providing opportunities for training, counseling, conflict resolution and other skills needed for transformation. The management would also make systemic changes in leadership, to promote compassionate values and adopt reward systems that supported these values as it had always supported technological excellence and business success.

The first day, soon after I got pad and pencil and established myself in the office I was assigned to, I made an appointment with Bill to meet with him later that week and discuss the vision we ought to create at

SRC. In the meantime, I visited some of my colleagues and talked to them about my new temporary assignment. Some teased me for the dreams I had, others wanted more details, and some were pleased by our plan and wished me success.

Several of them were still trying to apply the VDT and other devices to new configurations under government contracts. They were still hopeful that the device might work on helicopters, Vertical Take-off and Landing (VTOL) aircraft, or undersea vehicles, so I expressed a hopeful view that some of the devices they were working on may be very useful. I wanted to believe that they would succeed.

Passing by the office of Henry Mar, a kind-hearted and wise Manager with a PhD in the Materials group and a good friend of mine, I felt I had to stop and chat for a while. Henry had taken a trip to China once and enjoyed telling me about his distant relatives there. We used to go for lunch in the Chinese restaurants around our office and he had taught me what to eat and how, from the abundant Chinese cuisine.

"I heard you were coming back to work and I couldn't believe it," he said greeting me. "Are you going to make us more proactive, more productive, more prosperous or what?

"Too many friends to leave behind," I said, giving him a hug. I knew he was a thoughtful and restrained man and I couldn't miss the chance to show him that he would have to deal with a boisterous Greek again. It was always so calming getting together with Henry at my office, his office or for lunch.

I owed him a lot for the advice he had given me when my mother was sick. I postponed going back to Greece to see her, hoping that I would still find her alive when I went back in a few weeks. Henry insisted that I leave for Greece right away. "You will regret it big time, if you don't visit her right now," he had urged. I sensed that he had experienced the pain he was asking me to avoid. And he was so right. I went and saw my mother when she was still well enough and could talk with me about her future with her "Little Christ".

"I got my bag ready for the blessed rip," she said to me at the hospital. I left Greece having had a good chat with my mother and she left us a few weeks later.

"I owe you a lot, Henry," I said, and he turned his chair.

"I've got something for you," he said and went to the locker behind him and took out a large role of heavy paper. He unfolded the role of the two-by-four paper, filled with Chinese letters. "I bought this for you when I was back home. I meant to give it to you, but by the time it came, you had left this place.

"Thanks, Henry. What does it say?' I asked him.

"Beware of Greeks bearing gifts," he said with a smile that meant more than "welcome back". Henry's teasing was a gift.

As I strolled around the Department, I could see a group of engineers from the Control Sciences Group having a meeting in one of the Conference rooms and I recognized a couple of my old friends. I thought it would be a good idea to take a seat, listen and learn what they were working on these days. I knocked and opened the door, ready to sit at one of the empty chairs in the back of the room.

"I'm Tolly Kizilos, working part-time for Doctor Sackett these days, and I'd like to learn about the projects going on in your group," I said and waited by the door for a welcome response from the leader of the group,

"I'm Charles Feldman," the group's manager said, rising up from his chair at the head of the table. "I'm sorry, but this is a private meeting," Charles Feldman said and sat down ready to continue his meeting. I don't know what snuffed all thoughts in my mind then, but I wasn't my usual self. There was a numbing silence in my head.

"OK.," I said and turned around and left the room, humbled and shaken. I crawled into my office and tried to reassess my choice to continue this new job in the organization that I had worked for so many years until a year ago. "You can do this," was an uninvited echo from a small voice that replaced the silence in my mind. "I'll have to learn how to work with Feldman," I thought. I felt sad. "You must do that," my will urged me on, but there was no push for it.

In the following days I found other colleagues of mine who wanted me to listen to their decision-making problems and welcomed my suggestions for training and organizational changes. Several of them thought it would be a good idea to run a class with a communications expert and wanted to learn some ways of conflict resolution.

I had to stop at Joe Kilpatrick's office and see how hard it was for him to work on the most precious product of the Company, the Ring Laser Gyro (RLG) with all kinds of people throughout the Company and others. "I can't stop working for the best product the Company will have," Joe said, and the flame of achievement was burning in his eyes. I knew how healing that could be. I had been there. He had been working on that project for several years with the same zest and resilience. The responsibility he had was part of the joy of work.

"I'll stop by again and talk organizational transformation," I said and moved on, thinking about those who were immersed in their work, as I was once, and those who have had enough and want out.

Later that week, I saw Bill Sacket and told him what I had found out and some needs I identified and was beginning to work on. I also shared with him some of my frustrations. "I'm not sure I can break into this system again," I managed to say, as I explained that Charles Feldman had kicked me out of his meeting.

Bill looked disheartened, but was still in the fight. "Next time this happens, instead of going for the door, sit down and repeat your position and your responsibilities in this organization," he said and paused for some time. "If you cannot do that, you'll lose the war before the first battle ends," he said and his face had turned red. "And, there will be other battles; you can bet on that."

I knew that he wanted me to be strong, to take the blow, get up and stand my ground. He was expressing my anger, and I accepted his counsel. He was standing by me. "O.K. I'll stick around and do what we need to do, to make the world a little better place," I said and relaxed back on my chair.

"The hard part is to convince enough people to agree on what is better," Bill said, and folded his hands, perhaps, waiting for me to give him an answer.

"Don't we kind of know what our technologists want? I said after a while. "Tough problems to solve, inventions that make the world better, teams with friendly people, decent salaries, promotions for those who excel, compassion for each other, all that. . ." I said and stopped, embarrassed that I had told my boss what I was sure he knew best.

"Everybody wants to be happy and find meaning in their work, but they want different things." It seemed to me that he was looking for an answer that was better than what was in his mind. "We have to create a top technology organization that helps the company's business goals so we can be trusted with power to set our goals," he said weighing his words.

I wanted to add that this wouldn't be such a hard thing to achieve, but instead I said what I really thought. "Companies are not altruistic, Bill; they'll change because the old way of doing business doesn't work anymore." Bill was thoughtful. We just spent a few more minutes about the pain all people suffer, when they try to change the world.

Having a discussion with him was usually pleasant and often enriching. You had the feeling that he was shooting a few baskets in an empty basketball court and soon was going to throw one your way so you could have some fun too. But, Bill was always serious when he talked about the Research Department. No jokes; no clever comments; no slack; just problem-solving by brain-storming, hard facts and gut-feelings. It was apparent to me that we were already working a problem of great interest to a man who could be trusted to make serious commitments to those who worked with him.

"You got it right when you said 'there's got to be more trust here.' The company needs a robust Research and Systems organization to increase its overall business for the government marketplace, but most of our people are not attracted to the competitive marketplace that will win contracts for us. They want to do technical work, solve tough problems and innovate, not write proposals and sell ideas in the marketplace for huge contracts. To survive and thrive I found out yesterday that we have to change the system so we can do both. The Systems Department has already been formed, but we have to transform it, if we are to succeed."

"When was that decision made?" I asked. "It makes any change more difficult for us," I said with concern.

"It was decided yesterday at Corporate and they let us know that they need our technology to win these days," he said.

"Why doesn't the company fund our work, if they need us so much? Most of our people don't want to become marketers," I said having known dozens of engineers in my previous career at the Research Department.

"We get some support from the company, but most of the funds must be brought in by winning contracts. Especially now that the government wants bigger projects and the company wants to win some of them and grow."

"Bill, most of our people don't want to do marketing, or cannot do it. They are the best technologists one can find," I insisted, sure of what engineers wanted. They are happy with technology."

"You're generally right on that, but, there are some who can go in the market and win. You and some others were able to win several contracts, do good research work and support several engineers with the funds you brought in."

He was right on that, and I decided to keep quiet and listen, even though I didn't like where we were headed. Did I want to return to the work that had nothing to do with the arts? Did I want to devote my energies to empowering people so they can create better weapons, that incompetent leaders can use to fight unnecessary or unjust wars? Did I want to work for a virtual production division of the company, knowing how much I had fought to enter the research department in my engineering years? I felt a chill in my shoulders, a cold stream down my back.

"Perhaps, there are a few more nuts that can do what I was doing," I said. I had no enthusiasm for the old game of competition, winning and producing things that didn't have much meaning.

"If people can work in teams," Bill said with outmost faith in his words, "then those who can or like to deal with the market can find out what the customers want, propose solutions by their teams and get the funding to produce the technology needed by their entire team," Bill continued enhancing his vision, but my thoughts were drifting, trying to find reasons worthy of my commitment. "Then we can transfer any production work to the divisions," he added.

Who cares? I was asking myself. Bill kept thinking aloud. "Some scientists and engineers can work with the divisions, and bring more funding for us here, when problems arise." I shifted back my attention when I heard the last few words.

"If we are not in the market, our work will only satisfy the needs of the production divisions and we'll never be independent to pursue the ideas that our people and some visionary customers want us to pursue. To build the organization I am describing, our people have to be free to form teams to do work they choose, and that's based on freedom and trust," I said, but I had a lot more to say. Creative, free people, working in teams for meaningful things can make the world a better place, I thought and kept quiet. I felt that I was fighting with a master in jiu-jitsu and was being battered.

"We have to also hope that they'll choose to work on things that make us a stronger country than a deadlier war machine," I said, having at last found the right words to say, and shut my mouth.

"If people are free and learn to stand up for what they believe is right, we won't have unneeded invasions and costly mistakes of judgement," Bill said dismissively. Clearly, he wanted to talk about "the project", but I was sure that he was open to discuss further the kind of work we would go after and the people we would like to lead our efforts.

"It will take good communication skills, teamwork skills and a team decision-making system, as we were saying before. People will have to make decisions with everyone's participation, and by consensus," I said and I thought I should fight for the people more vigorously. "People will want to be rewarded fairly, get the power needed, so they can take risks and experience the fun of freedom to achieve their team's goals."

"I don't intend to promote dictators and neither do you." Bill added.

I kept up my stream of objections. I was driven to object as if, somehow, I knew this was my duty for the job I would have. "The people who do the marketing may become more powerful by the control they gain, than those having fun solving technical problems," I said, remembering the last few years of my engineering career. It was easy to assign others to do the work I didn't enjoy doing. "You got the money, you find the power," someone had said back then.

"That's fine if you care for the people in your team. Trust is not only good for teamwork," Bill said. "Now it is the crux of the operation. The work that we need to do cannot be done by people who are afraid to open up and tell each other and their managers what they really think, and what they want to do," Bill said, clearly disturbed. "People must prove their technology expertise before they can venture out in the market. That's the ticket for advancing, and people must not be afraid to go beyond what they already know."

"Some people are reluctant to stand up and speak their mind; but there are also some who don't follow orders blindly," I protested.

"The freedom to disagree should be the norm of this place, so we can unleash people's creativity and do the work their way, not ours," Bill went on. "Don't you do that when writing your fictions?"

I could see where Bill was going. "Technologists have real power too. We'll never know what engineers and scientists can imagine, create, invent and produce, unless they disclose it," I said with confidence that surprised me. "They have to believe that we support them," I went on, remembering stories we used to tell one another, back in the days when we were in control of our work-life, inventing, marketing and getting funded by the government. We had an unauthorized but well-oiled research-marketing-production line. Respect was a given. People know that they have a choice to express themselves and offer their ideas or just clampdown and do what we assign them to do. The engineer who reads the New York Times with his feet up on his desk at ten o'clock in the morning, may be the one who invents the biggest moneymaker for Honeywell.

"There is also the other advantage we get, if people can step up to it: when a decision is made by consensus in a team, rather than by a boss or some unseen 'management', the people feel committed to achieve the results," I said, remembering some ways I had discovered when I managed my projects.

Bill was thoughtful. "People expect a lot from their work and we have to help them achieve what they want to achieve," he said and turned his chair and stared out of his window at the shiny cloud puffs sailing by up high. Then he turned back and spoke to me, with conviction. "We do have many projects that benefit the company, bigtime," he said, apologetically, I thought.

"Do we have any projects that people started on their own initiative?"

"You bet we do: The Honeywell Ring Laser Gyroscope (RLG) will be one of the most significant technical achievements to come out of Minnesota and the United States. It will change the world of inertial navigation, guidance, and control, and is being developed by three of our top research engineers and engineers from Honeywell's production divisions. You know Joe Kilpatrick, right?

"I know Joe and Ted Podgorski, and just talked to Fred Aronowitz," I said.

"These Three guys and Mercer from Sperry love their work, and I would bet they'll be winners of the prestigious Sperry Award for the RLG long before it is used on most commercial and military aircraft, and space vehicles such as the Space Shuttle."

"I didn't know they were that far ahead," I said feeling elation.

"What else do we do that adds something useful to the world and leaves it in better shape?"

"Talk to Henry Mar about the superconducting materials his group is trying to develop for use in fast transport systems. The Pattern Recognition group is trying to read X-Rays to identify breast cancer automatically. It's a form of Artificial Intelligence. Talk to some of the computer guys who are working on robust operating systems for the years to come. There are, of course some systems the government would like us to work on that we have some doubts about, but our people know the benefits and risks and there is a good reason to hope for the best," he said and went no further. "When Artificial Intelligence becomes functional we'll have to be very alert," he added, as if he was instructing himself.

"When humanity's existence is at stake, we better have a human rather than a machine at the controls," I said. Then, a few words burst out of me: "He or she can pray and ask Jesus Christ to have mercy on us.'"

Bill smiled, surprised by my fervor. "I see you're still a Christian," he said.

"Always, and more so as time goes by," I said and let go of the discussion. I knew Bill believed the data more than any other way was the way to understand reality and he hadn't changed since the last time we argued the case of faith. But, he was interested in the spiritual life as well. There was a time when he encouraged a meditation group to meet in some conference room so people could learn to relax. And, in one of our discussions, he had told me that he liked Krishnamurti as a good theological-philosophical thinker. I didn't have much to say because I hadn't read him but I had read on a review of one of his books that he was interested in "illuminating the concepts of Freedom, Personal Transformation, Living Fully Awake and Much More. He was interested in spirituality and that was good, I thought.

"We hire people with a lot of good education, achievers with high expectations and imagination, and if we don't give them a chance to achieve their goals they will either be picked up by the divisions, or they'll leave the company for a better deal in a warmer climate. I want to find out how to make people feel that this is their own place. "There was silence for a long minute. "You can use your experience to help people adapt to this system we are talking about. Get some consultants to help you, trainers to improve oral communication skills, teamwork skills, negotiation skills. . . We have to take the risk of growing our way, if we are to avoid becoming the supporting department of the big company divisions. I don't like to fail," he said and looked at me with a question drilling into my mind.

"Neither do I," I said. I could feel his passion, but I wasn't sure what we could do to spread it around. Yet, I knew from my early years at school that I wanted to work for big ideas, impossible dreams, lasting improvements for all the people.

Kate came and asked him if he wanted to take a call from some divisional V.P. He said he would be back soon, and I was left to ponder our discussion and my developing career.

Bill was a builder of quality relationships, had managed groups of motivated people and was a helper of dreamers. I never knew where he stood on the Vietnam war, but he was never a hawk. He, like most of us, I suppose, wanted to win in Vietnam and wanted us to provide the morally correct technical help the divisions needed; but the time came when many of us sensed that the war was a lost cause. Too many of our people were being hurt for no worthy reason. There was a meeting I had attended with a dozen other engineers several years ago in which a big Division wanted new ideas from us to solve a problem in a product used in the war. No one offered any idea.

I found myself going back to my last years in engineering, as if they had something to do with the invitation I had just received from Bill. All of us who ever worked with Bill sought his advice and valued his company as a mentor and a friend because he was always ready to give rather than take. Even when he pushed you to do something you thought was hard to do, deep down, you knew it was for your own good. There was integrity in this man. Was it worth spending twenty years helping him to create a transformative organization with humanistic values? Was there a chance that their spiritual life increased and God's Grace was received when work lives flourished?

I thought that technology would make the world a better place, if people were enjoying their work and created things that mattered. I agreed with that, but I could never believe that any world of technology could be the purpose guiding my search for meaningful things to do, or the best guide for a human being's journey in life. I had a story published in a local magazine, in my "engineering" days, making the point with a computer scientist, who was suffering from depression because he couldn't create an algorithm that would make an advanced robot experience the joy of the flavor of a spumoni ice-cream cone.

As an engineer, I believed that I was doing valuable work. Technology could help us make the world a better place, but would never lead us to the Elysian Fields, Valhalla or Heaven. The end of our searches was beyond the material world. Someday, somebody might find the right place to use some of my inventions and the inventions of others. Or, they would never matter as devices, but they were important because we worked on them with all our knowledge and skills and formed relationships that mattered to us and supported our families -- a noble goal for all of us. The only things that last forever are always beyond the things made of matter.

I wasn't sure why I lost my zeal for engineering work. Perhaps, I abhorred the Vietnam War; or, I had reached a point where being involved with the intricacies of human relations at work was more meaningful to me than solving engineering problems. I stretched myself on my office chair and raised my legs up on my desk. Sometimes logic lets imagination run things and find the answers to life's problems.

Writing made me travel to the Soul and the Universe, and success might give me a chance to speak to a bigger audience, change the view of some people from the pursuit of wealth, pleasure and domination to happiness based on eternal realities. But, I was also moved by solving relational problems, organizational problems, counselling people with work and career problems, empowering people so we could build a better world. I wanted to find out what others did to overcome personal problems and become a kinder, friendlier, more compassionate person, than I was. This was the best chance I was going to get to learn how to love my neighbor. "Love God with everything you have and love your neighbor," were all that was needed to become whole, a human being, saved, united with God, become god.

And, if you want to serve others well and know how you discovered the purpose of your life, you show the steps you took. It is then that you compose a violin concerto, or barge into a Chapel and paint a smile on a serene Angel, or tell stories that reveal the meaning you found in creating something unique, or touching the soul's rush of undulations or the flip that turns a down into dare to survive. You have to relive the experience you had when you fought against the violent, the venal, the virulent and the variety of other evil doers and show others how to endure with the Spirit within. And, sometimes, you have to return close

222

to days of sorrow and grief, and act again the way you suffered your losses and your failures. And if you cannot act again all the meaningful moments of your life, tell someone else's true story to those you want to serve. Some writing serves a moral purpose. I didn't want to let go of that. I was beginning to see that going around and talking to people to find out what they were doing and how well they were doing, or if they had a moral code, or what was their purpose in life, so I could teach, or guide, was not only ineffective but also blameworthy. I had to love everyone I was going to help. And the "I" was the experiences that was revealing the human being I was supposed to be.

Bill came back to my little office and complained about the new goals he was asked to have. In truth, I thought he loved the new responsibilities he would have, because he would have a chance to sail his ship through the angry seas and daunting horrors of our world and bring it hopefully to Ithaka.

Driving home, my mind continued its exploration of my having landed on a job I hadn't planned to get. Had I been helped to arrive at that contentious meeting with Raymond and Bill so I could do this work at Honeywell? Or, was this a hodge-podge cavalcade of luck and chance? Some positions I had worked in the past run like a movie clip in my mind. I had travelled from MIT's rigorous Mechanical Engineering classes, lessons in my youthful foolishness and proper admiration of the friendliness of steel workers to my first job in Heat Transfer at an old factory in a blue-collar Ohio town, to a modern company working in Machine Controls and a Research position in Fluidics and Aerodynamics where I dreamed up devices and got patents. Full stop. I want to be a writer but there is no way I can afford that with a family I love and must support the best way I know how. Providentially again I win a Leadership Fellowship with money available for a year and a half to do anything my heart desires. How? Why me? Drop engineering and MIT and patents and research. Start walking on another path. Shift gears and go. Go! Go to College for Modern Literature and writing a novel that warned people of the evils in society and bellowing a moral code. Anger loses; but love wins. Then I walk into Dr. William Sackett's office and I am given a dream of a job that I know something about, a job that was no different than the life I had lived in my younger days, but not aware of it yet. Then Edgar Schein pops up in my mind and the group dynamics studies and Organization Development jump out of the box. I'm not that.

I am a Change Agent, providing ad-hoc solutions for work life, exploring and improvising, improving and imagining a better world and acting on that belief. I thought that someday I would put all these pieces of work and study together and prove that I was guided and helped in my journey by a mysterious person that I would call "God". Perhaps, everybody travels with a friendly guide now and then, or always.

31

Survive the Alaska Wilderness as a Team

With the encouragement of the Center Management Team (CMT) various groups were formed at the Research and the Systems Departments and started working on their respective goals. The members didn't have the needed teamwork skills, so making consensus decisions and acting on them wasn't easy. The people who had gained respect for their technical expertise were always having more power, and reaching consensus didn't change that. Sometimes I would be invited or drop by one of these meetings and facilitate the process by strengthening the opinion of a quiet participant, or confronting a strong manager who didn't let everybody have his or her say-so in the process.

I remember the time when three engineers in a Section meeting I was attending raised the issue of marketing and helping a company Division out of town. They reported that the three of them had worked things out and were happy with the outcome. This kind of collaborative work was exactly what Bill Sacket and all of us in the CMT had hoped would happen.

"What outcome is that?" came like thunder the voice of Charles Feldman, the Manager of the Section in that Group. "One guy does all the marketing work, and the other two have all the fun solving technical problems and take an occasional trip to our Division in Palo Alto with a side trip to Big Sur?" Feldman stopped and waited for an answer, but none came. "In this Group everybody does some work in the marketplace and the Divisions.

"The Center Management team made it clear that a team has to do its marketing, so some members can do marketing and others can do the technical work," an engineer said in defense of the three colleagues who had proudly announced their team's agreement.

"There are issues you know nothing about," Feldman insisted. "Have you asked the Division Production Manager, whom he wants to deal with?" It seemed that Charles knew something no one else knew.

"Charles," I said with authority I didn't have, but I felt was needed, "we argued the marketing issue extensively in the CMT team with both of us present and decided by consensus." I kept my eyes fixed on him ready to respond quickly to any further resistance Feldman might put up.

"We'll talk about this again. We voted on a guideline, not a rule. There cannot be a strict rule like that," Feldman said icily and changed the topic on the agenda.

"Place it on the agenda for the next team meeting and we can discuss it again," I said and felt like I had thrown my glove, challenging him on a duel.

After the heat of the moment left us all disoriented, I spent hours regretting my anger, but justifying my position. Isn't that what all prideful people do? I didn't know how corrosive pride could be. It was serious. Things that matter are never easy to resolve, I thought as I was trying to find an easier way to deal with the conflict.

It seemed that nothing could change from one day to the next. Time has to go by and people have to wrestle with their emotions, reconcile their view of the world with the view of others and move something in their view of the world. I met with teams almost every day, and heard arguments and verbal fights. I had some good days and some bad ones. But, as the wise janitor who emptied the wastebaskets in my office said late one evening, when I asked him how was his day: "Today is better than yesterday, but worse than tomorrow!" And so, I hoped, was the management process of our organization. I could see what was happening and proposed the appropriate training to help us all develop the skills needed to solve tough problems on our own. I was happy when several people said they wanted to participate in a training workshop.

With help from the consultants who kept in touch with me, I organized a Team Decision-Making training exercise in a nearby motel. Charles Feldman two other Managers from the CMT, along with a couple of supervisors and several Engineers and Scientists, including Martin Telford, one of the top technologists we had, agreed to attend.

Well-functioning teams produce outstanding results, not only due to the skills and experience of each member, but also because they create a heightened sense of affiliation in their members that strengthens collaboration, support for one another and unity to meet goals. To strengthen teamwork, I used an old but, always exciting training exercise titled, "Survival from Alaska's Wilderness". I won't describe the exercise, but the process followed was exciting and revealed many strengths and weaknesses of the participants.

As it happens most of the time, the exercise proved decisively that the team decision of the tools needed to survive was superior to the decision of any individual in the team, including the decisions of the best thinkers and the most successful managers.

After the meeting broke up, I asked Charles Feldman, if he had come to believe that the team could make better decisions than he could.

"'Hoi Polloi' had the upper hand today," Charles said as if the outcome was regrettable.

"I'll tell you a secret, Charles," I said in a whisper, "I always thought I could do better than any team I've been a member of, but it looks like I was wrong. Something happens to people when they work together and get to know each other. I don't know. . . it's like you add two and two and you get five," I said and thought I was bearing my soul. Feldman raised his eyebrows, clearly disapproving, but I wasn't sure of what.

"Two and two can become 22 sometimes," Charles muttered. I was pretty sure he would go around and around, but never respond to the question. So, I did what I have done all my life: explore, probe, find out what is there. I knew what to do because I had lived on the other side of pride long enough.

"What do you like about your management job? "I asked him.

"Getting done things that matter effectively and efficiently!"

"The people? The teams? The friendships? The fun of being united in some way with your subordinates, your colleagues?" I asked and saw the demeaning look in his eyes turn even darker, wilder, irreconcilable.

"I have nothing against teams," he said and took a long look at his wristwatch. "They are a good management tool when they work well. He stared at me as if I was flat on the ground. "Good job today, Professor! "he said and walked away, master of his own world.

32

Harold Gets Over It and Thrives

Harold came late one evening in my office and I stayed to hear what he had to say. I had a hunch he had a problem to discuss and I wanted to listen to him. Harold was a good engineer, but he was older, and he was neither a great skinner nor a born hunter. He knew he needed to be part of a team, but he hadn't found a match yet.

"Schmidt said, come next month, he has no work for me," Harold said as he came in. He took a seat at the round table in my office. "Every time I ask him to let me travel and market the command interface control system he tells me that it's a waste of my time. Instead of help, I get, "You'll be out of a job.""

I knew that Betty and the kids were waiting for me at home, so I tried to speed things up a little. "Does he give you any reason for what he wants you to do?"

"He says there is no money in the budget for the interface project. And now he says the Research money we get is already allocated, so he has to let me go."

"When?" I asked, to find out if we had any time search for an answer

"At the end of the month," he said and turned his attention to the Sketch of the Thinker that one of the Research Graphics artists had drawn some months ago.

"Have you tried to find a project to work on with somebody else?"

"Every time I contact somebody with a project, they tell me that I need some training to do the work of the project they have, but Schmidt says he has no money for training." He occupied the chair fully and relaxed. "He doesn't want to help," he said.

"it may be true," I said, thinking of a supervisor's pressures to find the funds and feed his people.

We discussed his predicament for some time and it seemed that his boss wasn't interested in helping him. Schmidt had been hired from an out of state manufacturing company for liaison with a Production Division and probably had no idea of the ways we cared for people at SRC. But, I still had trouble believing that a supervisor would let one of his people go without giving that person some help. I promised Harold that I would look into his situation next day, but he should know that he was working for a guy who wasn't familiar with the SRC ways and had deadlines to meet that were at times cruel. His group wasn't integrated to SRC yet, so I didn't know how much we could help.

"In the meantime, contact the people you know and offer to work for any project you have some expertise," I said. "And mention that you have some ideas for getting funding from a contract."

"I'll do my best. Tell my boss that you asked me to look around," he said, stood up and left, walking with both hands in his pockets. I kept thinking of a man in trouble all the way home. I knew so little about him. Was he sick? Was he married? Did he have any children?

I didn't want to feel compassion for him before I could help. I wanted to think of a way to change his boss' attitude.

Next morning, I found out that Harold had worked himself into this kind of needy situation before. If a person needs help too many times, it is hard to get a long-term commitment from any supervisor in a place with many achievers hunting for game. But we have to care for each other, I kept thinking, trying to convince myself that I was on the right track

I talked to a few managers who might have work for Harold and twisted as many arms as I could, but no one could promise help in a field that Harold's skills were needed right away. Dale Green said that he would ask a couple of his people when they got back from a marketing trip. They were all people who cared for others, but were also constrained by many obligations. Government and Production Managers expected the promised work and wanted deliveries on tight schedules. Would somebody see the need and help? I wasn't an adept negotiator, but I could press hard to make something fair.

I had heard some of his people talk about Schmidt's authoritarian ways before, and I knew what that meant. People said that Schmidt was running his group like a dictator. You just couldn't argue with him. Harold's colleagues felt sorry for him. "Schmidt used people for production results and zero people concerns," another engineer said, quoting the description we had taught people on a class of management styles.

I went to Fred Schmidt's office and asked to see him. The secretary told me to wait and I sat down waiting to be admitted. I decided to approach him gently, though I felt ready to attack his harsh ways. "Fred, what's the situation with Harold? I asked taking a seat in his office. "The man is worried about losing his job. Isn't there something you can do to get him to stay in the game?"

"He can't handle his job," he said abruptly. "I'm recommending his dismissal," said Schmidt.

"He has worked for the Company a long time," I said. "Do you know if something has happened to him recently?"

"It's none of my business," he said. "That's a personnel issue, and they'll take care of it," he said and started writing something.

"There may be projects around, where he can do a very good job and have a better work-life," I said but he didn't stop writing, "Come on Fred, give a hand to a guy who obviously needs some help right now. We all go through hell sometimes."

He stood up, and looking straight at me said, "Stay out of my business."

"I'm trying to help the situation," I said and waited. He said nothing. "I can't just let an employee with years on his job without trying to help him," I groaned and left his office wanting to strike back, but holding back my anger. I went to see Fred's boss in his office, hoping he could help.

I explained to Mort Johnson the problem we all had, and asked him to help. He said he didn't want to talk about the problem just then, but he would call a meeting with Schmidt and me and try to help us with the problem of Harold's employment.

I cannot remember the exact words Schmidt and I exchanged in Mort's t office next day, but I recall that when I entered Mort's office I felt that I stepped into a battlefield without a clue of how I could save Harold's job or step on mines for that matter. These people were working on big contracts and had the support of the people in the divisions that SRC could never counter. But, I knew one thing and that was enough for the moment: Harold wasn't going to be tossed out in the street with his dignity shredded by an autocrat and his friends. For reasons that were not apparent to me at the time, I felt totally invincible, totally irrational and I had no idea why.

"I hope we can settle this problem with Harold without making a big deal out of it," I said, directing my comments to Mort Johnson. He sat low behind his desk, as if to protect himself from incoming fire.

"What is the problem, anyway?" Mort asked moving himself closer to his desk.

Fred Schmidt took over and said "Harold can't handle his job and, as I told you, I'm letting him go."

It seemed to me that he had already discussed the issue with Mort and felt sure he could do what he said.

"Throwing a man out in the street after employing him for ten or twenty some years makes no sense at all," I protested as calmly as I could. "Harold may be having some personal problems we know nothing about. He may need some help to overcome them. I have a consultant who can help," I said and waited for Mort Johnson to help.

"You know, we are not a philanthropic organization here," Mort said sliding slightly forward on his chair until he reached his desk. I thought that Fred must have convinced him, probably telling him that they should do the "right thing" and get rid of a person in need whom they didn't need.

I was angry, but I remained silent. Mort was a good businessman and knew well the moves he could make to solve problems. He could transfer Harold to another section in his group, allowing Fred to have his way and giving time to Harold to find a way back to a meaningful job and, perhaps, a happier work-life. I wouldn't presume to tell him what to do. I had heard enough complaints about Fred's harsh treatment of employees, but they didn't dare confront Fred. They were afraid and I couldn't disclose anything known to me privately, so I could only be mute and give more room to Fred.

"Fred wants to proceed with the lay-off," Mort said. "The situation has been going on for some time, and we have to end it," he insisted.

"Mort, you can transfer Harold to another one of your groups and give everybody time to solve their problems," I said and waited for his response.

"We have decided that this is a long-standing problem and has to be solved now," Fred said, before Mort could reply. There were moments of silence. I knew then that the issue wasn't Harold anymore, but the management and work life values of SRC.

"Harold is probably going through a very difficult time in his life. Won't you regret it if something awful happens to him?" I asked, hoping that they wouldn't take the risk of tossing an employee out in the street without a better justification.

"We've spent enough time on this issue," Mort said straightening himself on his chair.

"You'll have to deal with Personnel," I said. "You'll have to have some reason to. . .

Fred Schmidt cut me off. "If you are so concerned about Harold, you can have him and solve his problem any way you want. He's laid off as far as I am concerned."

"Do you want to do it Fred's, way, or find out what reality looks like?" I pushed hard on Mort. "We could have a 360 Feedback Review for your group, if you want. . ."

"I said that we have decided that issue," Mort interrupted and stood up. "Now, Harold is your responsibility."

"Tell Harold what you want to tell him, and ask him to see me," I said, not knowing what else I could do. "I'll talk to him about any ways I can help," I told Fred and headed for the door, then stopped. "give me a couple f days before you notify Personnel."

"Done!" said Fred.

As I was walking out I realized that I had essentially accepted the responsibility for finding work or doing something helpful for Harold, somehow, somewhere in the Research Department or the Universe. I felt like collapsing, but only for a moment. I was angry. I felt defeated, humiliated. So, what? What about Harold? This wasn't the world we were going to build here. People without compassion didn't belong here, and I wasn't sure I did.

Fred was furious that he couldn't get rid of the "deadwood" in the Company; and Mort was confused and anxious about the state of affairs in his department, the ominous sounding "360 Feedback Review", which might expose inefficient practices and force unpleasant actions and I felt that I had achieved nothing.

Outside Mort's office, Fred stopped me and leaning against the corridor wall with an extended arm near my head, said that he knew my type. "You bleeding hearts are not helping people stand on their feet and feel their power," he said and let his arm drop down.

"That's exactly what I've been trying to do, Fred. But, not when the man is weak and, perhaps, depressed or sick in some way," I said and walked away, while he was still leaning against the wall. I went straight to Dale Green's office to find a job for Harold.

What did you do today, Apostolos? It didn't feel like I had done anything good for Harold. I didn't know enough at the time to ask God for help in prayer, but I did think that I had some help, somehow.

I didn't find Dale in his office, but I made an appointment to meet him late next morning. He was waiting for me and had good news. One of his supervisors could take Harold in, if there was some money for training him in the field. The work was different from the work Harold wanted to do in Command Interface but he could learn enough with some funds for training. And there was a chance of getting another contract that could use another engineer's help. Harold could have a job in one of the projects Dale had, if we could get some training funds. I thanked Dale, and told him I would see what we could do for training from the Department. Then I headed for Bill Sackett's office.

"I got myself in a tight spot," I said dropping down on one of the chairs in his office. Bill kept working on a sheaf of papers on his desk. I explained the problem I was trying to solve, emphasizing that it was an organizational values issue rather than a personnel problem, and ended up with the bottom line of my story: "Bill, I need $4,000.00 to retrain Harold in one of Dale Green's projects," I said and stopped. I had already spotted red on the face of my boss, and it wasn't a good omen.

"What the hell are you doing messing around with management and personnel issues in another group? You should have known that they have huge responsibilities with large projects and they still do things their way and it's not at all like your way." It seemed that Bill had enough of me.

"Harold needs help, not the cold shoulder of an autocrat," I said quietly. "The job of the supervisor is to care for his people," I preached to the man who knew compassionate management better than anyone else.

"You do have a problem," Bill said, and then thinking took another path: "the budget has no free money this year. There isn't a dollar that hasn't been allocated."

I was in a zoo cage. There was no exit here, no lock to pick. I stood up, ready to leave one way or another. "Bill, this guy has some problems and could end up in a bad way," I said and stopped. Time seemed to have slowed down as if it couldn't slide through the heavy atmosphere of the room. "Listen," I said and looked Bill straight on his red face in a way that I cannot forget: "One day you'll retire and go for a long holiday in some Florida beach to enjoy the sand the sea and the waves, lying on a reclining chaise-lounge with a cushion." Bill's face was getting red and ready to explode, but I felt I had to go on and get it done. "Your mind will be taking trips into your past including this building and the people here, at this time, in this lousy weather.

And, you'll be thinking of all the decisions you made and all the goals you achieved. What will you remember? That in 1972 you balanced the budget, or that you took a little chance and saved the job, the career or the life of another human being?"

"Damn it!" Bill exploded and pounded his desk with the sheaf of papers he held. "Take you four thousand lousy dollars and do some lasting good with it." He stopped and took a deep breath. "You did a lousy job making this place better with all your maneuvers and theatrics. I don't see anyone getting less fearful or more empowered or having fun doing his best at work!" he shouted at me.

"I know," I said. "I tried, but didn't make it," I agreed.

"Remember and do better next time," he said and the red vanished from his face. "Keep an eye on that man. He's your responsibility now."

"Thanks, Bill," I said, feeling restored as I left his office and headed for Administration to get the appropriation for Harold's training. "I always knew you have a heart, man!" I kept thinking, happy for the privilege to work for a man who would never stop trying to build an organization that cares for people doing their best. I never asked how I got to have such a good day that day. Somehow, I knew what happened.

I kept in touch with Harold as he familiarized himself with his new job and I was surprised by his growing interest in the new field he was working on. This was a day that had meaning because it was done for the right purpose.

33

The Serious Job of Interviewing Candidates

A ny organization that wants to sustain its excellence in mission and in quality of work life has to select both managers and non-managers with care and awareness of the benefits and the risks in hiring.

At the Systems and Research Center, teams of managers and non-managers decided by consensus a variety of issues affecting the entire operation, such as resource allocation, funds distribution, facility design and hiring. We believed that a team effort produces better decisions and reinforces the members' commitment to the goals we had set for business, leadership, culture and interpersonal development. Choosing managers and many non-managers by team consensus based on one-on-one interviews was essential in maintaining the personal, business and cultural values of the organization.

Rather than using interviews to gather only information on the career of the candidates, the members of the Center Management Team (CMT) tried to make them learning experiences by posing management, ethical and appropriate personal questions to assess each candidate's character and values and her or his chances of thriving in the SRC culture. We used anecdotes, explained what it takes to be productive and enjoy working at SRC, and how to succeed in our organization. We usually described the values that were published for all to see and explained how we practiced humanistic values. Candidates who avoided direct responses to our questions during interviews were asked to state their position and defend it, and those who offered diatribes were asked to give direct responses without pivoting to related issues. Strange exchanges would take place sometimes, with mutually satisfying communications, but there were other times that the most basic connection could not be made. Nobody asked me what made an interview experience meaningful, but, had they asked, I would have said that establishing a friendly relationship opened the door and daring to take a position based on a constructive value and defending it successfully against opposing values was owning the room.

Once, I was scheduled to interview a recently retired Lieutenant Colonel for a position in the Marketing Department, and I posed a problem to him during the interview. I set the scene asking him to suppose that he was hired here as a marketing representative and in one of his contacts with a senior government official, he was asked if his company would be willing to work on a contract to make a modification to the turret of a tank his company produces, so that it can be used safely in the dessert, something that was specifically prohibited for that tank now.

"Will you accept the contract?" was my first question. The Colonel wisely said that he would discuss the problem with his manager and the cognizant engineers and respond to the government officer after that.

"The engineers consider the modification wanted," I continued, "and unanimously decide that it cannot be done safely. The sand could get in the machinery and create dangerously high heat for the gears and the crew's safety. Your boss thinks that the engineers are being too conservative, and it would be foolish to turn down such a profitable business opportunity without further exploration. He asks you to negotiate the contract with the customer, explaining, of course, the concerns the engineers voiced. "If he is willing to accept the risk, we can proceed, otherwise, no," he says to you. After a pause, I asked him point blank: "Will you follow your boss's direction, elevate the issue for decision to your boss's boss, and follow his decision, or tell your boss that you cannot proceed with the contract unless the engineers agree."

"I will follow my supervisor's direction," the Colonel said without hesitation. "We tell the customer the truth, it serves the needs of our government and we get some new business. It makes sense to me," he said satisfied by his response.

The Colonel had given a good answer to my questions, but had not considered the hazards that the engineers had presented. Here was the situation of choosing between opposing values that I wanted the interviewee to consider. "We get the contract, the engineers do their best to satisfy the customer's demands in the contract, but never change their concerns, you and your boss feel satisfied that the responsibility for hazard lies on the customer who asked and got the deal he wanted, and all seems to be in good order," I said and gave him time to think over his answers, before continuing. "But, three months after the end of the contract, several tanks are deployed in a dessert country, and one tank catches fire that kills the crew of three of our soldiers. The New York Times prints a photo of burnt tank and identifies your company as the manufacturer of the tank," I said.

The Colonel said nothing for a while and then he responded to a question I never asked, "There are risks with anything we do," he said, and then added, "I'd never go over my supervisor to change his decision. Loyalty counts!" he said with conviction.

"So, does human life and the good repute of your Company," I responded and we talked a while longer, and I thanked him for his truthful answers.

The CMT, after a serious discussion decided not to hire this candidate because character manifests itself by choosing the better of two good things and he had failed to do that. It was a tough decision for the team to make, but that's the way we chose to build integrity in our organization.

There was another unusual interview I had with Harry Menzies, an experienced Scientist, recommended by his boss, Jim Clark, who wanted to be a manager in our Imaging Sciences Group. Harry Menzies had a reputation of being a top-notch Scientist and was known to some of our people from his published work, but I knew nothing about him and was interested in talking to him. I had known, his supervisor, Jim Clark, for some time, and I knew that he was a very demanding manager, but also a very good mentor. If he had found a top scientist for us who could become one of our managers in time, I wanted to meet him and welcome him. I was pleased when Jim Clark asked me to interview this high talented guy. We were always looking for the best in all fields of interest to us. But, first perceptions sometimes differ from those that an interview will yield. From the start, Harry Menzies told me that he would be "a good fit for our place" because, no matter what else he had heard about us, he was sure we were "tops in technology".

On one wall of my office, by my desk, hung an enlarged folder of the SRC Perspectives, which we had finalized after transforming the organization significantly and considered the views of all the people at the Center, as I will show below. The SRC Perspectives listed the Goals, the Culture and the Values of the organization and I used it as a starter sometimes for my interviews. Most candidates who came to my office for an interview, would scan a few lines as they sat by the display, but never asked a question about it. Harry Menzies, however, was the first to smile and ask, directly, if we "really apply these principles in real life". He had a hard time believing that "Respect for people who take the initiative", and "Freedom to express ideas and feelings responsibly" would ever be practiced in the business world.

"We try hard to practice them, even though we don't always succeed," I said, taken aback, but ready to affirm our culture and hoping to convince Harry that we meant what we wrote. Found ourselves in a debate, but I was also aware that Harry was able to take a risk and confront issues with sound arguments. He may be just the top talent we want to attract here. I had done some recruiting myself, using every means available to attract and retain top talent in the land of snow and ice dams.

I went through my routine of questions, such as what Harry wanted to accomplish at our place, what he felt was his best professional accomplishment thus far, the most significant event in his work-life, his worst failure on the job, and so on. Then I described our organization's goals and ways of management, and added a few criticisms of our place to show that we were always trying to do better. He seemed satisfied with my answers, but that smile kept coming on every time I mentioned one of SRC's climate achievements. Was it an ironic smile when I said that our culture values "Respect the dignity of the individual?"

I wanted to ignore what I perceived as a disapproval of some aspects of our culture and I proceeded with my usual interview questions.

I asked him what was his greatest personal strength and, without any hesitation, he responded that he was the person others liked to consult with work problems, because they knew he could always help them. The way he said it, with a smile of a daredevil soldier successfully disarming an IED, signaled to me that Harry was a leader who cared for his people and wanted people to know it and like him.

"Do you have many friends at work? I asked.

"I get along well with people; if that's what you mean," he said.

"Yeah; people who come to you to share problems or successes in their lives," I said pointedly.

"I'm always available to discuss any issue that bothers people I work with. I don't socialize very much," he added.

Then, I thought of the next routine question I asked everyone I interviewed, expecting some slightly negative answer, like, "I'm a little late for meetings, or I'm working on listening more carefully to people", so I asked: "What do you consider to be your most significant weakness?"

Harry Menzies smiled and pulled back on his chair. He was silent, weighing his answer, and then with a sort of sneer and conviction he said, "I don't have any significant weakness."

That moved me off balance. I gave him a chance to use a punchline and exit from his joke. "Nothing?" I asked in disbelief and with a smile.

"Nothing!" Harry repeated somberly, and leaned back on his chair and waited for me to recover from a shock.

"What about having any weakness?" I asked, trying to navigate out of this terra incognita we were in.

"I don't feel that I have any weakness," Harry replied definitively.

I really wanted to ask the bottom line question, but I would have been at the bottom myself, so I continued the interview by asking Harry, if there was anything he wanted to improve in himself, or anything he wanted to know about our organization or myself. I felt deflated, but I stayed with Harry for another half hour or so, responding to his technology questions the best way I could. He was sure that we would recognize his expertise in Imaging Sciences and sometime in the future we would consider him for a management position in that group.

I shook hands with him and wished him success in his interview process. I held his hand for a few seconds, wishing that he would ask me something about the interview and I would have a chance to give him the feedback he needed to have, if he wanted to fly with eagles. But he didn't ask and I had no business to shine a light in the domain where shadows dwell.

I reported the results of my interview to Jim Clark before there was a Management Team discussion on Harry, because he had asked me to interview Harry. It was a very difficult discussion, but in the end, Jim accepted the responsibility to help Harry understand the fact that he would have to grow, if he wanted to advance. Jim had never thought that his top scientist could be rejected because he was perfect.

I reported what Harry Menzies had said during the interview without any comments. The team assembled for the selection of key scientists in the Imaging Sciences Group and hired somebody I wasn't asked to interview. I kept in touch with Jim Clark, and with some mentoring, counseling and close teamwork with the people he had helped many times before Harry recognized the reality we live in and the journey we have to travel, if we want to use our gifts to make the world a better place than it would be without our life in it.

34

Inspired in Alameda

I t was a hot day and I was seating next to a window on the first floor of a big brick building in Alameda California with a dozen executives who had converged on that Company Division to find out what the problem was with the production of a critical part for the tank turrets used by the Egyptian Army in the Libyan dessert. I happened to be in San Francisco at a conference on McGregor's Y Management Theory and its comparison to The Japanese X Theory and Maslow's hierarchy of needs which underlies just about any system of people you want, and was asked to go to Alameda and possibly help the executives meeting there with process consultation. I listened to the technical issues that had been identified, but I had nothing much to offer so I drifted to thinking about the possible music show some of the other guys wanted to attend later that evening.

The local managers were defending the work they had done, but several of the people from other Divisions were not satisfied. Nothing like a conflict to wake up a curious person like me, snap back up and listen. The group of executives found a polite way to get the local managers out of the room, thanking them for the good effort they were making to fix a critical problem and urged continuous diligence.

"I've discussed the problem with two engineers in the project and I can't get a straight answer," said Daryl Simson as soon as the door was closed. "They keep telling me that there is a fear factor in the building and no one knows what to do about it."

"Nobody trusts anybody else in this place," someone I hadn't met before said with surprising finality. I chuckled, thinking that I knew what he must have been through.

"Lack of trust is always an excuse. It's never the cause of a problem," a manager, someone called Pat, said with disgust. "These guys need somebody to tell them how to earn a paycheck."

It took half an hour or so for everyone to discharge all the accusations they were loaded with.

"They just don't know how to lead," said Daryl Simson looking sad and dismayed. He expressed his feeling with truth and a spark burst inside me. I drew back from the creeping sun and said what flashed in my mind like a meteorite speeding toward me from far away.

"We should find a way to reward managers who do well not only in their business responsibilities, but also in the way they treat their people," I said, having had no intention to speak, no plan to present and no idea what I was talking about, but having a hunch that what I blurted out would make the world a little better.

"How do we get that done?" One of the executives from Canada asked with interest. It seemed that he was already past the discussion of the idea's merit and was talking implementation. I was scared and wondered how big a job I had committed to do.

"Everyone knows the managers who care for people,"

Daryl Simson said, "You guys seem to have some idea about a better way to lead. Get together and see what you can come up with." You can't take back a good idea, I thought and nodded in agreement.

The meeting lasted a few more minutes, scheduling further visits on the technical and business issues and then we broke up and headed back to our hotels or airports to plan another day. Gregory Platt, the Canadian executive who supported my idea, and I had a short discussion about what he called the "Honey-Money-Boss" project that day.

"Can you handle that project yourself, and call me when you need help?" he asked. I felt like a fish caught by a snappy hook cleverly twisted.

"I'll do the best I can," I said resisting the assignment

"Great," Greg said, tapped me on the shoulder and run after a passing taxi, before I could say goodbye. I never saw him again.

Now, several things happened that I had not foreseen. I proposed to Greg that the project should be about creating a Management Award with a significant honorarium of $5,000, by a credible process I would devise to find the best manager in any Division whose executives wanted to participate and make it known to others for future use.

"And how on earth will you find a needle in a haystack?" Greg asked, unable to guess what I had cooked under the Alameda sun.

"I know a lot of people I trust and I'll ask them to give me a list of the best managers they know. After that, I'll ask the top tier of people who were listed as the best managers to send me a list of the people who are in their view the best managers and keep going until a consensus develops. Then, some team of top-level managers selects a small group of winners." He looked at me with a sneaky smile.

"The best choose the best and the best of these choose the best and.... When the hell does this stop?" he asked still puzzled, still unable to buy into my scheme.

"When the same names appear over and over again, we'll ask the group that gave us the project to select the best managers from the final group. They will be known by most, because good managers make a lot of friends," I said and hoped that Greg wasn't a hermit.

"I think we can bring a couple of the people from our project team and the Corporate HR into the final selection, instead," he said with some apprehension. I didn't feel sure about mixing HR in the process I was preparing, but I thought it was wise to say nothing.

Roger Heimisch was my boss at the time, so I went to his office a couple of days later to share the progress I was making with the Award. He was enthusiastic and encouraged me to continue. As we were discussing the method I was using to select the best from the better, the phone rung and Roger picked it up. Immediately he set himself straight on his chair and started talking to the caller.

"He is here," he said and muted the phone with his large palm, and turned toward me. "Jim wants you to go and do some work at Corporate," he said. I said nothing. "Our President wants you at Corporate," he said, clearly worried by my silence. I had no intension to leave the people of SRC and spend my time attending HR's endless meetings.

"I'm pretty busy with the project, Roger," I said, thinking at high speed how to escape.

"Let me get this," Roger said clearly disturbed, now, "you want me to tell the President of this Company, now on the line, that you refuse his request to work at Corporate?" I hadn't seen Roger Heinisch, a Marine fighter pilot scared before, but he was now.

"Tell him that I'll go and try it out for a few months," I said and saw Roger take his hand from the phone speaker and speak with thankful sigh again.

"He'll be there next week, Jim. He's got some projects going here, so he'll be there part time." He thanked Jim for asking the Center to help with Corporate needs and ended the call. I didn't know exactly what we were going to do to help our President, but whatever it was I would have to do it and come back to SRC.

I worked on the project of the Award of the best manager and came up with half a dozen outstanding people respected by all the people who had worked for them sometime. Then I thought that I needed a name for this award, which would be accepted and be appreciated by all who won it in the years to come.

One afternoon I stormed the Minneapolis building where retired executives of Honeywell were given offices for a variety of philanthropic and civil support projects, and headed for the office of the man I had known by reputation but never met some thirty years before. I found his office, knocked and went in. He looked at me as if I had been lost, and seemed ready to help me find the office I was looking for. "Mister Lund?" I asked, and introduced myself and explained that I was looking for him.

It took me about ten minutes to explain to him that I was working on a project to create an award for finding the best manager or managers of the Company every year. I told him that Gregory Platt from Canada and others supported the idea and called the project, the search for the "Honey-Money-Boss" and he laughed jovially. He was delighted to hear that Platt was still enjoying his work. I told him that I had completed my report but I needed a name for the award. Then I looked straight at him and told him that I had heard many good things about his caring for people for thirty years, and how a lot of people who had worked for him had said many good things about the priority he gave to caring for people. I kept blabbing, not being sure of his reaction at a time when I needed help.

"Mister Lund," I finally said, "I would like to call this Award 'The Lund Award', if you don't mind."

The wise man who saw the better practices of management long ago, was moved and was silent for a few seconds. "I would be honored young man," he said and we shook hands. I told him that he would be notified by the Corporate HR as soon as I presented my report to top management. "Thank you Mister Kizilos," he said, as I was leaving.

Our President, Doctor James J. Renier, President of Honeywell Control Systems, had started Honeywell's process of change with the publication of "People in the 80's" report, commonly referred to as the "Self-Esteem Report", and had additional plans to encourage managers to care for people and their development, so I was asked to organize with Bill Sackett and Ray Brant a Management Guidelines Team made up of transformative and successful executives. I started right away, enthused by the interest of our President and we produced "The Management Guidelines Team Report", which was widely distributed and used for encouraging the practice of human values in all management practices.

I worked isolated from Corporate HR and did what was expected of me, living as a recluse. Several months passed since I had left SRC and had no news of the whereabouts of the approval of the Lund Award. In one of my visits back to my office at SRC, a fellow CMT member, showed me a small complimentary article in the back page of the Company newspaper, which mentioned that Tolly Kizilos had worked for the effort to produce the well-known Lund award. The Lund award had been presented a month ago by Corporate HR, without anyone inviting me to attend the presentation or even letting me know that it was a done deal. As long as people understood that the Lund Award with a $5000-dollar honorarium was created to honor transformative and effective managers and it was Honeywell that encouraged them to care for people, I was satisfied. After that we created other awards at SRC, like the hundred dollar "Alpha Award Program", for small kindnesses from one person to another over a period of time, "The SRC Technical Awards", for the best technical achievements. Some Divisions liked what we did and followed our ways.

As soon as I had completed my assignment at Corporate, I returned home to SRC and continued creating training workshops like the Marketing Workshop that made fun a tool of learning how to market, or the Career Development Workshop that was used by other Company organizations to develop people by setting them free of their fears and made people's work friendly and more productive.

The organization was thriving and the people were no longer afraid of anything they wanted to pursue, accepting the responsibility for it. The people were set free and made the world a little better place than it was. Everyone seemed to have found people to share work and life stories, to have lunch together, attend a friend's church and invite friends for a party. Step by step we were finding the bits of meaning that someday would help us answer the Life Questions. There were times when I wondered how long this would last.

35

Participative Management and Transformation

A year or so after I had rejoined SRC, I discovered a title that fit a part of the job I was doing and with Bill's consent I called myself an "Ombudsman." Most people know what an ombudsman is these days, but nobody knew anything about such a creature back then, except the Swedes who have a government person, an Ombudsman, to help citizens walk the government bureaucratic labyrinths we all have to travel sometimes. I saw my title as an employee "in management," but not "of management," who helps other employees operate more autonomously and deals with work life challenges in ways that have meaning for them and for the organization. To achieve this goal would take more training, and new guidelines for norms and systems that make work life open, ethical and rewarding. I did get the title of Director of Organization Development some years later, but it didn't quite fit me because it doesn't hint a change in humanistic values, which was always my goal. I wrote a paper, which was published as a bulletin, when I spent two weeks as a visiting scholar at the Stanford Research Institute and "On Organizational Change and its Agents." If I had asked Bill Sackett, to name me "The SRC Change Agent," he might have gone along, though no one would have known what that meant fifty years ago. We wanted to emphasize personal worth of the individual, the importance of human values and the creative, dynamic nature of human beings

I did suggest a title for my job one time, but I didn't really mean it. I had been on that job for close to ten years when one morning I heard on the radio a discussion on European politics which mentioned something that made me laugh.

Doctor Brant and I had just finished The Management Guidelines Team Report, written by a dozen top executives of our company, selected by the people, using a Selection System I created. I had worked hard on that report alone for several months, trying to identify Company managers, who scored high on both business and caring for people and trying to infuse some of the SRC culture in the report when we met and discussed all the issues they wanted to present. I was in a cheerful mood that morning, because the Report was published at last and I was taking a copy to Bill Sackett to scrutinize and tell me what page had a typo, or where I did well, beyond expectations. He was in a discursive mood and we talked about that and everything else for a while. This time he asked "what should we call you in this place that sounds like you're in management?"

I thought of the European politicians I heard in the radio that morning and said with a humorous intent, "I think what fits best is Manager without Portfolio."

"They still use that?" Bill asked.

"I just heard it on the radio," I said, ready to testify that it was the truth, but never meaning for the title to stick to me.

"It sure fits what you do. You can get the yearly visit to the Mayo Clinic and a free car rental, if we put this title on you," he said.

"Bill, it's a joke," I said and left to go to my cubbyhole, before somebody else stopped me and asked me to get into the labyrinth and kill the deadly bull once again.

A month later, Bill told me that Headquarters didn't like Managers without Portfolios. "They said it sounds like they are being punished." I started laughing. "Nicklebe said -- you know Earl Nicklebe, the VP of HR at Corporate -- he said that the title sounds like some boys had their portfolios snatched from them and are punished for being naughty."

"I told you it was a joke," I protested.

"And what do you think this is?" he said and we laughed for a while.

It was Bill's successor, Doctor Roger Heinisch who promoted me to the level of a Director of Organization Development, several months after he came to SRC. But, that promotion, almost cost me my job. A short time before Roger became our leader, he acquired a new overseer of the operations, who was a master technologist with great ideas for technology development. He was quick in making decisions and I rarely saw him smile. We tried to place him in some category we knew, but we didn't' know if he was a professor, an entrepreneur, a researcher or a cosmonaut.

All I know is that he found my promotion premature, unnecessary and alien to his experience. Our overseer asked for a meeting at Roger's office, and before we knew the purpose of the meeting, he was asking why I was doing what I was doing and doing it outside the auspices of Human Resources. "They are the people responsible for training, development, promotions etc., aren't they?"

I explained that I was helping people solve work and relational problems by building trust, developing teamwork skills and sharing the decision-making power of management. People want to find meaning in their work and be happy and effective in what they do, so the organization gets the benefits of their commitment."

"This is what people do without having to take classes or have a tutor for their work," he said, showing his annoyance. "As for training, that's what the Personnel professionals do, or ought to do, or be directed to do," he said showing his increasing frustration. I knew that this was going to be a long afternoon and I would have to translate everything I did before I could be understood. And I did try to do that for a couple of hours without any success or even a headway. Roger tried to stop the battle, but he was pushed aside. Suddenly, thinking of our superior's technological bent, I stumbled upon a word that I thought he might know well.

"To be frank," I said, "what I do every day is not that different from what many technologists do: I have stored a large amount of data and many algorithms and I use them appropriately in the kind of problem I'm solving.

"Algorithms?" our boss asked, as if the word had power in its spoken form.

"Yes, sir. OD is after all a process of changing the culture of an organization by applying behavioral science theory and tools. There are algorithms like the Managerial Grid by Blake and Mouton for managerial style, The McClelland dominant needs that underpin human motivation, McGregor's Theory Y, which explains the role of motivation in performance, or Maslow's Hierarchy of needs that explains human growth and societal trends. All these theories are mapped and provide guidelines to explain to people who are not familiar with the theory and the reason for using it."

"And what do you do with these algorithms?"

"When I face an organizational event, say decision making, or a conflict, or demotivated employees who never were encouraged to achieve anything great, or some other situation that is a problem for the people involved, or for our organization, I use the appropriate algorithms to understand the situation and help people to change it."

"I see, I see," he said and was ready to give an extension to my employment.

So, I kept doing what was needed to give people the tools they needed to fix their problems and make work a transformative experience. "Once people learn the way a solution is achieved they don't forget it." The way that process worked becomes a guideline, and a guideline can be modified now that people know its basis in theory and applied to solve problems in other situations. We help people learn any way we can, so the people are aware what to do without micromanagement or, sometimes, without any management.

When the leaders of the various groups have accepted the effectiveness of the participative process with consensus decision making, I and the other consultants we hire part-time now and then, would be asked to attend day-long sessions of various teams engaged in solving specific problems, such as "How can we enter a specific area of the market", or "How are we going to allocate the pure research funds we get from the company next year?" or, "Which of all the equipment we need are we going to buy next year?" Or, in some cases, when the managerial position was vacant, "How are we going to decide which one of us in the team will be our manager, if one or more of us want the job?"

"I understand, but I'll have more questions about the interplay of you and HR," our overseer said and told us he was late for a meeting

I sat exhausted in Roger's office and contemplated what we were doing with our minds hearts bodies and souls. We called this process of decision-making Participative Management. It proved to be effective and helped extend humanistic values and my workload increased. One of the most effective consultants was Doctor Alan Anderson, who became a good friend because we could work together and agree on principles and supplement each other's skills. In time I was given the overhead funds needed to hire Chris Jacobs, a young practitioner of OD, to assist me. Her values were similar to mine and her desire to achieve goals added to our organization's competency.

It was about that time that I wrote a Socratic dialogue, describing of all things, the process of Participative Management as we practiced it in our organization. It was the best way I could imagine to explain the dynamic interaction of this process. The dialogue was published in the Harvard Business Review and became well known in the profession.

The key to creating a well-functioning organization is building trust, feeling compassion for one's co-workers and practicing Participative Management, based on consensus decision making.

The team's leader has to trust the team members to recognize the leader's greater responsibility, without abandoning the expression of their best judgment or the confrontation of other members in the team. After a while, team members developed norms which they followed with consistency. One of the key norms was that members of the team may have to go along with the team decision after a rigorous debate, even if the decision wasn't their first choice; and, there were rare occasions when a team member, after debating the issue, could not accept the team's, or the leader's decision. Team members who on very rare occasions couldn't go along with the consensus decision of the team became known for their good judgment and were sought out for their opinion, if they were right in opposing the consensus; or were teased as sore losers, if they went their own way often and the consensus was proven right. I don't know how, but such splits were rare and the teams functioned effectively. When people know each other as persons and have a common goal, the process works very well because it is based-on trust.

Gradually, people established a way of working that allowed them to choose the research they wanted to do. This happened because they knew the business of the company and decided what work to do, what relationships have to be established with all the relevant divisions of the company, which people to hire and what risks to take by excellence in technology, marketing and teamwork.

Early in the development of the management process I developed a day-long Career Development workshop to give a thorough understanding of our organization's goals, its culture and the performance values we were committed to follow. This workshop was adopted as an effective training process by other organizations in the company, because the people who attended it at SRC spread the word by talking to their colleagues from other organizations.

Practicing with the guidelines we developed in this transformative process, we knew that the research engineers must first of all show advanced technical knowledge. Increasing technical excellence was the fundamental way of gaining the respect of one's peers in the organization. Good technical performers who could also market their work advanced in power and rewards. As time went by, older engineers who had reached an adequate level of technical performance but couldn't bring in funding from the market or the divisions, found themselves competing with the newbies hired with advanced skills, and ready to prove themselves at a lower cost.

The older engineers sometimes were stagnating at the technical level they had reached until they found a partner or a team that they could partner with and get their work funded. An informal system of "hunters" and "skinners" developed, giving both marketing wizards and technology stars the opportunity to grow in the way they could, or wanted. We also discovered that university students in technology and marketing fields could lower the cost of the work that had to be done and hired them in large numbers. This set up a Mentoring System of beneficial relationships between engineers and marketers as teachers and student aides, who found unexpected sources of learning from experienced engineers. Some of these students, were hired as regular employees after completing their educational goals. Giving opportunities to people to work where they found meaning was also a very meaningful experience for me.

After some years went by, we created guidelines for promotion of Engineers to Supervisors and defined the required leadership and interpersonal skills, and balanced the technical and marketing responsibilities. This was the first time such guidelines were published anywhere in our company, or any other company as far as I know. People with power don't usually like to commit important matters to public documents that might be loosely interpreted. I was happy to publish that booklet, authorized by the consensus of our Center Management Team, so people would know what was needed, if they chose to advance into management and have the support of their people. It took some vigorous debate to get a couple of the more traditional managers to go along with that consensus decision. Similar guidelines were used by the management teams in promoting managers at other levels. The healthy environment of our organization led to outstanding performance of various teams, valued by the company's Divisional and Corporate managements.

The story of the design of practices and systems we created to achieve excellence will have to be told in another book, but there are some events which gave everyone of us some exceptional opportunities to grow by experiencing the complex reality of meaningful work in a transformative organization, managed, essentially, by all its people. Bill Sackett was promoted to Vice President and the guidelines we introduced were extended and practiced with confidence and pride. After a dozen years of successful results Bill Sackett left our organization and assumed the leadership of the company's Advanced Research Laboratory.

One of the curious research engineers met me in the corridor around that time and asked me if I was leaving to go with Bill to his new position. "Why would I do that?" I asked him. He was surprised. "You always worked together," he said and, for a moment, stopped and asked "What does it take to do your job, anyway?" he asked with wonder. Having had enough of his interrogation, I said, "You have to be able and willing to pump gas," I said and I meant it. My job should never be understood to be permanent because telling truth to power is risky. If it ever became permanent in the Change Agent's mind, the agent would become a virtual mute.

Doctor Roger Heinisch was appointed by the corporate management to be our new leader. He, was a very competent, open-minded and jovial leader and all of us believed that the tradition of excellence in technology and our transformative culture would continue and be enhanced. Twelve years after Bill Sackett and I introduced the guidelines that gave people the opportunity to shape their work objectives and their environment, we started a process of selecting the leaders of a management team by the members of that team. I was a member of such teams when we, the members, had to choose our boss and I know that it wasn't easy. One decision took two days to make, but it was accepted by all and it empowered us because we achieved the excellence and were still friends.

Roger and I published an article in the Harvard Business Review, describing the process that was followed in selecting management leaders by their subordinates. When we were done with the paper and were going to send it to HBR, Roger stopped me and asked, "Shouldn't we ask for approval from headquarters?"

"Aren't we free to publish our publicly known opinions for a process we created?" I asked, and added, "it's the First Amendment, isn't it?"

"There's nothing classified here, so it should be alight," Roger said with confidence.

"We're trying to make the company more productive and the

workers' life meaningful and happier," I said. Then, it dawned on me that we had done something good in the world; that we had achieved what God had accomplished. Roger looked at me strangely. I was glad he didn't ask me to explain what I meant, because I would have to explain the way many theologians explain God's action in the world. "The company should give us an award for telling the world what can be achieved," I said, instead.

After thirteen years of crucially supporting the business performance of the Corporation, after having played a key role in developing the Ring Laser Gyro, which was one of the most successful products of the company, and having the top scores in human climate surveys, run by independent experts for the Company Headquarters, our Center Management Team decided to compose our organization's "Magna Carta", so-to-speak, which would state the reasons that we were having excellent results and the way we planned to proceed.

We all felt good working for SRC and decided to put together an outline of our goals, our culture and the performance values we tried to inculcate and publish it in the "Perspectives of the Systems and Research Center", all of it in a folded document with three tables on three pages of hard-boiled thought, teamwork and fairness. Everything we put in this document was based on the experiences we had, not merely the aspirations we hoped to achieve. We kept the doors of our offices open and invited everyone to stop by and give us their opinions for the composition of the document, describing the strength and weaknesses of our organization. I talked to dozens of people and got the good the bad and the ugly from them. We made clear to all that their opinions, needs and wants would be considered seriously and voted in or out of the final report to be published by the Center Management Team. Many people came and we had many discussions, usually after hours, based on their views of our work life.

It took many meetings over a period of several months in 1983 – 1984 for the Center's Management Team to debate divergent views and find areas of unity, collate the themes, discuss and debate the importance of the feedback we got from those who had been seriously involved in the process, agree by consensus on items to include and shape the meaning and the order of the people's and our own views. We finally designed an SRC jacket, which took an hour of debate to assign one of the team members to the project, and offer it free to anyone who wanted it. I cannot recall meetings that involved all of us so totally and were so productive and enjoyable.

"The Perspective of SRC", are the summary of 14 years of work we devoted to make the road straight for people searching for meaning in their work-life. We all had hopes that what we thought and what we did and recorded would guide others to build happy and thriving work organizations.

The slim folder of three pages with three tables served as a reminder for all of us in practicing our values. It was a presentation of the facts, and our aspirations and commitment to the organization. We used it to tell the stories of our work-life. An abbreviated version of the SRC Perspectives is shown below:

The SRC Perspectives

Goals of the Systems and Research Center
- Superior Technology for the Divisions of the Company
- Solve fast the technical problems that arise in the Divisions
- Provide an attractive work environment for the people of SRC
- Win recognition as one of he top research and development centers in the US

Culture of the Systems and Research Center

SRC's culture consists of values and practices which enhance our goals.:
- Respect for the dignity of the individual
- Trust as the foundation of all relationships
- Freedom to express ideas and feelings responsibly
- Conduct governed by the highest ethical standards

- Respect for people who take the initiative
- Challenging work for as many people as possible
- Rewarding relevant innovation by anyone
- Helping each other especially in time of need
- Placing high value on teamwork
- Sharing management's power to make decisions

Performance Values of the Systems and Research Center

Employee evaluation and rewards on performance based on:
- Accomplishments demonstrating excellence, creativity and sustained effort which further organizational goals
- Actions furthering teamwork, trust, high morale, caring attitudes, taking stands, and concern for people
- Helping people to grow: coaching, mentoring and helping others grow personally, professionally and in organizational leadership.
- Contributing to winning and performing relevant contracts in a timely, cost-effective and, above all, technically excellent manner.
- Contributing to the growth of relevant technical areas through a combination of technical, marketing and organizational skills.

36

Make Friends with Your Enemies

"Love your enemies, do good to those who hate you."
(Luke 6:27)

Saint Luke

I learned early on in my organizational life that the more friends you make the easier it is to innovate and give the organization new vistas to explore and grow. It was easy for people to try new ways of exploring all dimensions of human growth and modify them, shut them down or adopt them as their own. I could ask for help from some seasoned accountants in Administration, if an employee had difficulty balancing their budget at home, or saving money for retirement; and I could ask a nurse on some medical issue brought to me about an employee's wife's diet now that she had a baby. I did my best to do likewise, hoping that our relationships advance from being transactional and become friendships.

There was one manager however that I could never form a good working relationship with, no matter who that person was. There was always some opposition to originality and innovation which required a lot more effort to bypass the barriers they set up and try a way to improve our work life. There were times when I felt sad for the position of the personnel manager at SRC, having to deal with imaginations that tore things of the past to build greater things for the future, instead of working with fixed actions. I had sympathy for him or her and tried to maintain a good relation, but there were times when opposition couldn't be avoided.

One time, some people thought it would be an interesting idea to try the Maharishi's meditation with a mantra during lunch hour, but somebody wanted to clear it with Personnel. I had to ask the manager at the time, who wanted us to follow procedure and request his superiors if such a crazy activity could be allowed. The would-be-meditators gathered in a conference room near Bill's office and learned the fundamentals from one of our own guys who knew the method well. The number of participants increased the first few weeks and then the numbers went down until noontime meditation disappeared.

And then, there was the time when I found out from my secretary that there were three expectant secretaries working in the same area, who had miscarriages in the same month. They were concerned and I was ready to find out what the problem was. I sat down with Doug, the Personnel Manager at the time, and asked him to notify our Corporate Personnel Department and make sure they contact the CDC to find out if there was some substance or some condition that was causing the problem here or in some other similar work places.

"There you go again with the worst possible cause of something which may be a statistical fluke," Doug said. "There have been such cases before," he added.

"If I were you, I'd be on the phone right now," I said with enough conviction, I felt, to move him into action.

"You are sounding an alarm without a good reason," he said. I became angry. I called him to a meeting with Bill Sackett and explained that one of the women worked in one of my sections and I had a duty to find out if there was some kind a common factor causing the problem. Bill Sackett said that we should notify the Corporate Personnel and Medical Departments and they should do what was proper.

I thought we were avoiding the best way to get some answers because we didn't call the CDC right away, but I felt so strong about the situation that I had to state what I felt. "O.K. you inform Corporate as you say you'll do and I hope you are right. But, if another miscarriage happens here, I will personally call Corporate and the CDC and ask them to tell us what is going on. I feel we owe it to our people, to ourselves and to our Company," I said and added, "No one has done anything wrong here, but a bad thing can still happen if we do nothing," I said and walked out. I followed the situation closely and I'm happy to say that there was no other event in the months or years after I was there. I felt that I was right to be wrong.

My opposition to the ways Personnel wanted to treat people never got much better than I have already described. It did get worse at times, though. There was a time when we were mandated to prepare plans for a 5% to 10% force reduction at SRC. It was a sad time for all of us, but we were one team and we could take the hit together. Somehow the solution to the problem seemed obvious to me. I proposed to the Center Management Team, which had to devise the layoff plan, that we ask volunteers to take a small 5% or 10% reduction on our salary, so no one had to be laid off. We could all survive just fine getting a slightly smaller paycheck for a while. If there was a Personnel issue to fight for, this was the one, but compassion was required and there was no abundance of it at the time. I looked for support from whoever happened to be running our Personnel group at the time, but instead I found resistance and opposition. It seemed to me that Personnel was the opposition. The idea of building a caring organization was in general a repudiation of the status quo and all traditions of the very word "Personnel".

I could go on listing points of disagreement with every Personnel Manager we had, but, I have to say, that I never expected I would reach a collaborative relationship with a Personnel Manager. I had nothing against the Personnel function. I saw Personnel as an essential unit of a well-functioning organization. I was in awe thinking of the job they had to do with government regulations and laws, salary evaluation, equity and administration, and record keeping in various domains. It would be foolish to think that the Personnel function wasn't essential. Yet the Personnel Managers and the O.D crowd never saw eye to eye. It is part of this world to have snags, bumps and imperfections to be overcome.

And, after I had been at Honeywell for close to thirty years, I happened to meet a Personnel Manager that understood the function of personnel exactly as I describe it above. But we didn't get along as well as one would assume, given my exposition. Roxana Benton, you see, wanted to also do whatever O.D. is supposed to be. Now, there are many people who want to do the things we had been trained or somehow knew how to do in building a transformative and productive organization, but they cannot do them. My hunch is that Roxana Benton could do all such things in her own way. I had tried to convince Bill that we should try to sell the idea of Change Agents throughout the company, but he had a harsh answer. "I don't see anyone who can do your job," he had told me a few times. And once he said, "If someone tries to do the job you do, it will be a very different job".

For twelve years I had been solving aircraft problems. Then, I switched and worked with people for eighteen years finding ways to improve careers, empowering the reluctant and resisting the autocrats in this one organization of the company and proving that when people are trusted and free to use their skills and powers, the people are happy and the company more flourishing. The old timers knew the battles I had fought for us – single offices for scientists, participation in the selection of supervisors, counselling by a specialist in time of trouble for an employee, support of employees against autocrats, and courses to teach teamwork, marketing and decision making by consensus and more. Everyone was proud when the department was on the top spot in the company-wide surveys of the quality of human relations. We all knew what we had achieved and wanted to keep it going. Boring work or forced labor make work life meaningless and cause a lot of misery in life. Sometimes I took a seat by the round table in my office with a disgruntled employee and his or her supervisor and helped them find a way to resolve the conflict they had about a work assignment, or an alleged unfair rating of work evaluation and the salary increase to be expected, or the unfair treatment of certain kinds of people – foreigners, blacks, women, the disabled, the smokers, the new mothers and others. I wasn't wiser than anybody else, but I had gained some experience and developed some skills that helped others solve their problems. And, sometimes I was wrong and regretted it. There was no end to the distinctions some people were willing to make in order to reach their goals.

Then, one day, to top it all off, I received a complaint from Harry, an older man, that his boss, Kevin, one of the most successful supervisors around, was allowing some women to work at home, but wouldn't give him the same privilege.

"Really?" I said, meaning "There must be good reasons, Harry!" I said it trying to lessen the magnitude and the urgency of the accusation implied in the information Harry was passing to me. I knew the few women were cracker-jack programmers, working on coding aircraft control systems at that time, while Harry was having all sorts of meetings with government contractors and divisional managers.

"I knew you'd blow me off, but you'd do yourself a favor if you check that out," Harry said without letting up on his serious demeanor. "We got a lot of men in this place and we don't want to piss them off with biased rules that favor women," Harry said and stopped short of accusing me of a serious crime. A long moment passed by. "Right?" Harry fired his last volley. I thought that he was attempting to scare me by applying a law meant to protect women from discrimination, by turning it around so it could be applied to protect men.

"I'll look into the situation Harry, but I know Kevin is a fair man and wouldn't do unfair things," I said, equally serious now.

"I have many days I can work alone at home, but Kevin doesn't see it that way," Harry said disgusted and walked out.

Sometimes being alarmed and trying to calm things down at the same time doesn't work. You have to go through the hard work of exploring and asking questions before the dispute can have a chance for resolution. Labor, anxiety, planning, risk, humiliation – all the tools of handling every trial come out of the tool box before you can be ready to tackle the conflict. I had been the change agent of the system for eighteen years and I was still excited to get involved in resolving conflicts, repairing broken promises, straightening out distorted communications and making room for peace to reign. But, the process of getting to the solution of a problem wasn't as exciting as it was when I was creating the process. I felt the need to solve different problems, create new ways to make the world a little better

I also thought how good early retirement might be. So many more things to learn, systems to create, topics to teach at the University of Saint Thomas and at churches, battles to fight for a better world, people to enliven about life. I might yet fulfill the Adult Education career I had set aside for a while.

I had started making plans for my retirement years, but I still had to meet the age and service requirement. I had come to think that my boss, a brilliant young scientist wasn't as comfortable with the transformative management of the past and still wanted someone like me around to maintain our smooth operations. I was tired asking him to kick me out, but he would not.

There was plenty of work, and my boss was wise to keep me around even at my waning excitement. The next day I was in my office with Kevin, Harry's boss, trying to uncover why he wouldn't give Harry a day of work at home as he did with the women programmers.

"Harry can take as many days to work at home as he wants, if he trusts one of his younger team members to handle visits to customers who are in love with his helicopter innovations. He can do the same with someone else to take care of the guys from our Boston Division who are enamored with him and want him to connect them with his government acquaintances."

My mind was working in extra-sensory domains, taking me to an advanced holodeck, trying to rob me of my remnants of logic and give me great dreams to work on and enjoy. "Kevin, you got to let Harry solve his problem by himself," I said.

"He'll take off and we'll have to take care of a lot of people," Kevin responded, frustrated already.

"Harry is a fantastic market strategist and will decide which solution he wants to use. You try to nudge him to take a couple of days off on his marketing trip, or to Boston. Let him go to Cape Cod for a day and have fun. Then give him a few days of work at home if he will take them," I said and felt exhausted." I wanted to get back and finish the presentation of "Science and Religion" I was working on with books, articles and videos for a group of older citizens at the Colonial Church in Edina.

I got up from my chair and went to the window to stare for a moment at the multitude of parked cars gathering snow. I had more questions to ask and offer more suggestions, but I thought Kevin and Harry would do just fine on their own, so I stopped and thought about other approaches I might find to retire a little earlier than I was due.

"I'll try what you said and hope for the best. I have rules on how to use the privilege of working at home, and I won't change them. 'If you have customers coming, you have to be at the office,'" Kevin asserted.

"That's a good guideline," I said and wished him success.

I sat back at my desk and started reading one of the many Memos that were accumulated on that day's pile. And there was always the CMT agenda, which guided the topics up for discussion at the next team meeting. Perhaps my kind boss, will grant me my plea for a few months early retirement and I could get out of there and take a trip back to Greece and eat fried squid and drink retsina under umbrella pine trees.

Things were changing in the company. Globalization was gathering speed, investments in China were increasing, layoffs were discussed and people were asking questions to get some answers and stop the anxiety of not knowing what their work life may be tomorrow. It was a few months before that time when Roxanna appeared at the Center and took possession of the office of the Director of Human Resources, across the hall from mine. We had a similar rank as things stood at that time, but I was a sort of oddball Director, always claiming that I was "in management, but not of management" whereas she had her fingers on all the papers and the buttons that counted and claimed that she was into management deeply and permanently, while crawling toward its inner sanctum at Corporate Offices. Sometimes I would forget myself and watch her talk in a meeting of our CMT or just imagine her sail down the hall.

She was a beautiful woman, a tall warrior-woman with a fearsome black pony tail and a beautiful face with carbon black eyes that caught your glance and held it into a stare that could not twist, turn and escape from her gaze. When she strolled toward my office, I could hear the noise of a purposeful person on the move. I was always ready for combat and I had to do it while staying calm and in command of all my defenses. By the time we stopped arguing about every value many other noble souls and I had fought to establish in the organization, I was exhausted and ready for a scream that could not be uttered. Trust, support, empowerment, teamwork, collaboration, compassion, all these values and more seemed to be a waste of time to Roxanna. They were unproductive, irrelevant, expensive, wasting precious resources. It was like she cut a piece of my liver every time we argued and, after barbecuing it, offered it to me in a fork, Greek style, to make sure there were no hard feelings left between us. Her presence was a denial of my my and other people's work.

I was thinking of leaving a little early when I heard Roxana's characteristic walk on the corridor outside my office and decided to stay. She knocked at my door and came in to my office.

"Have you got a minute?" she asked and I invited her to come in and sit down. I thought about asking her to talk to my boss for a few months' earlier retirement, but I held back. The truth was that I didn't trust her. I couldn't reveal to her my problems and the solutions I dealt with every day because I was afraid she might undo some system or some way we did things after many years of looking for solutions that weren't in the books of Personnel.

"Did you know about this guy Harry who thinks his boss is discriminating against him because women can work at home?

"I know all about it," I said as if somebody had slapped me.

"I don't think he has any case. . ."

"He doesn't," I said stopping her abruptly. "That is a non-problem. I've talked to both Harry and his supervisor, Kevin, and I think they'll take care of it."

She came close to me, and directing her black piercing eyes toward me, she said with profound sadness, "Do you suppose that we must always have different views of the world?"

"There will come a day when the lion will sit with the lamb, but it may take some time," I said and looked at her, feeling sad for both of us.

"Do you get tired with people always having problems with one another? There are days that I think I was digging ditches all day long," she said with sincerity I had never seen in her before.

"You have to balance the problems you have with the problems you have no more, or the job will wear you out," I said.

"So, fellow dich-digger, what's the counterbalance today?

"Do you know Arti?" I said, and stopped.

"Arti, the Indian scientist at the Computer group?"

"Arti has just filed for Astronaut today!" I said.

"That's the good news, friend?" Roxana said and relaxed on her chair. "I'll go and congratulate her tomorrow."

"She's serving chocolate cake today," I said.

I'll go right now, then," she said and stood up.

"She's a top-notch analyst, so we have a potential win and a loss, if she flies."

"I still love chocolate cake," she whispered and took off.

Later that day Roger Heinisch, my old boss stopped by my office to see how I was doing these days, and in the midst of our discussion, I mentioned that I planned to retire early because I wanted to spend my time reading, teaching and writing. Time is coming for doing a few more good things.

"This is the best time to retire, my friend," Roger said with the instant burst of action he had when he was still running our place. I knew roughly what he was talking about, but I pressed him a little more. "The company is going to be sold and there will be big changes, different people running a different shop," Roger said and left my office. I decided that I would ask my boss again, telling him that I had done what I had dreamed to do here.

People knew what it means to be trusted, empowered, skilled, free to create with a team, ask for better work conditions and get them, assert their own initiative and implement it. They wanted to paint the walls of their offices with different colors and we saw no harm in that.

They wanted a building they could have an input in the design, and they got it. They were winners, all of them. They came up with diamonds, some of the best products the company ever produced. I felt that my thoughts were there to reassure me that the investment of time I had made at SRC wasn't a waste. The work was fun and had meaning. What else could I want from my work life? The train of thought stopped and all sorts of projects got loaded up.

The last couple of years I had added "retire early to teach, preach and fly a kite on the shore of Lake Minnewashta with my grandchildren, or write a book on 'God and the Problem of Evil' and tell the world that God is Love, loves all the creatures he made and doesn't do evil, even when something looks like evil at the time." I didn't know if my boss would accept any truths that Science couldn't prove. He might. He was a very brilliant scientist. I'll remember to talk to him about the book I'm writing. We'll start nice and kind, but sooner or later we'll disagree on some law of physics or some spiritual truth and we'll be off and going down the rabbit hole that leads to "no early retirement" for me yet. But, who knows? That may be my negative view projected on him. The war is still going on, I cannot be a veteran, not yet. There is no Captain McNeill here to bail me out.

It wasn't that bad, really, though some extra free time would have allowed me to think more broadly and find out what I could really do to make myself acceptable to myself and my loved ones. I'm getting angry more frequently these days with my wife for no reason at all. I need more time to help my children navigate the torments of the college world and what I'm supposed to do with the grandchildren, beside flying kites. I'm tired of staying calm when managers refuse to include their people in decisions, or address their complaints, or pack the work day with agony when I know that they could change their ways and let peace reign.

A couple of days after my meeting with Roxana and Roger's flyby, I had just filled two cups with coffee, one for me and one for my secretary, and I was walking toward my office when Roxanna saw me, came behind me and asked if I had a minute for her.

"Are you the service man here as well?" she teased.

"I told you the old rules don't hold in this place. My secretary makes my work easier and my life simpler. She's precious"

She came to my office, sat down and crossed her legs as if there was nothing difficult to deal with. "I was looking at your file last night and I saw that you have retirement in your career plan," she said and turned her eyes on me. "Is it true that you want to take early retirement?"

"I've been trying to do that for a while, but my boss loves me and won't let me go," I joked.

"Let me see what I can do," she said and stood up. "I'll let you know, if I come up with something."

Three days later, Roxanna gave me an envelope and explained the conditions for early retirement. I read the document over once again with my wife, and the next day I announced my farewell. I thought of giving Roxanna a hug to thank her for her kindness and was sure she would have been O.K with it. But, she was so happy already to achieve something that made someone else happy, that I didn't think it was necessary. Has she started up the road of loving her neighbors? I just thanked her, shook her hand and sat down to enjoy the last few days of work. I made sure my secretary had a job with us and I thanked her for all the things she had made possible for everyone in the department.

It was snowing again, but this time I let myself wonder in the sky's ever-shifting cloudscapes, searching for the source of it all.

Was our work to build an organization with a meaningful work life worth the effort? Did the work we encouraged people to have result in a better life at home? Have our values and our actions steered our people to seek more spiritual values and reduce the lust for wealth, power, pleasure and honor that people often seek in the world around us? The true stories I have written for SRC, linked to the stories I have written for the other six stages of my life provide partial answers I will have for the "Life Questions" when the time comes to answer them. I hope that they will help others to link the stories they have lived and benefit themselves by the self-knowledge they acquire and the joy of their life's work.

G

ENJOY, SUFFER AND REJOICE

37

Hinged, Unhinged and Rehinged at Rehab

Right after retirement I felt quite motivated to continue teaching at the University of Saint Thomas in a creative way all about the transformative organization. I wanted students to experience the right way rather than learning it from my instruction. I told the class that I would never give them any short exams in class without announcing them in a previous class. And I kept my word for a few weeks. Then, I started a class by announcing that tonight we'll have a short exam, and distributed a paper with four questions. Everyone in class proceeded to solve the problems. Five minutes later, I stopped the class and asked my students why did they not protest when I violated the rule I had set. Most students understood the real problem I was trying to teach them, so we discussed what one ought to do in the unfair world we live in.

Then I felt the need to present to older Christians a variety of topics covering science, literature, theology and philosophy. I organized courses which introduced some controversial topics in a way that gave people the option to choose and strengthen the beliefs they already had, or change to newer or deeper views. That way I was able to present topics in evolution, Islam, cosmology and the anthropic principle, the evolution of Christianity, theories of Salvation, "God and the Problem of Evil" as a Socratic dialogue and so on, without forcing people to cross their comfort zones. I used video lectures from the lecturers I could find with permission and added written materials wherever they were needed.

Betty and I worked together in preparing the materials and discussing the growth-producing questions and answers. I enjoyed the objections and the debates that ensued because I feel the mind is one of God's precious gifts and "Thinking the Faith" (The title of the series I presented) is part of a Christian's educational obligations. It was a great time until Betty and I started developing medical problems which limited and finally ended these joyous efforts.

My ordeal started when our family physician said that there was no way of fixing the pain on my leg without a hip replacement surgery. Adding another frequent pain to the pains I had suffered from time to time on my wrists for many years was too much to put up with. At least this doctor knew what the problem was and how it should be fixed. I always wanted a diagnosis that comes straight at you, out of the blue, like a dazed drone ready to fix your worn-out body with a single deep dive. I didn't argue much with my doctor. The doctor who had worked on my wrists was never able to diagnose the disease. He was trying to fit me with gloves and some ineffective drugs. I finally had found a rheumatologist named Erskine Caperton who had finally found a drug that stopped the pain. He had told me that I had more than 50% chance of getting rheumatoid arthritis after ten or more years. I told my family physician that I was going to find an orthopedic surgeon and have the hip replacement operation right away.

I left his office and searched for the best orthopedic surgeon in the area. And, there was a man of the hour in the daily paper, with a procedure that had some advantages when compared with the standard procedure. I went to see doctor Heller and was promised minimal discomfort and a speedy recovery from what is an intricate operation with minimal cuts, least recovery time and shortest time of immobility. I spent some days comparing the advantages and disadvantages of the procedures, consulting with friends who had a hip replaced and decided that Dr. Heller was the doc for me. I saw him with Betty near me and we decided to go ahead.

The operation went very well, I was told, and after three days of hospital stay, I was put in a van and taken to the Masonic Rehab Center.

Betty wanted to escort me and take care of me, but I was still a proud and staunch warrior who didn't accept help easily. I would find out later how hurt she was that I didn't let her help me, and how much she wanted to take care of me, but wasn't allowed. I cut her out of the recovery process because she wasn't doing so well herself, walking around with a liquid oxygen bottle for breathing and struggling with a killer pain on her back.

I was recovering well, doing the necessary exercises and keeping my leg totally still., even when asleep. There were some days when I felt drained of energy and the doctor ordered a second transfusion to boost my hemoglobin level. It seemed to me that other patients were progressing while I was struggling. The thought that I would have to remove the shell which protected my leg from moving while taking a shower terrified me. I would have to lean on somebody strong and he or she would have to hold me tight so I wouldn't slide out while covered with soap. I postponed taking a shower as long as I could, but I finally gave up and agreed to go to what seemed to me to be a torture chamber, held by a brawny Iraq veteran. I felt better and tried to execute my recovery routines more energetically than ever. But, slowly, I felt my digestive system bothering me in ways I hadn't experienced before. I could only stand a spoonful of soup, a couple of bites of meat and a bite of some of the deserts they offered. I was losing weight and nothing was helping me feel healthy. A kind of helplessness was dumped on me and I became a sick person by the circumstances.

I finished my week at the Masonic rehab center and went home to recover and return to my normal self. That was my goal, but it wasn't happening, and I went to the doctor to find out what was wrong with me. He diagnosed me with diverticulitis and placed me in a harsh diet and strict antibiotics regime to recover. Betty was doing everything possible to take care of me, but she was already on an increased liquid oxygen container for breathing and her back pain had become severe from the arachnoiditis disease she had, so I couldn't stand her trying to take care of me and add to her suffering. I followed the diet and the complex schedule of drugs the doctor had ordered, but I wasn't getting better. At the next visit to the doctor's office I had an MRI to explore my situation. The answer came back with unusual speed: there was no sign of diverticulitis, but there was a bit of ominous news in the form of kidney cancer, found accidentally, which needed to be examined.

One day with a snowstorm warning coming at us, a cold and onerous day, nothing was going well. A much-needed light bulb went out and made the stairway difficult to climb up to our bedroom since neither one of us could climb up a ladder to replace it. Then the truck delivering Betty's liquid oxygen tank was stuck somewhere in the highway and they called and told us that they didn't know when it would come and deliver the stuff that kept Betty alive. I got up from my lounger and tried to straighten out a picture on the nearby mantle, stretching my leg and my arm like a discus thrower has been doing on his Greek statue for eons. One more tiny stretch and I was struck down by a thunderbolt of pain on my new hip bone and fell back down on the lounger. An indescribably intense pain on my hip joint kept me pinned down on the very same place I had fallen. I had just suffered the worst thing that can happen to a person with the operation I had: a dislocation of the hip.

My wife called my son, Paul, and the police to help us. They all came and saw the horrible position I was in. The slightest move made me scream with pain. The move of bone against bone was unbearable. But the strong policemen who came to help us knew exactly what to do. I couldn't quite grasp how they placed me on a stretcher and carried me to the ambulance. The presence of people who knew what they were doing filled me with confidence. I don't know how they synchronized their moves, but they carried me to an ambulance keeping my body as if it was one cast iron piece without a hint of disturbing the hip joint. My son Paul sat next to my stretched-out body and I felt that as long as he was there everything would be alright. I was happy that I had served as a police commissioner in my city for six years and had contributed to the quality of the Police force with selection and training. It was some time ago, and I don't think anyone of these officers recognized me

As we made our way toward the hospital the date came to my mind out of nowhere: it was Tuesday, August 13, 2013, which happened to be exactly 60 years since I stepped on American soil, at Hoboken, New

Jersey. That day apparently was reserved for testing my endurance under multiple challenges. It was a strange concurrence of adverse events that made me suspect evil intervention. The liquid oxygen would last for another day, and then Paul would act if the truck was still stranded. His wife will stop by at the house and replace the burnt-out lamp. I don't know if anyone would find me in Hoboken, but I met some distant relatives I never knew I had and made it to New York, then the Boston YMCA, a restaurant in Copley Square as a bus-boy, arranged by Greek compatriots, and then to Cambridge and MIT, until I realized I was travelling in an ambulance with a very loose leg.

The EMTs took me to another hospital because the one where my surgeon practiced had no rooms available. My first impression was that I was in a hospital for the indigent. The walls had stains, the couple of chairs in the room were scratched and discolored, and the ceiling was cracked all over. The two or three people milling around the room had no idea what to do with hip dislocations, let alone with the complex, one of a kind, most imaginatively conceived hip surgery I had selected to have. Nobody knew what exactly was upsetting me. They were used to improvise and make do and fix the best way they knew how. I was flat, but I could see the general reluctance to push hard for getting anything started. I kept asking Paul what is going on, and he would do whatever he could to gather some crumb of information. "I need to empty my bladder," I kept asking the nurse that would appear occasionally in the small storage-room-looking Emergency Room.

"Soon," she said a few times, but no action was taken.

"They need to bring a catheter here and empty my bladder, or it could burst and injure somebody," I said injecting a little black humor in the scene. She paid no attention, Paul requested action many times, but he finally accepted that the hospital would do something because they knew there was a problem and hospitals solve problems.

After some time of waiting for a doctor to come and change the situation, a small woman, young and diminutive, approached me and introduced herself as "Doctor Helen Park," and reported that Dr. Heller would be unable to come and work on my dislocation, because his poodle had died that very same day, at noon, and he was bereft.

It was August 13, wasn't it? I thought and my intended scream was choked. I tried hard to believe the present moment.

"So, what is going to happen to my dangling leg?"

"I'll call Dr. Heller in a short while and he'll give me directions," Dr. Hellen Park, the young, probably, recent graduate, woman doctor would fix my tangled hip bones. I stared harshly at my son, but he was emotionally far away, Kansas City barbecue or Timbuktu, knowing that I was about to detonate. It's still August 13, I thought.

"My bladder!" I shouted at the proper doctor, who was already two steps away from me.

"I know," she said calmly as if she had the controls of all events happening around her. "We'll take care of it as soon as possible," she said and left. The fact that a small, female, newbie doctor had my life in her hands with no idea of the surgery I had, and only a couple of minutes training by a doctor, grieving for his dog started me praying. If God was going to help me, this was the time to do it, I thought, and prayed that my need happened to coincide with God's will. Hours passed. Paul was standing nearby giving me hope that there was action in the back room. They were talking about my situation. I felt exhausted.

Suddenly, the door of the back room was kicked open and Doctor Hellen Park burst in the room followed by a fat man in a nurse's uniform. Hellen Park seemed taller, animated, wilder than before. She seemed to move within a pre-determined plan and took her position where my feet were. She turned sharply toward the fat man and ordered him to come closer and stand by.

"You are the weight!" she shouted at the fat man, and with no other instructions, she jumped up on my flat medical bed, took hold of my dislocated leg while the fat man fell hard on my body, and she pulled my leg, twisted it and guided it back into its proper position.

The young newbie is an Amazon, I thought. Tears blurred my eyes. Lord, we see so little, I thought, and asked for forgiveness. I moved my leg just a little, and felt no pain. Doctor Hellen Park had healed me. "Thank you," I whispered to her, and watched her gentle face smile. "It wasn't that difficult," she said and moved on. And, from that time on, sincerely, I lost all distinctions I had prejudicially made about women and men. This MCP was now extinct. As a matter of fact, I had a feeling of comfort when a female doctor was there to listen to me and heal me. In time, all distinctions will vanish, and we'll know each other as we really are, children of one God.

I was moved to a hospital room and asked immediately for a doctor to help me with the bladder that, by this time, I felt, was holding much more than three times its normal volume. After asking for help and getting no response, I asked my son to look for a doctor. He came back and said that there were no doctors around, but some intern would come by in a little while. I was angry at him for not becoming enraged, but I owed him so much that I kept most of the whirlwind within me. Paul was a kinder, perhaps, wiser man than I was. The intern appeared and I spoke to him as calmly and agreeably as I had ever spoken to anyone who, in my opinion, had been so aloof. He had a nurse catheterize me. She couldn't believe I had accumulated three and a half times more liquid than it is normal. The young intern left before the nurse apologized on behalf of the hospital and proceeded to work on me.

Then, I found that I had at least one roommate. I couldn't see him, but I could hear him cough fitfully, talk loud on his phone, listen to a raucous hockey game on his TV and put up with his own jeering or cheering, and smell his cigarette smoke wafting through the curtain toward my slightly open window. The Medicare Rule required that I had to stay in the hospital for a total of three days, before I could return to the Masonic Rehab center. I didn't think I could go through that ordeal and I asked Paul to talk to the administrator about leaving first thing next day. Paul came back distraught and told me that I had to spend three days there, or pay a lot of money and then I could leave for rehab. I told him that I was leaving next morning and I would pay whatever it was. I was in a limousine with my leg safely protected by a hard sheath and stretched out all over the back seat, headed back for a second round of rehab to my familiar shelter.

The day that had gone by was an endless series of troubles. I was relieved that the day had passed. Yet, an omen of more trials and tribulations was in the air. That was the date when I had achieved my goal of coming to America, a goal I believed had been achieved with God's help because of all the things that happened without a specific effort to achieve them. Was now time for pay back? I prayed.

They sent me to the second floor of the same Rehab Center I had spent my first recovery period, and I knew right away that this floor provided fewer services than the first floor. It made sense. I was supposed to be doing better, even if I wasn't. Betty wanted me to go home so she could take care of me, but I knew that it wasn't easy to care for me with my problems.

I was using a walker to get from my room to the dining room and I started to notice that my shoulders and my neck were hurting more every day. I switched to a cane, but the pain didn't improve; it just spread to my wrists. The nurses on this floor were late or early, but rarely on time. I couldn't take the sleeping pill at seven o'clock when I planned to go to sleep at twelve, but my nurse had all kinds of reasons that I should take the pill and go to sleep at the time she was present and could watch me. She had to fit me to her schedule and that was slavery to me. We spent a lot of time negotiating, pleading and arguing. There would be another reason for antagonism because whatever I asked for could not be done to my satisfaction. When you are thirsty you have to drink water, but it took a long time for a request to be done; and, when the water stayed in the room for the better part of the day, it was warm and you had to wait hours before the nurse or some assistant would bring you cool water. If you were being difficult taking your pills, or keeping the yogurt in the refrigerator in time before it turned sour, you were causing disruptions in the operation. I knew I needed help, but the nurse made sure I felt my subordination all over.

Then Jenny became the assistant nurse assigned to me and schedules became guidelines for helping the patient. She was a wonderful person, who made it her business to make my life as comfortable as possible. I think that she had a mild down syndrome which turned any deficit she might have into a healing virtue. I remember one day when she was telling me how much she enjoyed working at rehab. It was a hot day, with a scorching sun outside, when suddenly, Jenny quit our discussion in mid-sentence and left the room. She returned a few minutes later with a jug of cold water in one hand and a bowl of ice- cream on the other. "These will help a little – the air conditioners are not enough today," she said and picking up my old warm water jug she left the room.

The dislocation was a constant presence of fear and alertness in my daily struggle. It could happen while sleeping, or walking, in the dining room, as you tried to get by, or it could happen, where it almost happened -- in the bathroom, when I was trying to get from the toilet to the sink and my cane fell down, and bounced beyond my reach. I had no idea which move would cause the dislocation. I was too far from the red alarm cord, so I couldn't pull it and get help. I hobbled to the bowl, pulled the cord and stood up leaning with both hands against the wall. I thought of turning and sitting down on the bowl again, but I was afraid of the maneuver and committed to remain pinned on the wall with my arms stretched out, as long as it took.

Pat, one of the least compassionate nurses came in and instead of helping me to reach the sink and then help me go to bed, she picked up my cane and hung it from my arm. I thought she was about to reprimand me, but instead she said with an icy calm voice, "You've got to get hold of yourself. Couple of weeks ago a young 'dislocator', who had been here three times, killed himself. It's a difficult recovery, so be careful."

I was about to have a combat with her when Jenny appeared at the bathroom door. Somehow, she understood what was going on right away, perhaps she had fought other battles with Pat, and moved quickly toward me. She grabbed me with both arms and walked me to the sink and then to my bed. "Let him learn how to walk on his own," Pat called out as she left the room.

"I'll go and get you your Ensure from the refrigerator," Jenny said, straightening the covers of my bed. I waited pondering my situation. Why did this young woman with so many responsibilities of her own care for the wellbeing of a strange, cranky patient like me?

I don't know how many days I had been in the rehab center, perhaps three or four, but one morning I woke up and couldn't move my hands without screaming. I had some pain in the past, when I strained my wrist working in the house, but now the pain was excruciating and affecting every bone I had. Nobody knew what the problem was, so I tried to get Pat to contact Dr. Caperton. It took some time to convince her and more time to talk to the doctor. Jenny helped me sit on a wheelchair and took me to the dining room. I wasn't hungry, so I watched the news of the war in Syria, holding my arms up. I tried to enter the battle and follow the troop movements and the controversy of the Red Line that our kind-hearted President was trying to set as a limit for the use of chemical weapons. I knew the snakes would bite him and the good he was trying to do would be twisted against him. I was upset at the raging debate on the TV and in discussions among the patients, so I asked a server to push me to a table with only one guy, who looked like he cared nothing about this world. I was afraid that the wrist pains I felt wouldn't let me use a spoon, if I happened to get some appetite. With grinding teeth and muted pain, I tried to eat some soft food and drink a glass of milk.

"I can help you get rid of the pain, if you believe in God and pray with me," the man said softly, calmly and in earnest.

I was surprised, but rejected his offer. "I have been praying, but we don't always get what we pray for," I said.

"You are a Christian, aren't you?" the man said smiling as if I had welcomed his offer.

"Yes," I said and stared at him. The man, touched my hand, intending to hold it for a prayer.

"Ouch!" I screamed and he drew back. "My hands are hurting bad this morning," I said, and caressed one of my hands with the other.

"Lord, help my friend get rid of that pain that cripples his hands," the man said with closed eyes. "He's hungry and has trouble to eat; he's had an operation on his leg and now his whole body is in pain," he prayed with folded hands.

"Thank you," I said and tried to eat something holding the spoon as if it was a shovel to reduce the pain on my fingers.

"I'm in Room 246," the man said. "I'm Clay, and here is my card," he said, handing me his card.

I gave him my name, but didn't volunteer any other information. We talked about our beliefs and I found out that Clay believed he was given various difficult assignments to perform thousands of years ago. He believed that God ordered him to cut up in tiny pieces some idolaters he had killed a long time ago. Not a word about Christ's self-sacrificing love for our salvation. I thought the man was travelling on another road. "My friend Bob is always with me. I couldn't do it alone," he said and looked at me like a sergeant at a recruiting office.

Jenny appeared with a glass of water and a pill and said that it was already past the time I was supposed to take my pill. I took it and asked her to help me get back to my room. I told Clay that the events of the Old Testament are very hard to understand. Jenny was already moving me out.

"I'll be here for a couple more days" he said. "We can pray again. You know, pain doesn't exist; it is the sins in our mind."

"It's hard for me to talk about anything right now," I said, waiting for Jenny to get a glass so I could take it.

"I know you are hurting and I want to help you," Clay said and pulled back his chair. "I have to go right now but, we can pray tomorrow. And, you got my number. I'll come to your house."

"Thank you," I said. I didn't want to debate him. He got up tapped me on the shoulder and left.

It was early, and I looked around the room for anyone who might help me spread some butter and jam on my toast while we talked for a while. I saw a man seating nearby and I thought he was kind enough to do me a favor. He had surgery on both knees at the same time and some people had talked about him, saying that it was a very smart thing to do, kind of "killing two birds with one stone," while others thought it would be very difficult to have both legs out of commission and feel double the pain. "He must be brave enough or totally nuts to do that," someone summarized the situation.

I knew right away that Mark wasn't nutty at all, so I asked him, if he could reach over and put some butter on my toast. He was a very friendly and very smart professor. We agreed on the few topics that came up in our brief talk, but they were enough for both of us to sense that we could become friends. We looked for each other in the dining room of the Masonic Rehab and continued to meet once a month for brunch, until COVID 19 split us up. Clay stopped by the next day and said hello, but he understood that Mark and I were talking about something that he didn't care about. It was theology, and I was trying to convince Mark that God exists, indeed.

Dr. Caperton was looking for the right therapy for me, but time was passing and the pain was wearing me down. He recommended cold and hot water five-minute hand baths for me, and every day I kept up the prescribed procedure. It had no effect. I was driven to his office in a limo again and he started an aggressive prednisone therapy which began to make some difference. But, my abdominal pain and the lack of appetite had weakened me. I had started to think that the devil had something to do with my sickness and was preparing for a confrontation of some kind. It seemed that all life-supporting systems of my body had been affected. I watched some religion programs on TV and started to think that there were too many bad things happening to me. I talked to my wife on the phone and told her that I was not doing well and was looking forward to getting back home and being with her. She wanted to come and see me, but I explained to her that, no matter how I wanted to be with her, it wasn't possible just now. I felt bad to have troubled her this way. Yet, listening to her voice and her advice strengthened me. I was starting to think that some evil force was out to get me, and Betty replied, "Pray and know that I love you.". I started praying and asking for help from God. A Protestant minister who came to see me thought that providential help was needed, indeed. And he prayed with me. The Orthodox priest came and helped me to strengthen my faith. I asked him to perform an exorcism, so he put on his cassock and prayed with me. He was one of the most compassionate people I knew and never stopped smiling. There were times when I wanted to help him bear the burden of pain he was carrying from his visits to suffering and dying patients, but I knew he could handle it all well.

Every time I felt that I was getting better, I thought of my wife, alone at home, suffering the pain of her thirty-year-old spine disease and her forty-year-old lung disease which was reactivating itself after an extended quiescent period. How will I be able to help her when I get home and she wants to help me instead, carrying an ever-increasing oxygen bottle on her side? I would stop trying to guess the future and think of the day they would sent me home again, when the comparatively trivial hip problems I had were a thing of the past. Love doesn't make life easier, but it makes living meaningful.

It was Saturday evening when I found out that there was a Protestant service offered next morning in the underground chapel of our building. I had visited the chapel on my first visit to the Masonic Center and was attracted by its mysterious underground entrance and the solitary gold cross standing on a small table, deep inside the tunnel-like entrance. I decided to go and join the ad hoc congregation for a communal service. It has always been hard for me to get up early in the morning, but on that Sunday morning I didn't feel sleepy, lazy or dutiful. I felt a desire to go down to the tunnel chapel rolling my wheelchair, as if it was the center of all comfort and healing. Jenny wasn't there mornings and Mark didn't go to church, so I started pushing the wheels of my wheelchair with whatever strength I had left. I headed down the tunnel with the heavy golden cross still sending rays of light in my mind.

When I reached the entrance, the chapel was almost full with old people on wheel chairs. I paused, wondering whether I belonged there. An old man, one of the deacons, I assumed, came on a wheel chair and handed me a flier for the service. Standing by, another deacon came over and guided my wheelchair at the end of the rows of wheel chairs already arranged to face a pulpit. An amphora filled with red and white flowers stood next to the pulpit table.

I hadn't expected the gathering of so many people in this tunnel chapel. They were all recovering from something that had threatened their limbs, their organs their very life. I felt a sense of belonging there that I hadn't experienced since I was a child crouched in a crowded bomb shelter seeking protection from another enemy's fire and fury. There were no explosions to be heard here, no crashing of windows, no blood on the street, but there was the same sense of safety that Lena's bomb shelter had given me. This was my cohort. We were the same people, praying for protection from the same enemy of mankind in a different form. I opened my bulletin and started singing along the hymns I had heard on radio programs without paying attention to the words:

> Amazing Grace, How sweet the sound
> That saved a wretch like me
> I once was lost, but now am found
> I was blind but now I see...

A sense of mysterious calmness permeated my body, mind and soul. The golden cross, deeper inside the tunnel glimmered with reflections from a candle. I felt that I was stronger in this fort of wounded humanity and prayed that my wife and I would be saved.

My hip was still hurting, but it was healing well. My digestive system and the pain in my wrists and shoulders which was diagnosed as Rheumatoid Arthritis made me feel exhausted and lost. When I told Jenny that I would be leaving the next day and thanked her for her love and care, she wished me God's blessings and said that she would pray for my complete recovery.
I was discharged and started physical therapy at home. I felt cut off from the world, and my remoteness and lack of interest in everything didn't help me to be close to Betty. When I saw my doctor, he said that I needed to go and have a urologist examine it.

The urologist, Dr. Bernard Hahn, was Vietnamese and had studied in Paris and Oklahoma, but was also interested in the Greek culture and gave me the impression that he had a good understanding of Greek history and traditions. He wanted to know more about Greece and I talked about the food, the dances and the songs of the various islands, plains and mountains. The doctor had a good heart and wanted to help me. I decided I didn't need to do any research for a top-notch urologist.

When he told me that he liked the popular songs of "Zorba", I promised to bring some CDs next time, if I was still around. He laughed, but not heartily, and I felt a little cloud, grey and gloomy fly by.

"We don't know if we have to do something now for your cancer, but we could operate and get it out – it isn't hard," he said. I wanted to know if we could go on without any operations or biopsies. "We could follow it for a while and see what it does," he said. I really appreciated his willingness to wait. He examined the scans on his computer and verified his decision to do nothing now, but we would have to watch it periodically and act accordingly. I went home and lay on my lounger and kept trying to escape from tangled dark thoughts for three weeks.

One morning, I woke up and tried to walk but my ankles were locked and I couldn't move. I lay in bed and looked at a small TV screen, but I couldn't watch and follow a story. A couple of days later I went to see Dr. Caperton, the rheumatologist who had found a way to keep me well for two decades, and he told me that he had secured a biologic drug for my case. I started the injections and my problem literally disappeared. I started writing poems, cooking for Betty and myself, and talking to some friends about my three-week long depression. The poems were dark, people told me and I agreed. The reason a depressed poet writes poems is to discharge the poison that has gathered inside him. I would love to write joyous poems, but I have to fix some other things first.

When I came back to my normal state of discontent, I thought it might be interesting to consider moving to some nice Independent Living apartment and benefit from having some of the labor-intensive and time-consuming services, like house cleaning and cooking done for us. Betty stared at me as if she was lost in some noisy toy store and couldn't make out what I was talking about.

"You see my feet right now?" she said her eyes piercing my daze. "They are nailed to the floor," she said and the exploration of other residences was stopped dead on its track. I didn't appreciate the wisdom of her choice then, but after she died and I was left alone, I also decided that our home backyard with a forest further back, crossed by deer and turkeys and squirrels was better than a senior apartment of a twenty-fourth floor high-rise, as long as I was able to take care of myself with some help for house cleaning.

So, we decided to find a helper for house cleaning and any other service that the person could provide. We had several women come and clean house, but no one fit the qualifications my wife had stored in her mind. Then we found Elizabeth and Betty gave her thumbs up right away. It must have fit the algorithm Betty had in mind. After a few visits it became increasingly apparent that Elizabeth was indeed a rare person, and Betty had discerned her qualities. After Betty's death, Elizabeth became my housekeeper and my helper and friend. She is hard-working, smart, and caring person who stays optimistic even with a pandemic raging around us

She is one of the people I came to trust with my life when COVID 19 forced me to a lockdown of indeterminate duration. A daughter in law of mine learning about the help Elizabeth was providing to me with groceries, medications and cleaning said that she was a gift left to me by Betty, to see me through the tough times of grief and isolation I would have to travel. I know she is right because Elizabeth is one of the few truly happy people I have met.

38

The Strange History of My Kidney Cancer

My kidney cancer gave me no problems, but I had to go every year to the urologist, have a little chat about the CDs I had brought him, talk about this year's Greek festival and its music, and waited for his diagnosis, as he read the scan of my kidney on his computer. I noticed that Dr. Hahn wasn't too eager to use a knife in my case. "You can come and see me a year from now, and we'll find out what we'll have to do, if there is anything to do," was his standard reply to my question about my cancer's whereabouts. I felt that a weight had been lifted off my back for another year and I was ready to flap my wings and get out, up and away.

Year after year three times in a row, I went for "the cancer check" and got the same good answer of "No change" uttered with ever increasing conviction by my friendly doctor Hahn. By that time, I was convinced that he was joyous with the static status of the kidney cancer situation. I was sure he had many other people he could work on and was glad he didn't have to work on me. Though by that time I had learned how to put up with the MRI ordeal with a prayer and pill, I still found it to be an unpleasant procedure, so I asked the doctor if he could get similar results reading an ultrasound scan instead of a n MRI.

"It would be much easier for me and we really got nothing to lose by trying." The doctor stopped; he froze looking at his screen. He thought and decided on the spot:

"Next year we try ultrasound first; I think it'll tell us what we want to know". I thought that the answer came too fast. Am I muddling up the facts designed to save my life? I was anxious again.

"Are you sure it'll be O.K.?" I said regretting my suggestion.

"It is good to try, so we'll do it," the doctor said, defending the innovation as if it was his own.

"Thank you, doc," I said and left feeling lighter than before.

On the fourth year of our well-established-by-now kidney relationship my urologist studied the Ultrasound and expressed his surprise at the clarity with which he could study my cancer. Bye-bye MRI, hello Ultrasound. He compared the two different scans and they were the same. He was happy that I would be happy with the change and with the fact that the cancer had the same size. No need of procedures, hospitals and operations, recoveries, possible spread to other parts of the body, inoperable organs with twisted situations and a truckload of grief rolling on a road with a single lane toward me. The doc said that he had learned some Greek dances and was finding that they are very joyous and great for his exercise program. I wanted to ask some questions on this subject, but I decided I wasn't the keeper of the Greek culture and let the subject fade with a nice smile of total approval.

The fifth year I went to see my doctor, I told him that my wife had died and I couldn't take any more bad news. He understood my grieving and offered me a consolation, saying that sometimes death becomes a good thing when life is filled with suffering. Then he studied my scans on the computer and said to the screen, "the cancer is smaller."

Turning toward me, he announced: "The cancer is smaller now than it was last year."

I wasn't expecting anything different than before, but the good news surprised me. I felt a little breath of hope passing past my face, but it wasn't a good time for dwelling on good news either.

"It will be better for you next year," the doctor said in a small gentle tone, as I was leaving. I thought it was a kind comment, but I didn't attach any diagnostic value to it. A couple of months later, I saw my regular doctor for the continued problems I had with abdominal pain and mentioned to him casually that my cancer had shrunk a little. He looked at me with sympathy and asked how I was fairing under the load of grief.

"The cancer has shrunk," I repeated, attempting to elicit a response from him, and planning another theological debate.

"There are inaccuracies in scans sometimes that we must take into account," he said and left the room.

The August of the sixth year came suddenly. My calendar was crowded with visits to medical specialists for problems with Rheumatoid Arthritis, throat infection and voice warping, regular therapy for my worsening back pain with Osteoarthritis and a nasty bout with sciatica along with a regular bimonthly appointment for podiatric care. I was also working on a book of poems, building friendships with people from two different Christian congregations, and participating in discussion groups; but as I had done the previous five times when the August appointment for the "cancer check" popped up on the calendar, I prepared myself for it with the same care as I had always done before. But this time, I sensed a strangeness inside m and around me; something was making me cautious, apprehensive, as I got ready for the appointment that morning. I felt that, perhaps, the test wasn't as necessary as the doctors thought it was, and I wanted to be done with it and pursue the things I had a say-so. I timed the water drinking quantity and drinking times carefully for the ultrasound, and left the house an hour ahead of time.

I had visited the Park Nicolet Clinic dozens of times for various tests and treatments over many years and I knew I could be there in fifteen minutes, so I never plugged the Clinic's address in my car's navigator, as I usually do for important appointments, because I have trouble locating addresses and changing routes. But, as I said, I was ready to get the test done and left home an hour early. The street which I knew was the key to getting to the Clinic was blocked and I followed the indicated detour. A minute later I found myself at a fork on the road with a car tailing me and I took the side that seemed to be closer to the location of the Clinic. Another turn a minute later and I realized that I was lost. Somehow, I found myself turned around on the way back home. There were several blocked streets and I couldn't read the street signs. I asked one of the workers holding the blocking sign, how could I get on the street he was blocking and he threw both hands up in the air and pointed ahead, to the direction away from the Clinic. I felt the drizzle of panic blossom on my forehead and ducked into the parking area of the first Gas Station I saw. I tried to remember the address of the Clinic and type it into the navigator, but I couldn't remember enough of it.

I turned off the car and tried to clear my mind of all thoughts and fears for a couple of minutes. It was no use. The time to the appointment was passing and I was static. I was totally lost. A strange feeling of despair got hold of my body and mind and I rested my head on the steering wheel. "Lord, I need your help," I said, holding the steering wheel with eyes shut. I received no instructions from God, but when I opened my eyes and started at the car again, I was absolutely sure that he, the God who had helped me so many times before would guide me to the Clinic.

I left the Gas Station and went past a couple of streets away from the direction of the Clinic, and then I turned. I turned again, went straight, I had no idea what I was doing, but ten minutes later I saw the back side of the Clinic and headed for it, straight to the ultrasound department. "Urology has moved to a new building" the ultrasound nurse told me as I was leaving after the ultrasound scan.

"I hope that there is no barricade between them and us," I said. The young woman smiled and said that it was easy to see it. But that day I didn't know where I was going, God did. I parked in the wrong parking lot and went to the wrong building. They pointed to a building that was a movie theater once, and I had gone there with one of my grandsons many years before. Someone said that it was Urology now. I got in the car and parked in the old theater's parking lot. I went to the door, but there was nobody there. "The entrance is on the other side," a man headed toward McDonald's across the street called out. I arrived at the Urology Department, gave my name and took a bottle of water to drink, feeling exhausted, but not dehydrated yet. I was shown to the doctor's office and sat down, drinking the water, as I waited for the doctor to come in and read the scan on his computer. If he only knew what I had to go through to reach him.

Doctor Hahn took his seat with a smile and a friendly plural greeting. "How are we doing these days?"

"We'll know pretty soon," I said.

"Of course, we will," he said staring at the scan on his computer screen. He moved closer and murmured some word I couldn't understand until he uttered the word "Fantastic!" and then explained it to himself.

"Your cancer has shrunk again!" he said.

"Thank God!" I shouted before I could think of anything at all.

He turned his chair and faced me. It seemed to me that his eyebrows were bunched over his nose as if he was about to accuse me of something unfit for a person like me.

"Do you pray?" he asked in all seriousness he could convey.

"I sure do!" I said, already dashing for the barricades.

"I have never seen this before," he said. "Last year it was 3.4 cm. long and now we have come down to 2.4 cm.". He turned back toward the screen and said something in French, I don't know to whom.

"My family doctor doesn't think that cancers shrink, so could you, please, send him a note telling him what's happening here?"

He looked at me puzzled. "Sure; I'll do that," he said. Then, with eyes still bunched up and glaring at the screen, he said:

"It cannot happen, but it shrunk!"

I couldn't resist repeating the words my family doctor had said, "There are inaccuracies sometimes," I mumbled. He let the remark go by without a comment.

"We'll see what happens next year, won't we?" I stood up ready to head for the door.

"I'll be here, but the cancer may be gone," I said and reached for the door.

When I got back home I thanked God for whatever was good in my life. I had faced many tough times, and I had done well. I didn't ask for a miracle this time. A "static" condition was plenty good, but if my God wiped out this cancer, who was I to stop him? I asked four doctors, friends of mine, if cancers can shrink on their own, and they all said that they hadn't seen or heard anything like that before. A fifth doctor friend doubted the fact that what I had was a cancer. "Probably, a growth," he said. He wasn't going to believe that it was a cancer without a biopsy, which couldn't be performed without risk of making things worse, if the growth was a cancer, indeed.

"It's probably a cyst!" he said irritated. "It cannot be a shrinking growth or a cancer; it has to be a cyst!" I didn't argue with this friend. There could be many reasons that I knew nothing about what made him doubt so vehemently the shrinkage of my cancer.

39

Nana's Best Birthday

Betty was the wonder-woman of our family, a gentle matriarch loved by everyone and the favorite of her children, their wives, her seven grandchildren and me, her husband for fifty-five years at the time. of her seventy fifth birthday. The whole family was waiting across the street as the snow continued to fall, bundled in their parkas and woolly coats, ready for me to turn the lights on so they could rush the door and surprise her and hug her to feel her heartwarming joy. It was a night to remember because the daughters in law had prepared wonderful food, I had created games to play with the kids, and the whole family had games to test each other's humor and persistence, insistence and humble character, after the special birthday cake was cut and everybody sung to the woman we loved a Happy Birthday song.

I remember how moved she was that night, with a sense of wholeness in her eyes, as she sat bundled in her periwinkle jacket, and raised her glass and drunk the champagne I had picked with great care and all of us raised ours and drunk wishing her many happy years to come.

We all knew that Betty had been suffering with two incurable diseases that caused pain and could change and threaten her life, but Betty had a way of facing all challenges with a brave and dismissive attitude that didn't hint that fear or trouble would ever get the upper hand.

It was time to open the presents and read the loving cards, and for everyone to remember some happy day they had spend with Nana baking ceramic dolls in our oven, or silk-screening deer or creatures of their imagination on bath towels or large handkerchiefs. She was a grandmother somewhere in some of those children's minds, but she was Nana, in every way, the loving friend who always gave so much more that she got. There was a time when I used to check what the children carried away, because Nana could give away whatever the children may have been playing with, like memorabilia and little dolls and silk-screened images of magic dragons along with her loving heart. She was happy on that birthday night as if she knew there would be a few heavier snowstorms and deeper treks ahead.

It wasn't more than a year after that blessed evening of family togetherness and love had gone by that the two diseases, manageable for many years, began to act up. Sarcoidosis had struck Betty almost as soon as we landed in Minnesota, some fifty years before, and started working at Honeywell as a Research Scientist. A slight pain one night, a few misdiagnoses after that, and finally a full-blown sarcoidosis diagnosis, an incurable disease of unknown origin, started working on her lungs, destroying tissue and making the lungs less able to provide her enough oxygen for breathing comfortably. Nobody knows how one gets the disease, but there is research at the University of Minnesota going on to find out and save others. Betty had an operation, and for more than thirty years the degrading of the lungs was almost stopped.

The other disease she had, arachnoiditis, happened from an operation Betty had soon after we got to Minnesota. She loved to slide on the snow with our boys each on a saucer outside our house. One time she hit a bump on the snow and suffered a chipped vertebra that tore the lamina close to it. We went to the hospital sure that the tear would be fixed easily. A laminectomy fixed her problem and she felt good for five or six months. Then a new back pain appeared and it was diagnosed as a vertebral break, requiring surgery. I remember when the doctor came by her bed and explained to us that he had to visualize the damaged area of her spine by injecting a chemical substance before he operated on the spine to fix it. There was no MRI or CT scans at that time.

"There is a one percent chance that the chemical used for visualizing the spine could create a painful reaction on your back and I want to know whether you are willing to take the risk," he said and waited for her answer.

"How long would the pain last?" Betty asked.

"It could last a long time, or forever, but it is, as I said, a very rare thing," the surgeon said and left the room, saying that he would be back for our decision. The operation would be easy the doctor had said, and the risk was only one percent. We talked for a while and both of us thought that one percent wasn't a bad risk to take. Betty decided to take the risk and fell in that horrible one percent which inflicted pain on her for the rest of her life. We visited more than twenty doctors, clinics, practitioners of all kinds, including a couple of visits to Mayo Clinic for two body casts, and with another doctor a fusion surgery on her lower back, but nothing could stop the pain.

The only relief she found was from concentration on her writing, her art and crafts. She wrote eight books of poems and religious books for children and created many silk screens of images for everybody in the family, for her hometown festival, for our house and for the church food shelf and children's summer bible school of the church.

When she focused on a project, she never quit. She had become an experienced photographer during her high school days and figured out complex ways of reproducing large icons at the church and use them for bookmarks and greeting cards for distribution by the church. Later, she became a Photoshop expert to render the images in her mind in stunning colors using her computers, scanners and printers.

Once, she decided to create three original icons of Christ for Thanksgiving, Christmas and Easter, and produced 100 to 150 copies by silk screening them in the early years, or printing them in a laser printer later on. I remember them as she spread them out all over her studio, then glued them on brown bags we bought from Costco and carried home in bundles of 500 at the time, then took them to the church to give them to all parishioners who might want to fill them with food items for the food-shelf of the church. Betty did this project for nineteen years because she loved to help the poor with her work. People appreciated her work. She was so surprised when she found out that some parishioners kept the icons and donated generously using their own brown bags. She also made calendars filled with funny and wise quotations, cartoons small sketches of things she liked and gave them to her Bible-Study friends, other friends who would ask for them. And, for the family she printed photographs she took at the many family gatherings we had, to celebrate the meaningful events of the year. Her work was commemorated with thumbnail prints of all the 57 of her icons of Christ on the proper church wall. A little space for roughly ten thousand original icons of Christ for his beloved poor. I bet that she would be angry with me for creating the panel with them that still stands there.

Sometimes, as I go around the house and see something she made hanging on the wall, or one of her books in our living room bookcase, I stop and imagine her at her computer composing, sometimes unfolding one of the little notes she tucked in her pockets, to remember a jewel of a thought; or I watch her painting the face of a bear doll, that she had just made, making with a body of rope and little clothes fashioned at the sewing machine table in her workroom. When she stopped driving because of the oxygen machines she had to carry, she would often ask me to buy more rope from the hardware store because she was going to make some more dolls and she needed a little more rope and a better stand for resting the little dolls.

After that wonderful seventy-fifth birthday night, the sky seemed to come down and press upon us a little more every year. Betty had trouble with breathing and we started using portable oxygen machines, and as the oxygen needs increased with the decrease of her lungs ability to work, we increased the size of the machines. Using liquid oxygen was working fine for her for months. She would wait for the technician who brought the huge new tank of oxygen every week and chat with him for a while asking him about driving in the snow to bring oxygen to the people he was looking after that day.

We were able to function with the liquid bottles even when we had to increase their size. I would cook and do the dishes, serve her lunch or dinner, refill the oxygen bottle eat and watch the news or some of her favorite TV series, like "Northern Exposure," or "Monk" or "Doc Martin". She would watch with me all the videos I downloaded on discs for my lectures on the various series on "Science and Religion," I presented in Churches, critiquing my style and content, and often sharpening the focus of my message.

One winter season we decided to go all out for heady videos and watched the entire series of twenty-four videos from Yale Professor Shelley Kagan's series on "Death" to reject the logic that led him to have no faith in God and followed it with the entire series on Euclidean Geometry from our well-stocked Hennepin County library. She would get around the house using one of three walkers I had placed for her in every floor, and she would go up and down on the three floors of our house, using the three chairlifts we installed. She would sit down when she was done with her crafts or writing work and we'd discuss everything under the sun.

But, there were times when I just had to stop the routine that kept us going, and if the weather was friendly I would propose a night out at our favorite restaurant where there was no more cooking I had to prepare, or plates to serve, or dishes to wash, but only the two of us with no care in the world. I knew that she was more comfortable at home, but she would go along for dinner sometimes to our restaurant for her favorite pasta. I remember the night when we were there at the right time and sat at our favorite table and ordered the red wine we both enjoyed and our favorite plates came at the right time, and we quit attending to the oxygen concentrator and the seating preparation, and saw each other again as we always had, a couple living with each other a meaningful life scarred and smoothed, scratched and sanded back. She could converse without a word and I, who usually said too much was muted. She was smiling a question at me, asking me something that I should know, but did not. I was lost on her eyes and that impossible, yet real, smile. Time had stopped running out. We raised our glasses and drunk again, and let love stayed with us. She was looking at me as if we were going to be apart and wanted to remember. She wouldn't say anything, though I kept questioning her with my eyes, which I never knew how to do. "What is it?" Her gaze didn't change, as if what was could not be spoken; but, it was there as real and yearning as we had always been for close to sixty years.

In time her back pain became intolerable and she had to take injections at a pain clinic, then she started taking pain medications even as the oxygen requirements increased. I had started praying after the rehab operation and kept praying as Betty got worse. Sometimes I would pray for healing her as she stared at the ceiling of the family room and I knew she was in touch with God. I waited for her to scream sometime and ask God why he was allowing these two monstrous diseases to torment her. Surely, she knew he loved her. She had told me years before that when she was a little girl she was sure of one thing that I had never heard: "Jesus loves me," was the most real thing she ever knew. So, why now all this pain? What did I know of this God of love that she was talking about?

"He is here and suffers with us," she would remind me.

"But he has the power to heal you and doesn't," I would protest and add that I knew all that, but in our case, I couldn't imagine a purpose for her suffering. "Remember, I wrote the book on Theodicy," I would say.

"There is a purpose to everything he does."

"I wish I knew what it is," I said and tried to imagine what it was this time. I went beside her, hugged her and laid my hand on her silver hair, and asked our Lord Jesus Christ to heal my suffering wife. I waited a few minutes for something to happen, but nothing did. I had been looking for a bona fide miracle all my life and I thought this might be the time I would see it. But, once again, after many indications of possible divine interventions, after some possible providential action, meaningful dreams and unexpected help from above, all sorts of mysterious favors in my work, my career and the rest of my life, there was no restoration of her eyesight, ceasing of her back pain, and no new lungs created. 'You're probably right dear," I said. "If we could know what God plans to do, it would be a sign of our divinity, and I know

I'm not there yet," I said and kissed her forehead. Jesus said that if one has faith he could move a mountain, and I was trying again to make a deal with God, having no idea what faith was. The time of learning about faith was near, but I didn't know that yet.

"Let's arrange the medications for next week," she said, the pain raging in her, or she wouldn't ask for help. "You do a good job," she added, and thanked me with her eyes. I knew that things were getting worse. It was getting hard for her to move around the house without dropping her oxygen level or the heartbeat in the oximeter. I had to follow her and make sure she didn't fall.

At night I thought of how I spent the day, and if I had taken all the measures needed for the sustenance of her survival. If I couldn't hear her breath, my anxiety would rise and I'd get up and go near her and listen as she slept. One time she fell and had a trace of blood on her head, so we called an ambulance and went to the hospital, with two of our sons and one daughter-in-law following. The nurses moved her to another room while we were checking the CAT scans and we got back and found her without oxygen connection, minutes away from irreparable damage or death. Danger was hiding all around us. So, I bought motion detectors and placed them around her bed to signal her getting up to walk, but they were not reliable and I had to dismantle them. Then I hired a nurse to lift her from her bed, if she could not, so she wouldn't fall again. The nurse was interested in action but had no compassion. Having no action, we felt as if we were to blame and we let her go next morning. Betty's breathing tube got loose one night, probably because I didn't tighten it enough around the humidifier and she couldn't breathe, and if my son Paul hadn't rushed from his house to come and turn on an auxiliary oxygen bottle I had bought as a backup, and supply oxygen until I felt the oxygen fill her lungs and fixed the connection, she would have left us.

What kind of care was this? You mustn't care too much if you want to give good care. Yeah, it felt like a paradox was been brewed. Where did I get my caregiver's license? They replace people like me, don't they? There were times I wanted to escape, get rid of the responsibility I had, but nobody could ever chase me away from her side. And all along, through anxiety, fear, anger, sorrow and doubt, I felt closer to her than I had ever felt before. That "her" I was in love with now, wasn't to be felt or seen but only to be taken in between heartbeats in random drips of grace. Caring for her was the most meaningful series of events I had ever experienced.

She was often present in my reveries, the stray thoughts of days and the substance of my prayers. And, she was there when I went to bed, just as she was that night of her seventy fifth birthday party, dressed in her periwinkle jacket, raising her glass of champagne to spread joy to our family with her warmth and her smile. Perhaps, she was also raising her glass to thank God for bringing her to this party with people she loved and sustained for so long.

For four years roughly, she lived with the little things she could work with: the bits of rope from the hardware store, the inks for her color printer, the bags for the food shelf food. She wanted so much to produce the last year's calendar, and tried, but couldn't. I felt so useless when she asked me to help her with putting it together, and I didn't know how to arrange the pages. I was ashamed of my inability to help her in one of the few things she cared a lot to finish. But, she did finish the icon of Jesus Christ she painted with love and pain.

Some weeks later she had trouble walking with her walker and we had the nurses come and discuss the situation. We had gone to the hospital to discuss the worsening situation three times before, but we had come back every time because she still wanted to fight. This time she told me she could no longer go on. She could only go four or five steps before sitting down. We found a truly caring hospice house nearby and she lived there for a few days, the most beloved woman of the family that she had always been. She laughed and talked with the dozens of relatives and friends that came to draw strength from the person who always had more than she could give away. I believe that she went to meet the Jesus she had loved all her life, and he was there to greet her and show her the wonders waiting to enrich the life of his beloved people.

40

A Prayer and an Encounter for All Time

A lone now, I move in silence from room to room of our empty, crowded house, pushing myself to bygone happy times and scenes of pain and conflict I didn't care to remember, but it is all I can do. The one who added meaning to my life was gone and no prayer or hope could bring her back. Death was here to resurrect all memories of discontent and burry the warmth of her embrace so it could hurt the part of me still moving in a daze of loss. Death is our enemy and is supposed to be gone, but not quite yet.

I was far from being right, even when I thought I was; when I relented and lost an argument, I didn't feel it in my heart. We would travel to Tyros by the sea and swim on the pebble beach and drink ouzo, eat octopus and find joy, until the sea at Samos turns to wild furies smashing against our sailboat, bent to upend us. I'm confused. Where will I go now? Should I get an apartment to limit my choices of lonely rooms and my useless freedom? My memory shifts and leaps up to the trees of a mountaintop in Portaria, and I see you in your happiness with the children at the beach. I felt joy with you around and I wanted to leap up, to take off and go down the mountain, running until I lose the future and the past and fly in the moment and fall by your side with a broken arm bone. Run away from the brokenness in the city and leave for Meteora, high up on the monasteries sculpted by monks working for eons and for God to build them and see you now holding on the side of a foot bridge up high, ready to join the eagles in holy adoration.

Something happened to me on the way back, when you heard hymns flowing out of the town's Cathedral in the street and wanted so much to go in and listen, pray, thank God for helping you live with elation, but I said I didn't feel like going inside and being squeezed in the sweating crowd. I said no more of the priestly perorations I had been bound up with since birth. You were like a rosebud that wilted from my foul breath and all your delight shrunk and we became two bodies rambling in the dark, back to our hotel room.

Then, we left the land of myths and landed back in our cloistered home and fought against your illness, you with arts and crafts and prayers and I with cooking, poetry, and meditation. You were so easy to care for, so content with little effort from me. She's never coming back. She's forever in the glorious now, and I'm trapped in a hole in the ground too deep to crawl out of it. All I can do is pray that somehow, I'll stop the assault of broken promises and accusations with sorrows of some impossible intentions. I felt totally and everlastingly lost. I had the sense that something had happened that could never be reversed, or fixed. How could I be so lost?

I see the past I forgot, the errors I cannot correct, the moments of creative force that pierced through the solitude of myself, the anger that broke the links of life's connections, the help I gave and the joy I got and then forgot. What am I doing under the MESTA Machine's Underbelly now? I'm tossing out oil-dripping rags and dead rats hidden from the world. I'm sorry I didn't know that the more I won the more I lost; the more I could do, the less I could be. Now I can see that the bad outweigh the good in my soul and I repent.

You have wanted to judge me all my life, and I was afraid of you. I cannot run, walk or see anymore. I thought you were mighty and angry; I knew nothing of your love. Give me a hand and get me out of this mess and judge away. Come and pull me out; my God, come!

Before Betty's illnesses started to impact the normal flow of our life I had been trying to find solace with a prayer to the God who has the choice of giving punishments or favor to those who appeal to him. I had started with the Jesus Prayer when I was sick at the Masonic Home, three years before and I didn't experience the hoped-for enlightenment or peace. I remembered the small practical nurse who cared for me more than anybody else in that organization and thanked God for her presence. I was terrified of dislocating my leg again and dying in pain. She was my defense against being a phantom. I couldn't get rid of thoughts that interrupted my praying and I had to persist, which got me nowhere. I had learned how to pray with the method of Thomas Keating, which is a method designed to facilitate contemplative prayer and I started using it.

Three weeks or so after Betty left us, I remembered that she said she grew up knowing that "Jesus loves me, this I know," so I started praying that I would find solace starting with that thought. I went to the room I designated as "Prayer Room" in my mind, sat down and settled on my seat. I closed my eyes and said the secret word I had chosen as the method guideline of the prayer indicates, as symbol of my consent to God's presence and action in me.

I let my imagination set me down at the grassy shore of a small river while boats go by, pushed by the water flow. Every time a thought appears in my mind I put it in a boat. "Heraclitus. . ., call the gas company. . .," put them in the boat. The purpose is to keep the mind as free of thoughts as possible. God will not approach you, if you are thinking about the day's concerns. Everything is put on a passing boat and flows down the river. Quiet, till the next thought. It was my Dark Night of the Soul, and thoughts and feelings were put on the boats, going smoothly, slowly, loaded with pain and thought after offensive thought . . .

Into a boat I see passing down the river and watch it not for long
because another thought and I stop and turn and I'm up walking
Up on a grassy hill a dozen feet behind a man I haven't seen before

The troublesome thoughts are gone, but I'm upset I don't follow the rule
And if a thought or two were to come at me right now, what would I do?
I slow down, and he stops, turns and I see his radiant face, his long golden hair
A man in loose white pants, a white loose shirt with long sleeves like a hippy I think,
I know I thought, and he said,

"Are you going to put me in a boat, too?" he asks with a smile, his eyes wonder
His eyes are bright, soft and calm, and the voice is clear, steady, pure
He's asking me to choose, what path to follow as I take my load uphill
"I commit," I said and knew he was true, no doubt in it, no hesitation
That very moment I knew I'd never be the being I had been before.

He raised his arm and waved me to join him with a welcome smile
Jesus Christ the everlasting God of love wanted me, the lousy me to come near
He threw his arm around my shoulders, I was aware, and it was no ploy.
How can I explain walking next to Jesus, in a shower of light full of joy?

I wrote the few words above as I experienced them in the moments right after my encounter with Jesus, feeling a kind of liberation from all darkness by the love I had for his presence. I hadn't known such separation from the confusion of the world except when Jesus asked me to approach and walk side by side with him. How did we communicate so many decisions with so few words? I was sitting on the same chair, but the chair was in another world, engulfed by peace and a sense of knowing that I could do whatever came up next, without any further exploration.

In that mysterious moment of Grace from Jesus, my life changed with a transcendent response of faith in him. I committed to do what he asked. I had no doubt whatsoever that the man who called me to walk with him was Jesus Christ and that he loved me the way I was. I know that my decision wasn't made using any cognitive processes, and there was no trace of transaction in my mind. It was a very unusual way for me to make decisions of any magnitude, let alone a life decision like this, without analysis and finding the pros and cons, the gains and the losses, and the certainty of having got the best deal around. None of that happened this one time. That's the way I should act in from now on. It won't be easy, but it must be. I don't know how material the image of Jesus was, but I felt his arm around the back of my neck and there was nothing ghostly about the person I saw. In retrospect, I am convinced that it was Grace that drew me to him. And I knew that my job was to continue transforming myself by being what Christ had told us to be and do what is needed for building the Kingdom of God.

Almost simultaneously I felt that for the first time in my life I was absolutely free to do anything I wanted to do because it would be the right thing to do, given my closeness to God and trusting his Law. I hadn't been a particularly serious student of the bible, but now, it seemed to me that I could remember what Jesus said in various situations and it was congruent with my thoughts. It was a joyous experience to know what to do without being afraid of breaking a commandment or a rule of some churches, or following manmade instructions or rules.

Some time later, I felt sad and angry at myself for having needed eighty-two years to grasp the purpose of my existence. I had always thought that I was a brainy and street-smart kid, able to see how to win a game. How could I have missed the goal post of the most important game ever? But, I had figured out that living for meaning rather than pleasure, money, power or aimless happiness was a good preparation to finding the ultimate purpose: moving close to God. Then, I thought of the ways people come to the same conclusion, and I knew that no matter what we do, from the best to the worst, God finds a way to bring us home, if we are lost and use our say-so.

41

Acts of Transformation

You must be the change you wish to see in the world.
Mahatma Gandhi

And we know that in all things God works for the good
of those who love him, who have been called according
to his purpose
St. Paul, Rom. 8:28

A few days after the transforming presence of Jesus, I started thinking of the actions I wanted to take to fulfill the commitment I had made to him. I continued praying, hoping for further contact with the divine, but I couldn't even concentrate for a few minutes. I felt that I should be somehow working, doing something good for the Kingdom of God, but I didn't know what. I had already written a few poems in the moments of grief and love after my wife's death and thought it would help to write some more and collect them in a book from which I could recite and talk about my faith. But, was writing poems a way to build the Kingdom, or was I trying to make myself comfortable and, perhaps, publishable? As I was searching for answers to the questions, it occurred to me that my encounter with Jesus had cemented my love for God, but had done nothing for the second greatest commandment of "Love your neighbor as yourself." I had never understood how to experience that for every neighbor I met. How could I love somebody

I didn't really know? And what kind of love are we talking about? I was alone now in the house and didn't have a way to test any effort I might make.

I tried to pray, but it wasn't any easier to concentrate now, yet I kept at it, hoping that I could have another meeting with Jesus and get some guidance. Talking to Christ and listening to him was a flow of thoughts at times, or a perception of my being without logical thinking. Watching, being aware of things happening around me and waiting for the unexpected I thought would help. Then Jesus' response to the smart-alecky Pharisee who asked "And who is my neighbor?" came to my mind. It is a tough command to obey, but as a follower of Christ I had to know more. Could I really love my neighbor? I knew that I was respectful, helpful, even compassionate, but, am I really able to love strangers? I remembered how good I had felt with the team members I worked with, my high school classmates, the steelworkers at Inland Steel, and the people of SRC I had worked with. The Samaritan, a strange neighbor showing love toward an Israelite, is equivalent to an American showing love for a Taliban soldier by bandaging his wounds in Afghanistan. How far could I travel on this road? As an O.D. expert and an agent of organizational transformation in the corporate world, I felt that it was important to lead by being a servant of the people. It was always satisfying to help people with the difficult problems they faced in the workplace, but was that good for them as it was for me? Those who want to be leaders had better follow Christ and be servants first.

Since, at the time, I hardly left the house, I didn't have a lot of chances to meet and talk with strangers or other people, I decided to make a special effort and get to know better the servicemen who came to fix things in my house: the plumber, the cleaning lady, the cable man and others I worked with. I greeted people with a smile and acknowledged their presence by starting conversations, tried to help any way I could with the work to be done and later talked about the difficulties of their work. Then, I offered water, pop or coffee and carried the drink to them. I realized that they welcomed discussion and forming a cooperative relationship with me.

When we see people as persons whose existence is much greater than the skill for which we hire them or the services they provide for us at our house or the grocery store, we show respect for their uniqueness and honor their life beyond their work. I was amazed to discover how much they wanted to do the work with excellence. The plumber had to make several visits tracking down old parts for my old washer. A Cable TV technician fixed the Cable TV and gave me his personal calling card and urged me to call him, if the TV had any new problems. My cleaning lady turned out to be an unusually trustworthy and cheerful person, and I found myself waiting for her to come for work so I could snap out of any pending gloom. I wasn't sure how these new "neighbors" of mine would respond, if they happened to read the poems I wrote for them, so I showed the respective poems to all of them that I saw again. I was relieved that they were pleased, even thankful. A few poems came out of remembering strangers who later became friends for life. Trust and a feeling of well-being are always present when "neighbors" become friends.

A long time ago, when I was a college student and worked as a steelworker in East Chicago, Indiana, for several summers, as I have already mentioned in this book., I learned more about relationships and helping others than I ever learned as a student at M.I.T., or a college professor, later in life. I felt a sense of brotherhood, devoid of contempt or superiority for others, illnesses people often contract when they let the ego have the power it always craves for. I hoped that my poems on the strangers I tried to befriend give a hint at the connections I hope to make. I began to see the good side of others before I spotted their flaws. I have a long way to go, but I won't give up. I called these poems "Love Your Neighbor," combined with some poems I wrote on Grief, Love and Truth and published them about a year after my wife's death, with the title, "Trips to the Soul."

When I recited some of the poems at a church gathering, I had a chance to testify and tell everybody how exhilarating it is to be close to God. I emphasized that we all need to remember that God is a person and welcomes a serious discussion with him, or bringing him in the thinking and emotions of the moment. He knows us better than we'll ever know ourselves and is ready to guide us, help us, discuss our requests, and be our friend, our teacher and our healer. There are many thoughts in this book that came out of nowhere and I thanked him for the inspiration. I was amazed at the opportunities that were available for doing something good for the Kingdom of God, both by actions I took and by changes in the ways I responded or engaged others. I discovered in a hurry that my almost innate tendency to judge people, for whatever relationship I had, was killing the possibility of compassionate love. I couldn't both judge and love, so I've been trying to stop judging the moral or spiritual worth of others.

My tangled relationship with an actual neighbor started to bother me and I wanted a way to improve it. So, when UPS delivered the neighbor's package to my door I took it over to him and gave it to him. He was very thankful, and I used the moment to express my regret for any problems I caused in the past and a desire for a better relationship between us. He responded in a similar way and we started waving at each other going by in our cars. Was that UPS package left at my door by accident or by divine intervention? We could all mention such events, if we happened to notice them and wonder if they belong to a divine plan for molding a softened heart. Now, I pay attention and I am thankful for any help I get. Now, I know that God is involved in everything we do.

The reason I was able to feel compassion for my neighbors wasn't due to my efforts, but rather to the fact that I was closer to God. I felt that the fact that we were both human beings united us in some way. I felt the same way as when I met another Greek person in my early days as an immigrant. The connection united us. It seemed to me that I knew what I was doing, and I didn't worry anymore about what would happen if any of my moves were rebuffed, or I was humbled or humiliated. I had overcome fears that had inhabited myself without my permission. And I had the feeling that God was happy with what we were doing together.

So, why was I so afraid of God when I was a child and stayed away from him later on, or stopped trying to find him and behave as he wanted? If I took a step to get closer to God back then, it would bring back the damnation I was afraid of. Moving closer to God was threatening, unpleasant and I remained undecided. If I broke the law, the punishment would be great. My defenses would rise up and try to confront God: if he was all good why would he toss me and every other human being to the everlasting fire? Jesus mentioned many times the torment we would suffer if we didn't follow him.

It took time, and pain and loss to understand that God suffered for our sins, rather than judged us. God's purpose has always been to bring us close to him, because only then we can follow him and get control of our lives and walk on the road that he has made straight for us.

I asked for more work to come my way, and somehow, I came up with the idea of studying the Parables of Jesus. Enthused by the wisdom I found there, I studied them for a couple of months downloaded or bought some exemplary videos and taught a course based on them to a combined group from an Orthodox Church and a Congregational Church. I tried to go deep into the wonders Jesus was trying to teach his audience and I feel that I succeeded conveying their meaning in all of them and their wisdom in several. I could sense the emotion and the surprise of getting the message that we all are looking for when we listen to the wisdom of Jesus. Teaching, becoming a member of community organizations, mentoring, helping people in need by giving generously out of love were deeds to be enjoyed. Doing good things should be a joyous deed, not a difficult duty. I knew that there were things I was enabled to do now, that I couldn't do before.

I'm aware of some of my shortcomings and I don't let go when they intrude in my life. I worked on patience, a fruit of the Spirit that builds relationships and brings peace to mind. I'm surprised that I don't find it very difficult to be patient now. I had been so impatient with my wife's unhurried enjoyment of whatever new scenery we came across, that I felt the pangs of guilt digging in me again. Being aware of such changes in alertness is helpful when trying to acquire any gift of the Spirit.

Thinking about Kingdom work, I became an active member of three groups, one being a bible study and the other theology discussion clubs, and tried to influence the group members to stand up for whatever faith in Jesus had taken root into their hearts, as opposed to always holding on to the literal meaning of the words in the bible, or to the traditional ways of thinking about the faith. I was pushing myself hard for taking risks to cause a change within our hearts and in the world, even when that was not the customary thing to do, or the polite thing to do, provided my faith in Christ pointed also to what I did. I did go overboard some times, and I would ask the Lord later if I had been too intrusive with my friends. Not to my surprise, I sensed that next time, I should be silent and listen more than talk, and other times I felt that he approved of my work. When I muted myself, people sometimes wanted to know what I had to say, and sometimes they went on without my interruptions. The days of the ruler landing on my hand bones in grade school were gone, and I could be quiet without intervention. Was that progress? I learned to be kind to myself also.

Being part of this effort to built a new world for ourselves, everything is in play and there is nothing that can escape our attention. I was watching TV about the grandeur of the greatest mall in America, and I began to feel a distaste for the world of glitz and glaze we have created in this world. It is not where I want to worship; or where I want to relax. Not where I want to have fun. I was angry that we let so many people drive us to these simulated cathedrals of wealth and pleasure where our grandchildren will go to get blessings from the hawkers of megastores. I got a pen and a piece of paper and wrote:

The world groans for change, a gene of transformation made with care
Its hardware needs no chips, its software is hope, love and what's fare.
(Excerpt from a poem of my book "Trips to the Soul".)

Then the news came up and they showed the starving children of South Sudan, and I knew that he was looking at me and expecting a response to the starving little girls putting to sleep their paper dolls and the boys kicking a football made of worn out socks. It's only a trip to the computer and some donation which isn't yet a sacrificial giving and it's not getting to that level unless I try harder. Then, I continue with another couple of lines in the poem that seems to will itself into existence:

We live for something, wait for a miracle or a guru with a bright aura
With no idea what it is, we walk with eyes shut, ready to hug Pandora.

I have to make someone listen to Jesus before the devil grabs the seed from the path of the sower. The changes within and my effort to add a little goodness to the world came together and happened increasingly ad hoc by my reactions to the events I confronted. It seemed to me that my reactions were more spontaneous and irrevocable now. Before COVID 19, I found out that I had a spiritual experience when I went to church in the evenings with few people, lower lights on, and without all the formalities of some palatial churches. I felt present in every beat and word of worship. It made me feel that we were in communion with the God who let the world crucify him so he could save the world.

I've been on a pilgrimage a long time. I've searched for the Holy Place until I pleaded with God to find me and I found out that he was always with me. He was with me, and he achieved everything good that I did at work and in my life. I'm now working to make myself friendly to anyone who wants to come with me in the most exciting journey they can imagine. All are called, some will choose the ardor of the journey and others will find reasons to avoid it, or find it in a night-club, a bar, a dive or a climb of some kind of ladder, or another stuffing that fills the emptiness we all arrive on the planet with. I do all I can and pray to the Lord to help everyone to discover our purpose. I befriend people from all walks of life, all faiths and many who lost their faith, or never had any, and pray for them to come and enjoy a life with faith that doesn't die with death. Come as you are, and you'll get some good answers to the life questions we all must answer as we approach the end of our struggle. There is an end to strife, if God is the Purpose of life.

42

An Act of Grace

B y mid-August of 2020, most people were beginning to express their restlessness with the COVID19 pandemic and all the demands it was imposing on their "once upon a time" normal life, whatever that meant to every person who dared to weigh in on the discussion. I had never realized that so many people relied upon a group, a company, a gathering, a diversion of some sort to live their normal life. I wasn't relying upon any group to add any necessary elements to my normal life, especially now that I was alone, my sons were approaching one of Social Security's Magic Numbers and my grandchildren were digitally, professionally or erotically involved with people I didn't have the chance to meet. What I'm hinting at is that I was alone and the pandemic wasn't close enough to my normal life to affect me. But on that particular mid-August evening, rain was coming down steadily, persistently in the darkness, and I was feeling down because my family was re-positioning themselves on the American map, and I had no chance to get the feel of summer beyond the couple of sunny days I had on my backyard deck

I was getting close to finishing this book, and I went down the basement looking for a hefty book of quotations to find some epigraphs, hoping to happen upon one or two "good" ones and say something more profound than I had been able to achieve thus far. I found the 1000-page-long "The Oxford Dictionary of Quotations," and dragged it upstairs, noticing that my arm muscles were weak because I had stopped my muscle-building exercises and vowed to restart as soon as possible.

I felt the same loneliness I had heard others talking about and watched another video on the existence of reality. There was a nearby lightning followed by a crackling thunder and the TV was about to quit on me.

I didn't belong to any group, and now wasn't a good time to be alone with the overhanging COVID19 hinting at more action as the winter was coming upon us. The furnace, the toilets, the humidifier, the dishwasher and all the other machinery that kept me going were hungry for maintenance and I was inert, afraid to break the lockdown I had started since COVID19 rolled into town months ago. I took "The Oxford Dictionary of Quotations" under arm and stated up, toward my bedroom. As I was passing by the icon of Jesus Christ, the icon that started and ended my days, I felt that he had abandoned me.

"Where Are you Jesus?" I thought. The summer is disappearing and we are still with necks laid on the block waiting for some British Tower axe to come down and call our departure. "I am afraid Lord," I said and bit my lip, remembering that he had said "Do not be afraid," seventy-three times in his gospels. What happens when the winter dives temperatures down to thirty below and I fall down again? I'm afraid of my waning strength and the way things go bad so fast so invisibly deadly. I know you are with us all and doing what is possible to do for us, but we have got enough suffering from COVID19 alone and being battle-ready all the time. Good night Lord and thank you that I'm still able to head upstairs and reach my bed.

I went to the room I have designated as my prayer room, sat down on a chez and dropped "the Oxford" down on the floor. I was glad I could still climb up. It was comfortable up here. I'm in a safe space and getting ready to devour all the pages of "the Oxford," somehow. I picked the book up and opened it sticking my finger somewhere in the middle of the book. It was then that I glanced at the text, a bible verse, and read the page title: The Book of Common Prayer, page 397:

> *There shall no evil befall thee, neither shall any plague come nigh thy dwelling. For he shall give his angels charge over thee, to keep thee in all thy ways. They shall bear thee up in their hands, lest thou dash thy foot against a stone – (Psalm 91:10 -12) KJV*

I read the first verse several times, doubting that it said what it said, but it was clear that the verse was a direct response to the fear I had confessed to Jesus Christ. And, a plague is a pandemic, if it is anything at all! So, I was safe in my house. I offered my thanks for the love and care with which Jesus had responded to me. But was I certain that God had given me an actionable direction in the psalm? Was I ready to proclaim the house a COVID-free zone and call any family and friends I could gather next day and have a safe party in the house? My doubting mind wouldn't bow down to the verse of promised protection. Seventy years have gone by since I was looking for miracles and a year since I met Christ in fact and sensible reality, and I am still looking? My faith was strong enough to penetrate the first line of logic's defense, but I was still ashamed, not exactly guilty, of getting stuck there. I was amazed and I kept repeating to myself that the probability of finding by chance a verse that fit so wondrously to my prayer for help from Jesus was awfully low. I heard the echo of the father with the child tormented by a mighty demon, who asked Jesus: "If you can do anything, take pity on us and help us." And Jesus saying, "If you can?" Why can't I believe entirely the fact that God wants to help me? I was exhausted and fell asleep.

The morning was bright, and I decided to make an omelet with a couple sausages and cheddar cheese, instead of my quick-fix breakfast of oatmeal with blueberries, milk and maple syrup. It looked like a good day to relax and write the last few chapters remaining in the book I had been working forever and six months in the COVID 19 lockdown. I made a cup of coffee, and started working on the omelet in the frying pan. Suddenly, I forgot that I had skipped taking my morning pills and, turning, I opened the fridge to get the bottle of Orange juice, skipped a step to shut the door, pivoted and changed direction to reach the pills on the countertop. My shoes stuck on the floor while the rest of me took off and left the kitchen floor, airborne, headed for the countertop, veering off past it, barely clearing a chair and the rear of the countertop and landing like a sack of potatoes dropped from a truck on the hard floor.

The fall alarm system I wear was shouting at me to respond, loud, if I had a fall, if I need an ambulance to come, repeating things I had heard before, just as I was checking my legs, then gently, what about the backbone, the coccyx I knew from grade school all about the coccyx that was down there on my back.

"No ambulance; I think I am alright," I said.

"Are you sure?"

"No Ambulance," I said and thought that I sure didn't want to have strangers breaking the near-total lockdown I had been under for six months. But was I alright? I could press help and have them come. I raised myself slowly and it seemed to me that everything was working. I had a tiny scratch on top of my right hand as I cleared the back of a chair, and my left foot had an almost imperceptible twist but, I could walk fine. I saw now that my body was dropped in the narrow gap, formed by the countertop edge and the table and a displaced chair arrangement.

As I stood up and thanked Jesus Christ for saving me from what could have easily been the dreaded 'fall of old men" in living alone at home, I remembered the psalm verses and started going upstairs where I had left "the Oxford." The second verse made sense now:

> *For he shall give his angels charge over thee, to keep thee in all thy ways. They shall bear thee up in their hands, lest thou dash thy foot against a stone – (Psalm 91:11 -12. KJV)*

I believed that this was a providential assurance. I had a sense of being protected. All would be well now. I thought of Jesus trying to reassure the biblical father of the demon-possessed boy he had just healed that "Everything is possible for one who believes," and the father praying "I do believe; but, help my unbelief."

Made in the USA
Coppell, TX
12 May 2021

55572221R00198